TRAVEL GUIDE TO RUSSIA

Books by Irving R. Levine:

TRAVEL GUIDE TO RUSSIA
MAIN STREET, U.S.S.R.

TRAVEL GUIDE TO
Russia

by

IRVING R. LEVINE

Garden City, New York

DOUBLEDAY & COMPANY, INC.

1960

Library of Congress Catalog Card Number 60-6890
Copyright © 1960 by Irving R. Levine
All Rights Reserved
Printed in the United States of America
First Edition

To the memory of my mother

EMMA RASKIN LEVINE

CONTENTS

CONTENTS

One ought to see everything that one has a chance of seeing; because in life not many have one chance and none has two.

JOHN MASEFIELD

CHAPTER ONE

To Go or Not to Go and How to Get There

As a place to spend a vacation, Russia is interesting, surprising, engrossing, expensive, charmless, hospitable, thought-provoking, and often drab, uncomfortable, depressing, and exciting.

Russia is the world's newest vacationland, having in fact become easily accessible to tourists only in 1956. It is still something of a frontier with the adventure and lack of refinements that are expected of frontiers.

Russians are a friendly people who are delighted to welcome foreigners to their long-isolated land. A serious people, Russians also manifest a sense of humor about themselves: "Even the inmates at the insane asylum have a Seven-Year Plan. This year they built a swimming pool. Next year the Plan calls for putting water in it!"

Russia is the place to see a controversial way of life where everyone from architect to zoologist works for an agency of the government. There is no competition, for there is no other employer.

Russia is a country where you can visit schools, farms, factories, streets, parks, and mountains named after Lenin, and then go to see Lenin himself on public exhibition—embalmed!

Russia is a land so northern that on a June "white night" in Leningrad you are able to read a newspaper without artificial light at midnight; and winter days are

11

so short that a furnace-red sun, dimmed by a veil of frosted haze, slides down behind the ice-covered Moscow River by four o'clock in the afternoon.

Where else but in Russia will you find all hotels, restaurants, and stores owned by *one* management—the government.

What other society would consider it necessary to rewrite George Bernard Shaw's *Pygmalion* so that the portrayal of Eliza Doolittle, the uneducated Cockney flowergirl, does not offend the Soviet common man who sees little humor in a comedy about class society and who shares her faults of bad grammar; in the Soviet version Eliza's transformation is from eccentric to conformist rather than, as Shaw intended it, from proletarian to lady.

Come to Russia if you want to see a society as ancient as the 800-year-old Kremlin and as new as the Luniks; as efficient as the jet and as annoyingly inefficient as construction which neglects to include closet space; a people, warmhearted, outgoing, emotional, and generous who are denied the right to choose between candidates in elections because only one person is listed for each office.

The best way to know Russia is to go there and see for yourself.

The next best way is to read about it.

This book is intended to help both those who travel in person and by proxy.

In some respects a trip to Moscow is like a journey to Mars or to the moon. In most ways, though, it's no more difficult to go to Russia today than to travel to Alexandria, Athens, or Amsterdam—and hundreds of thousands of Americans, Canadians, and Britons visit those cities every year.

A variety of airlines now fly to Moscow. Visas to Russia are easy to obtain. More and more tourists from non-Communist countries are traveling to Russia. In 1955 several hundred adventurous Americans secured visas to travel to the U.S.S.R. These returned home without being sentenced to Siberian salt mines as many of their friends and relatives had half-jokingly warned them they would be. The number has steadily grown. In 1956 there were 2000 tourists, and the next year, even with the atmosphere poisoned by the Soviet intervention in the Hungarian revolution, the figure climbed to 2500. By 1958 the figure had more than doubled, and during 1959—with the added stimulus of the American National Exhibition— more than 10,000 Americans visited Russia. The number of tourists from Britain and Canada is smaller, but also is on the increase. Two thousand British citizens went to Russia in 1958. The fact that travel to Russia still is of minor dimensions is demonstrated by the statistic that, in all, 2,000,000 Britons went abroad that year as tourists. Thus, travel to Russia constituted only one tenth of one per cent of all British tourism. The Soviet newspaper *Pravda* has estimated the number of British travelers to the U.S.S.R. in 1959 at 5000.

In 1955 not a single Canadian registered at that nation's embassy in Moscow. In 1956 there were 86 names in the register. This climbed to 145 the next year and to 300 in 1958. Embassy officials estimate that at least 50 per cent more Canadians came to Moscow who did not bother to register at their embassy.

IS A TRIP TO RUSSIA WORTH WHILE?

Several people we've known have turned around and flown home or to the night spots of Paris after only a day or two in Moscow. But these tourists came expecting attractions that Moscow doesn't offer. The overwhelming majority of travelers to Russia find it a thoroughly worthwhile experience, completely engrossing, and a source of stories, anecdotes, and political observations for many, many months afterwards.

Like it or not, Russia is a—perhaps *the*—major force in shaping the course of world events and is likely to do so for years to come. Whether there is war or peace depends in large part on the Russians. This is reason enough to make it important, but there are many other reasons why a visit to Russia can be fascinating. Here is a land that is different in so many respects from the United States, Britain, France, Canada, and other countries of the Western world that it really is akin to visiting another planet.

The Soviet Union has much to offer the tourist in hospitality, in art, architecture, ballet, drama, history, theater. A trip offers unforgettable glimpses of Soviet people, their spirit, surroundings, mode of life, and interests.

Don't come to Russia if your primary tourist objective is fun. There's not much fun in a visit to the U.S.S.R. There *is* great, moving beauty in a performance of the ballet *Romeo and Juliet* at the Bolshoi Theatre. It's a spine-chilling and unforgettable experience to descend into the dramatically lighted tomb to look at the remarkably preserved bodies of Lenin and Stalin. You'll feel transported into the days of Tamerlane, the Mongol conqueror, when you walk amid the blue and green enamel tile corridors of the Shah-i-Zinda in Samarkand, one of man's earliest known cities.

These experiences and more you will find in a trip to the U.S.S.R., but disappointment awaits you if you seek the elegant comfort of Claridge's of London, the excitement of gambling at Monte Carlo, the sheer joy of quiet, relaxed basking in the sun on the rocks at Capri, or the high fashion and low fun of Paris. Russia offers none of these attractions.

Russia for fun, no. Russia for a plethora of unique, fascinating experiences, by all means.

HOW TO ARRANGE A TRIP TO RUSSIA

There is one organization in Russia, and only one, that handles tourists from abroad. That organization is called Intourist. Intourist is a word created from two Russian words—*Inostrani* (meaning "foreign") and *tourist* (meaning just that). Intourist describes itself on the sign at its headquarters at 1 Gorky Street, Moscow, as the Organization for Travel of Foreigners in the Soviet Union. It is the sole travel bureau in the vast land, and of course is an agency of the government.

One special feature of travel to Russia is that it is imperative to use the services of a travel agent. It is through a travel agent that you must obtain the visa that permits you to enter the U.S.S.R., and also the coupons for your room and board in Russia. These coupons are purchased in advance for the number of days you intend to be in the Soviet Union. The travel agent gives you a receipt or voucher. This voucher is presented at your hotel to a clerk in the so-called "Service Bureau," an office you will become well familiar with during your stay in Russia. In return for the voucher you will receive coupons for three meals a day (plus, for De Luxe Class clients, a coupon for, of all things, afternoon tea).

It is possible to make a trip to Paris, Rome, or Andorra without ever consulting a travel agency. The traveler to these places can write ahead for reservations, and make all the other necessary arrangements on his own. But not in the case of travel to Russia. The travel agent is not only helpful for a trip to the U.S.S.R.—he is almost essential. (By way of an exception, we know one American girl who was working in Tokyo where Intourist had no representative. She applied for a tourist visa at the Soviet Embassy, got it, made airline reservations, and arrived in Moscow without having ever heard of Intourist or of meal coupons. However, in the case of countries where Intourist does have arrangements with travel agents, a person who applies directly to the Soviet Embassy for a tourist's visa will be referred to a travel agent anyway with nothing gained and time wasted.)

Intourist does business with travel agents in many countries of the world. It has several hundred "corresponding agencies" in the United States, Canada, and England—that is, a letter from any of these independent agencies containing payment for a would-be tourist's trip to Russia eventually will be honored by Intourist.

Besides such "corresponding agencies" which include almost any travel agent, there are "contract agents"— travel bureaus with which Intourist has entered into a contract or agreement. These travel bureaus are authorized to take the necessary steps to obtain a visa for the traveler and to issue Intourist coupon vouchers.

It ordinarily takes six weeks to two months for the "contract travel agent" to conclude arrangements and to hand you your visa and tour documents. If you want to pay for an exchange of cables (costing about $12) between the agent and Moscow the waiting period can be cut in half.

In other words, *any* travel agency can make the necessary arrangements for your trip to Russia, but there are a number of travel agencies which are equipped through contracts with Intourist to do it faster. In the order in which Intourist lists them, these agents in the U.S.A. are:

> *Cosmos Travel Bureau, Inc.*
> *45 West 45th Street*
> *New York 36, New York*

> *Union Tours, Inc.*
> *1 East 36th Street*
> *New York 16, New York*

Lanseair Travel Service, Inc.
1026 17th Street, N.W.
Washington 6, D.C.

American Express Company, Inc.
65 Broadway
New York 6, New York

Hemphill Travel Service, Inc.
Roosevelt Building
727 West Seventh Street
Los Angeles 17, California

American Travel Abroad, Inc.
250 West 57th Street
New York 19, New York

Maupintour Associates
1236 Massachusetts Street
Lawrence, Kansas

Safaritours
7805 Sunset Boulevard
Hollywood 46, California

Gordon Travel Service
220 South State Street
Chicago 4, Illinois

The Intourist travel agents in Canada are:

Overseas Travel, Ltd.
1052 Eglinton Avenue, West
Toronto 10

O. K. Johnson and Co.
697 Bay Street
Toronto 2

University Travel Club, Ltd.
57 Bloor Street W.
Toronto

These are the travel agents in Great Britain which Intourist lists:

L. W. Morland and Co., Ltd.
5 Whittington Avenue
London, E.C.3

Progressive Tours, Ltd.
100 A Rochester Row
London, S.W.1

Workers Travel Association, Ltd.
Eccleston Court
Gillingham Street
London, S.W.1

Thos. Cook and Son, Ltd.
Berkeley Street
Piccadilly
London, W.1

Polytours, Ltd.
73–77 Oxford Street
London, W.1

Wayfarers Travel Agency, Ltd.
20 Russell Square
London, W.C.1

Cox and Kings (Agents) *Ltd.*
Kings House
10 Haymarket
London, S.W.1

WHAT WILL IT COST?

A trip to Russia does not cost as much at it used to, but it is still too expensive. Until a few years ago the Russian ruble (the basic Soviet monetary unit) sold four to the dollar. That meant that one dollar would get you four rubles. More recently the rate for tourists has been improved so that one dollar will now buy you ten rubles upon arrival in the U.S.S.R. That makes one ruble worth ten cents.

Canadian dollars do a trifle better. One Canadian dollar will buy you ten rubles and 30 kopecks. There are 100 kopecks in a ruble. Thus, a kopeck is approximately one-tenth of a penny.

Similarly in the case of pounds sterling the rate has been raised from 11.2 rubles to the pound to a much more realistic 28 rubles to the pound.

This increase in the ruble rate makes an enormous difference when it comes to buying a ticket for the opera or for the circus, or purchasing a jar of caviar or other souvenir to take home.

(For the sake of completeness it must be reported that rubles can be purchased at highly advantageous rates— 20 or 30 rubles for a dollar instead of the official ten rubles—at currency exchanges like Perera's in New York. Although this has long been normal practice in traveling to Spain, and in fact, has been quite legal for some countries, it is a violation of the law in Russia to bring in any rubles. It is risky business, and definitely *not* recommended. There have been a few rare cases of tourists who got only as far as the Moscow airport customs official before they were turned around and sent back out on the next flight when rubles were found in their baggage. It's strictly illegal to bring any Russian money in *or* out of Russia.)

Most of the cost of your stay in Russia must be paid ahead of time. When you apply at a travel bureau for a visa you will probably be asked to make a deposit, usually $50. Most travel agencies oblige you to forfeit your deposit if you change your mind and decide not to go to Russia after your visa comes through. When the visa comes through you will be required to purchase coupons for the number of days that you plan to stay in Russia. There are several rates which may change from time to time:

	IN SEASON (May–September)	OFF SEASON (October–April)
De Luxe Class	$30 per day (£ 10.14.4)	$25.50 per day (£ 9.2.2)
First Class	$17.50 per day (£ 6.5.0)	$13.13 per day (£ 4.13.10)
Tourist A	$12.50 per day (£ 4.9.4)	$ 9.40 per day (£ 3.7.2)
Tourist B	$10.00 per day (£ 3.11.6)	$ 7.50 per day (£ 2.13.7)

There is no choice of rate for the *individual* traveler. He *must* go de luxe. In fact, although the regulations are subject to changes, Intourist usually requires that there be a group of fifteen or more in order for each person to obtain the lower rates. The nature of your hotel accommodations, the amount of food you will be entitled to for your coupons, and the number of hours you may use a chauffeured Intourist car (if at all) and a guide depends on whether you are a de-luxe tourist or a lower-rate class.

Specifically, the de-luxe traveler is met at the airport or railroad station by a private car. He is entitled to a single room (double room for couples) with bath. He may order just about anything on the menu (vodka and other drinks are extra). The de-luxe rate entitles the tourist to use a chauffeured car three hours a day. He may keep the car longer, but will be charged for overtime. He has the services of a guide-interpreter for two excursions a day—which, in effect, means all day.

The First Class group traveler moves from airport or station in a bus, he enjoys a private, single, or double room with bath. His meals may be chosen from the first-class menu which offers somewhat less variety than the de-luxe menu. His daily excursions are in a bus accompanied by an interpreter-guide for the entire group.

The Tourist Class A and Class B travelers have the

same deal as the First Class tourist except that the Class A tourist must share his double room with another member of his group, and the Class B tourists sleep three or four to a room. Class A tourists have a bath or shower in their room; Class B tourists do not.

There is also a "businessmens'" rate of $12 (or about £4) per day. This covers only hotel room and breakfast. This recently introduced rate is intended to satisfy the needs of an increasing number of businessmen traveling to Russia to negotiate contracts. These businessmen found that they seldom used their meal coupons because they often ate as the guests of the Soviet authorities with whom they were negotiating, and rarely had time for car and guide to see the sights.

PENSION PLAN

The newest Intourist arrangement is called the Pension Plan. This provides the tourist with a room and bath and ample meals on the Intourist first-class menu. The Pension Plan traveler is met at the airport and transported to his hotel on arrival and taken from the hotel to the airport on departure. However, the tourist is on his own as far as sight-seeing is concerned. No interpreter-guide or car is provided as part of this pre-paid arrangement. Under the Pension Plan, you may hire a guide (at 15 rubles per hour) and a chauffeured car (at 23 rubles per hour) for as many hours as you wish, but you will be billed for these services. Many tourists may prefer to see the sights by themselves, perhaps with the aid of a guide book. This arrangement should serve to dissuade those who consider Intourist a sort of "spy organization" which never lets a tourist out of sight. The cost for this independent type tour is $16 (about £6) a day per person.

HOW TO GET A VISA

As far as the United States Government is concerned anyone who wants to go to Russia as a tourist has permission to do so. Restrictions on travel by Americans to the U.S.S.R. were lifted on October 31, 1955. An American passport can be obtained by applying by mail to the State Department, Passport Division, Washington, D.C., or at the Passport Offices which the State Department maintains in New York and other large cities. The *passport* is the document issued by the United States Government that permits you to leave the country and return. A *visa* is permission from a foreign country to enter that country.

It's a simple, almost automatic, matter now to obtain a visa to enter the U.S.S.R. as a tourist for a period not exceeding 30 days. It's a rare case, indeed, when an applicant for a tourist visa is turned down.

The best way to get a tourist visa is to write (or go in person) to a travel agency for copies of an application form. This should be filled out in duplicate. One passport-size photograph is needed of each applicant. (Some agents ask for two photos.) The photograph should be signed on the front, under the picture, by the applicant. These are returned to the agency, which then sends the application, the photograph, and the applicant's passport to the Soviet Embassy. The agency also submits a copy of the applicant's proposed itinerary.

Persons wishing to visit relatives in Russia stand the best chance of success if they apply for a tourist's visa, stating "tourism" on their application as the purpose of their visit.

Also, journalists would be well advised to obtain visas through the normal tourist channels. It ordinarily takes a long time for Soviet authorities to act on a newspaper-man's application for a special journalist's visa. However, a journalist who goes to Russia as a tourist can usually do almost everything (and in some cases, more) that an accredited correspondent can.

(There are cases when a traveler's schedule requires him to leave his home country before the Soviet visa comes through. Of course his passport is returned to him. Sometimes such a tourist is assured that he may have the Soviet visa stamped in his passport in, say, Copenhagen, Helsinki, or Paris, en route to Russia. This seldom works out. Once the customary routine is changed the wheels of Soviet bureaucracy don't seem to function properly. Our advice is to get your Soviet visa *before* you start out on your trip or don't count on getting to Russia at all.)

HOW TO GET THERE

The biggest blow to your bankroll will come right at the outset of your trip when you purchase your airline ticket. Round-trip fares (subject to changes) run approximately like this:

	FIRST CLASS	ECONOMY CLASS
New York–Moscow	$1,147.70	$768.50
Montreal–Moscow	$1,122.50	$759.50
London–Moscow	£ 142.04	£118.16 (Tourist Class)

It is possible to travel more reasonably by ship or rail to Moscow. There is almost daily sleeper train service from Helsinki, Berlin, Warsaw, Vienna, and Belgrade. Less frequent ship service is available from London or Le Havre to Leningrad. The comfortable if less-than-luxury Soviet ships that make the run include the *Baltika* and the *Mikhail Kalinin*. It's possible, too, to travel aboard a Soviet ship from Istanbul to the Black Sea port of Odessa in the U.S.S.R., or from Iranian port of Pahlevi to Baku, capital of the Soviet Republic of Azerbaijan on the Caspian Sea. In fact, it may be possible before long for tourists to board ship in Japan and travel to a port on the Soviet Pacific coast.

You can drive your own car to Russia, too. Several routes are prescribed by Soviet authorities. Russia may be entered by private car from the north, west, or south.

The northern route leads from Helsinki, Finland, to the border city of Viborg and on to Leningrad.

From the west you drive from Warsaw or Prague to the border crossing point of Brest and then on to Minsk, Smolensk, and Moscow—the main invasion route followed by Hitler's army.

From the south it is possible (if you can get a Romanian visa as well) to drive from Bucharest to the Soviet frontier city of Chernovtsy, and then to Kiev, Kharkov, and Moscow. (It's permissible on any of these drives to detour down to Yalta on the Black Sea Crimean coast, but this must be approved in advance when you are making arrangements through a travel agent.)

Roads are narrow by Western superhighway standards, but there's very little traffic. Also, less fortunately, there are few gasoline stations along the way. Of course, severe Russian winters make it impractical if not foolhardy even to consider making the drive after October. In fact, as late into the spring as April it's dangerous to drive because thaws and mud often block highways, and during the winter Intourist does not permit tourists to drive in by car.

A guide-interpreter furnished by Soviet authorities will meet you at the frontier and accompany you on the trip. Keep a seat open for him or her. Usually the assignment of interpreters works out very well, but in at least one case a French-speaking interpreter was waiting at

Brest for a group of Americans who spoke only English. The mix-up occurred because the Americans had hired their car in Paris and had made arrangements through a French travel agency. However, this case is an exception.

All in all, our recommendation, unless time is no object, is to go by plane. Train travel is so slow in Europe, and especially in Russia, that you will spend precious and not very comfortable days in travel that could be profitably devoted to seeing the sights. Also the scenery is pretty repetitious over the flat Russian plains.

You can get current schedules for plane, train, and ship from the various lines or from a travel agent.

The quickest way, of course, to get to Europe is by jet. Pan American World Airways, for example, flies jets from New York to the principal cities in Western Europe which have connecting flights to Moscow. Pan American flies jets to London, Paris, Brussels, Amsterdam, and Copenhagen, and from each of these cities there is regular service to Moscow. The schedule for Pan American's Boeing 707 jet is approximately seven hours from New York's Idlewild Airport to Le Bourget Field in Paris. Aeroflot, the Soviet Government airline, makes the run from Paris to Moscow in just about three hours. It is entirely possible to leave New York one evening and have dinner in Moscow the next day.

Although it's not generally known, the quickest way now to get from New York to New Delhi is by way of Moscow. It's jet all the way—Pan American from New York to Paris and Aeroflot from Paris to Moscow to Tashkent to New Delhi. A businessman or tourist can obtain a visa valid for one day through a travel agent for the trip over U.S.S.R. territory.

Having flown on the Pan American jet, we can recommend its smoothness of flight, lack of vibration, and absence of noise—all factors which make for a restful, comfortable trip. Passengers in the economy class section sit

three abreast on each side of the center aisle. In de luxe
class the seats are two abreast and very roomy and an
elaborate meal is served aloft including several kinds of
wine and champagne.

From London, British European Airways provides
flights to Moscow via a stop in Copenhagen; from Paris,
there is Air France service; from Brussels, Sabena; from
Amsterdam, KLM Royal Dutch Airlines has regular
flights to the Soviet capital, and from Copenhagen (as
well as Stockholm and Oslo), Scandinavian Airlines System flies to Moscow. It is also possible to fly to Moscow
from Vienna, East Berlin, Belgrade, Bucharest, Budapest, Prague, and Helsinki.

We've usually made the flight in and out of Moscow
on Scandinavian Airlines to and from Copenhagen and
have invariably been pleased with the courteous, per-
sonalized, efficient service both on the ground and in
the air.

SAS was a pioneer in flights to Russia, being one of
the first airlines to conclude an agreement with the Soviet Government. We can recommend SAS for good
flying. What's more, if your schedule permits a day or so
in Copenhagen en route you will find it one of the most
charming, friendly cities of Western Europe, frequently
overlooked by tourists.

This section on flying to Russia would be incomplete
without a few words about Aeroflot. The Russians now
fly big turboprops and jets, mostly TU 104s, on most
foreign and many domestic routes. Although passengers
seated near the tail of the plane are subjected to noise
and vibration, the Soviet TU 104 jet has proved itself to
be a reliable aircraft. It is not as comfortable as the
larger American jets, however. Meals are served aloft
and invariably include a generous portion of caviar. In
flight a printed form sheet is passed around indicating
the weather, wind, temperature, arrival time and so on in

several languages. It makes a fine souvenir and the Russian hostess will be glad to let you have a copy. Although the Russian jets are pressurized to compensate for the thin air of high altitudes, the hostesses usually hand out cellophane envelopes to protect you against ink stains from a leaky fountain pen. Be sure to ask for an Aeroflot sticker for your luggage. They are available at the baggage sections of Soviet airports.

Seat belts are used on the jet planes but are frequently tied behind the seat on older propeller-driven models. Soviet stewardesses will tell you that seat belts are not necessary because the pilots are so good.

WHERE YOU CAN GO IN THE U.S.S.R.

The traveler to the Soviet Union now has a wide choice of cities to visit. Many places still are closed to foreigners. In retaliation for the restrictions on American travelers, the State Department has closed certain areas of the U.S.A. to Russians. However, the U.S. has repeatedly proposed to the Kremlin that both countries lift all such restrictions on travel. So far the Russians have been unwilling to agree to this.

The tourist must plan his itinerary *prior* to departing for Russia. He may choose one of the standard tours offered by Intourist or he may plan out his own combination of cities. In either case the travel agent submits the tourist's itinerary to the appropriate Soviet authorities for approval. It is difficult to make changes once you get to Russia. In fact, it's usually unprofitable to try. More than one tourist has wasted two days in negotiations with Intourist in Moscow trying to revise his itinerary in order to spend, say, an extra day in Sochi. During off-season months when there are fewer tourists in Russia it *is* sometimes possible to alter the number of days you spend in a particular place or to eliminate or add cities. But don't count on this. It depends on how heavily hotel space is booked and on the mood of the Intourist representative you speak with in Russia. In short, it is good advice to plan your itinerary carefully before setting out and to stick to it.

These are the cities usually open to foreign visitors: Moscow, Ivanovo, Leningrad, Kiev, Minsk, Riga, Lvov, Odessa, Kharkov, Stalingrad, Chernovtsy, Gorky, Kazan, Ulyanovsk, Uzhgorod, Kuybyshev, Saratov, Rostov-on-Don, Tbilisi, Gori, Sochi, Sukhumi, Yalta, Borzhomi, Batumi, Baku, Ordzhonikidze, Yerevan, Tashkent, Alma-Ata, Samarkand, and Stalinabad.

STANDARD ITINERARIES

The itineraries offered by Intourist change frequently and it is important to consult with a travel agent to get the most recent information.

Here is a representative list of itineraries being offered by Intourist through travel agents in the United States, Canada, and England:

Tour Number	Number of Days	Places Visited and Length of Stay in Each	Cost in Dollars Per Person While in the U.S.S.R.
1-A	5	Moscow, 5 days	$150.00
1-B	7	Moscow, 7 days	210.00
2	5	Leningrad, 5 days	150.00
3	10	Leningrad, 5 days—Moscow, 5 days	300.00
4	8	Kiev, 3 days—Moscow, 5 days	240.00
5	7	Minsk, 2 days—Moscow, 5 days	210.00

Tour Number	Number of Days	Places Visited and Length of Stay in Each	Cost in Dollars Per Person While in the U.S.S.R.
6	6	Odessa, 2 days—Kiev, 4 days	180.00
7	12	Leningrad, 4 days—Kiev, 3 days—Moscow, 5 days	412.50
8	12	Kiev, 2 days—Leningrad, 5 days—Moscow, 5 days	412.50
9	12	Kiev, 2 days—Kharkov, 2 days—Moscow, 5 days—Leningrad, 3 days	410.00
10	14	Moscow, 4 days—Stalingrad, 3 days—Steamer on the Lenin Volga-Don Canal, 2 days—Rostov-on-Don, 1 day—Kiev, 3 days—Time spent on train, 1 day	467.50
11	18	Moscow, 3 days—Tbilisi, 3 days—Sukhumi, 2 days—Steamer on Black Sea, 2 days—Yalta, 3 days—Kharkov, 2 days—Kiev, 3 days	715.00
12	18	Odessa, 2 days—Yalta, 2 days—Steamer on Black Sea, 2 days—Sochi, 3 days—Rostov-on-Don, 1 day—Lenin Volga-Don Canal, 3 days—Stalingrad, 2 days—Moscow, 3 days	632.50
13	14	Leningrad, 3 days—Sochi, 3 days—Tbilisi, 3 days—Moscow, 5 days	567.50
14	16	Moscow, 4 days—Stalingrad, 2 days—Lenin Volga-Don Canal, 3 days—Rostov-on-Don, 1 day—Kiev, 3 days—Leningrad, 3 days	580.00
15	16	Leningrad, 3 days—Kiev, 2 days—Odessa, 1 day—Steamer on Black Sea, 2 days—Sochi, 3 days—Moscow, 5 days	627.50

Tour Number	Number of Days	Places Visited and Length of Stay in Each	Cost in Dollars Per Person While in the U.S.S.R.
16	23	Leningrad, 3 days—Kiev, 2 days—Odessa, 2 days—Yalta, 3 days—Steamer on Black Sea, 2 days—Sochi, 2 days—Tbilisi, 2 days—Kharkov, 3 days—Moscow, 4 days	890.00
17	19	Kiev, 2 days—Odessa, 2 days—Steamer on Black Sea, 2 days—Batumi, 6 days—Sukhumi, 1 day—Sochi, 1 day—On train, 1 day—Moscow, 4 days	676.25
18	9	Leningrad, 3 days—Moscow, 4 days—Ivanovo, 2 days	297.50
19	16	Moscow, 4 days—Ordzhonikidze, 2 days—Voyenno-Gruzinskaya Road, 1 day—Tbilisi, 4 days—Sukhumi, 2 days—Time spent on train, 3 days	632.50
20	9	Tashkent, 3 days—to Moscow, 1 day—Moscow, 4 days—to Tashkent, 1 day—(This tour can be arranged Moscow–Tashkent–Moscow)	432.50
21	14	Tashkent, 3 days—to Moscow, 1 day—Moscow, 4 days—Leningrad, 5 days—to Tashkent, 1 day	617.50
22	13	Moscow, 5 days—to Alma-Ata, 1 day—Alma-Ata, 3 days—Tashkent, 3 days—to Moscow, 1 day—(This tour can be arranged Tashkent–Moscow–Alma-Ata–Tashkent)	605.00
23	13	Irkutsk, 1 day—Moscow, 7 days—Leningrad, 5 days	561.25

Tour Number	Number of Days	Places Visited and Length of Stay in Each	Cost in Dollars Per Person While in the U.S.S.R.
24	11	Riga, 2 days—Leningrad, 4 days—Moscow, 5 days	350.00
25	13	Leningrad, 3 days—Riga, 2 days—Kiev, 3 days—Moscow, 5 days	443.75
26	11	Leningrad, 4 days—Riga, 2 days—Moscow, 5 days	350.00
27	15	Uzhgorod, 1 day—Lvov, 1 day—Chernovtsy, 1 day—Kiev, 3 days—Leningrad, 4 days—Moscow, 5 days	527.50
28	14	Chernovtsy, 2 days—Lvov, 2 days—Kiev, 3 days—Leningrad, 3 days—Moscow, 4 days	485.00

SPECIAL ITINERARIES

Many tourists prefer variations of these standard itineraries. In fact 80 per cent of clients of the Cosmos Travel Bureau, one of the most active in Soviet travel, have requested and obtained "tailor-made" itineraries that differ from those proposed by Intourist.

It's well to note that the tourist who goes with a group tour is *not* obliged to sight-see with the other members of the group. In fact, if he wishes, he will see the other tour members only at meal time, and can spend the rest of the time on his own, going where he pleases.

Also a member of a group tour may remain in Russia for a number of days after the group leaves if he makes arrangements with the Intourist Service Bureau. Once the group departs, the individual must pay de luxe rates.

He may travel under the de luxe plan to cities omitted in the group tour if he wishes.

Maupintours of Lawrence, Kansas, specializes in Group bus tours of Russia.

A number of airlines offer "package" tours in co-operation with travel agents.

Intourist itself now offers several out-of-the-ordinary tours for travelers with special interests. Not to be outdone by African safaris, Intourist even provides big game shooting for the tourist. Here is the Intourist description in a recent letter to travel agents:

"Hunting Tours. Hunting tours are arranged in Yalta where tourists can stay at the Oreanda hotel. Minimum stay is 5 days.

"Price of all-inclusive service is $22.50 per day per person.

"Price of game: $200–$700 for a deer and $30–$100 for a roe—in compliance with the Madrid scoring system. Part of this price ($150 for a deer and $25 for a roe) is paid simultaneously with the payment for tour. The rest of the sum and also the cost of the preparation of antlers ($15 for deer's antlers and $7.50 for roe's antlers) is paid after the hunt in foreign currency."

Low-cost camping tours are also offered by Intourist. Campers must travel by their own automobiles, but rather than sleep at Intourist hotels, they pitch tents in specified camping areas. To quote the Intourist announcement:

"Tourists traveling on camping tours are accommodated in camping grounds situated in the vicinities of the cities included in the itinerary. They are provided with places for a car and a tent, with water supply, electricity, toilet, and washing-stand.

"Excursions included in the cost of the tour provide sight-seeing in the cities, visits to museums and exhibitions.

"The prices do not include meals, which tourists can get in buffets in the camps, paying for these meals in cash. For cash payment tourist can also hire tents, beds, mattresses, bed clothes, crockery, cutlery, etc.

"Between cities tourists travel by their own auto transport."

A sample camping itinerary lasting 15 days takes the tourist along this route: Vybourg (on the Finnish-Soviet frontier)—Leningrad—Novgorod—Kalinin—Moscow—Kursk—Kharkov—Kiev—Chernovtsky. The very low cost for camping facilities is $40 per person for this entire itinerary.

If you plan to drive a car to Russia, be sure to obtain an International Driving License at any Automobile Club in your home town. Russia honors these licenses.

WHEN TO GO TO RUSSIA

Russia looks most like Russia *should* in wintertime. With snow on the ground, flakes flecking the sloping walls of the Kremlin and veiling blemishes of most other buildings, and with Russians wearing bulky coats and fur hats—this is Russia as Currier and Ives would have depicted it if Currier and Ives had produced Russian scenes.

If you have your choice, make your trip to Russia in the winter. November is the best month. Then the temperatures, although below freezing, have not fallen below zero fahrenheit, as a rule, and there usually is snow before the first of November. November 7 is an interesting time to be in Moscow, because it is the anniversary of the Revolution that brought the Communists to power. The holiday, which starts with a military parade, followed by a longer parade of hundreds of thousands of civilians carrying placards, portraits of the leaders, and floral decorations, is a sight that will be a highlight of your trip to Russia. A similar demonstration takes place on May 1. Another month of May attraction is the elaborate Russian Orthodox Easter service held in churches.

Another advantage of a winter trip (besides the reduced off-season rate) is that the top stars of the famous Bolshoi Theatre and of other companies will be performing whereas they are on vacation in midsummer. (Occasionally, even in January, the top performers may be out of the country on tour.)

With fewer tourists in town you will get more personal attention from Intourist, particularly in the choice of rooms.

Winter is our preference, but it's just a slight preference. A trip in the summer is certainly more comfortable although if you plan to travel into the central Asian regions—Tashkent, Samarkand, Alma-Ata—be prepared for brutally hot weather, often over one hundred degrees. Moscow and Leningrad, although pleasantly warm in the daytime, always cool off to light-blanket temperature at night.

Certainly the Russian people look more attractive in spring and summer. Then they shed their predominantly black winter garb and put on brighter prints and colors.

To sum up: a trip to Russia is well worth while in any season.

CHAPTER TWO

Questions You May Have— Travel Tips

A travel lecturer named Richard Thomas had a wonderful idea for remembering his friends at Christmastime. On a November trip to Russia he brought with him 1000 postcard-type Christmas greeting cards specially printed in New York with a photograph of Red Square and the unmistakably Russian St. Basil's Cathedral. He planned to stamp and mail them from Moscow. Soviet Customs officials at the border of Finland and Russia went through Mr. Thomas' baggage and pounced on the cards.

Although the Red Square scene looked familiar to them, they could not understand the English language message of holiday greetings. The quantity of cards seemed to stun them. The train was held up past its scheduled departure time while Mr. Thomas tried to explain his innocent motives, and suspicious officials consulted among themselves. Finally the train departed for Moscow *with* Mr. Thomas but *without* the Christmas cards. In Moscow he explained the situation to patient people in the Intourist office, and on the day of his departure Mr. Thomas got all 1000 cards back. By that time though it was too late to buy postage stamps and mail them. The cards were carried back to America by the disappointed Mr. Thomas.

Mr. Thomas' experience was unusual. More often than

not Soviet Customs authorities are easygoing and try not to inconvenience the tourist. Foreigners have brought copies of Boris Pasternak's banned-in-Russia novel *Doctor Zhivago* without objection from Customs men who went through their luggage. However, when a German friend of mine was found to have six copies in his bag the Customs inspector asked for an explanation. The German said the books were for non-Russian friends and they let him through.

Anything in *quantity* worries Soviet Customs officials whether it be six copies of *Doctor Zhivago*, 1000 Christmas cards or 12,000 small bottles of perfume (shipped in by a French fashion house as souvenirs during style shows held in Moscow by a French designer. Customs held up the perfume).

Customs men seem most suspicious of printed material, apparently worried that it may be circulated as anti-Soviet propaganda. By the same token, recording tapes and phonograph records sometimes must be played at Customs to make sure they contain nothing subversive. Before foreign airlines land in Russia the stewardesses are required to gather and lock up copies of magazines distributed during the flight. (However, magazines brought in by passengers themselves are never stopped.)

It's quite natural to feel nervous and apprehensive about going to Russia. Almost everyone does.

After all, Russia is a nation that has been closed to non-Communist visitors for several decades, a country with a form of government that tolerates no minority voice in its politics, a land where sudden arrest and imprisonment without trial were a documented fact for many years. Much of this has changed since Stalin's death, but Russia is not a free democratic country in the Western sense by any stretch of the imagination.

The butterflies-in-the-stomach sensation is not made

any easier by friends whose eyebrows raise when you say you're planning a trip to Russia or by acquaintances who rejoin with "what do you want to go there for?" or "don't go, those Communists will never let you out."

Even with the increasing numbers of Westerners going in and *out* of Russia, there's still a tendency to feel like a pioneer. There are bound to be scores of questions, and this chapter seeks to answer those we've been asked by travelers and intended-travelers to Russia.

IS THERE ANY DANGER IN GOING TO RUSSIA?

A tourist in the Soviet Union is completely safe. Of course it's possible to slip and fall in the bathtub in Leningrad or get hit by a car in Moscow (in fact, many Moscow drivers seem determined to run down pedestrians without discrimination between native and tourist). However, except for these dangers, which are also present in Minneapolis, Montreal, and Manchester, the tourist is safe from harassment or arrest.

The Soviet leaders who succeeded Stalin have decided to let in tourists for a number of reasons. To arrest them is not one of those reasons. Soviet authorities see tourism as a way of winning friends for the hammer and sickle. Many people carry away a much better impression of the U.S.S.R. than they had when they came. Also tourism is a source of foreign exchange.

There have been cases when tourists have been asked to leave. This occurred, for example, when Soviet authorities suspected that they were really in Russia for purposes other than tourism—such as representing a foreign intelligence network or an anti-Soviet propaganda radio organization. These "invitations" to leave were accomplished with a minimum of fuss and inconvenience.

You will find Soviet policemen courteous and helpful. It may come as a disappointment to some tourists to find that they are *not* followed. It seems unlikely that Soviet authorities would expend personnel and time in tapping the rooms of every visiting tourist. Certainly the Russians *do* have the facilities for monitoring conversations, especially telephone conversations. And the tourist with some special information of national security value should certainly use exceptional caution. But the ordinary tourist need not give this a thought. That goes for mail, too, although residents in Moscow have evidence that their mail is opened and read.

IS IT SAFE TO GO IF YOU WERE BORN IN RUSSIA?

The Soviet Government does not recognize that a person born in the U.S.S.R. may change his citizenship without a special act of the Kremlin's legislature, the Supreme Soviet. This has led to a fear on the part of some naturalized citizens of other countries, born in Russia, that if they return to Russia as tourists they may not be permitted to leave again. However, if the tourist holds an American, British, Canadian, or other foreign passport this is a needless worry. Nonetheless, the State Department has contributed to this fear by replying to inquiries from Russian-born Americans with a form letter intimating that the former Russian would best stay at home and warning that the Soviet Union does not recognize a change in citizenship. Legally this *is* the case. But in practice, Soviet authorities have treated Russian-born American tourists no differently than any others and all have been permitted to leave Russia whenever they wished to.

CAN YOU VISIT RELATIVES?

Before you set out for Russia for the purpose of seeing relatives make sure that your relatives want to see you. During the era of Stalinist terror any contact with a foreigner was dangerous for a Russian. Now many Russians are ready to renew ties with relatives living abroad in non-Communist lands. Many have done so. However, there have been heartbreaking cases when Russians have simply refused to have anything to do with even brothers and sisters who have traveled 5000 miles to see them. The attitude of these Russians is—"leave well enough alone." Recalling that during Stalin's time they were discouraged by threats and jail sentences from having any contact even by mail with foreigners, these Russians are worried lest the same sort of atmosphere reappear. They prefer not to expose themselves to possible similar accusations in the future.

Such cases are the exception. In most instances Russians are willing to assume that the present more civilized climate is here to stay. They receive relatives with open arms, and accept their gifts with thanks.

Out of thoughtfulness for your relatives write to them, at first dealing only with nonpolitical affairs of the family and suggest that you'd like to come to Russia. If you receive no answer don't impose yourself on them. It can only cause grief to them—and to you.

If your relative lives in a city open to tourists it is easy to go there as a tourist. If the relative lives in a closed area, you may apply for a visitor's visa but this often takes months or years. In such cases it is best for the relative to arrange to meet you in Moscow, Kiev, Odessa, or some other convenient open city.

WHAT TO TAKE

Besides the usual items you would pack for a trip anywhere—clothing, toilet articles, rain slicker—there are a number of things you will be glad to have brought along to Russia:

Soap. The red bars of sweetly disinfectant-scented soap manufactured in Soviet Government factories probably won't appeal to you. (Pre-moistened paper towels sold under a half-dozen different trade names such as "Wash-'n-Dri" are very useful for travel on Soviet planes.) Also bring along enough tooth paste and shampoo because chances are you won't care for the made-in-Russia kind.

Cigarettes. Russian cigarettes are strong, and foreign brands (except for those from Bulgaria and other Communist lands) are not sold. Soviet Customs authorities won't object to several cartons.

Toilet tissue. The Soviet-manufactured product is even coarser than that produced in other European countries. It's also a good idea to pack a small box of paper toilet seat covers because sometimes public facilities lack sanitary amenities.

A bottle of cleaning fluid, or better still a nonliquid dry, push-up stick which can't break. (Since dry cleaning takes such a long time this can be a life saver if you spill *shashlik* sauce on your shirt or skirt.)

Film and flash bulbs. Take along as much as you plan to use, because the Soviet products are not always available in the proper sizes and are usually of inferior quality.

A bottle of whiskey. If gin is your favorite drink before dinner take that along, or scotch or bourbon or whatever. Unless you're a vodka fan you probably won't like Russian mixed drinks—if, in fact, you can even induce the waiter to try mixing a drink. Russians like theirs straight. Soviet Customs officers won't object to three or four bottles in your baggage.

A sink stopper. You may not need this at all, but if you do you'll be happy to have thought of it. Try improvising a sink stopper sometime! The farther you get from Moscow the more likely it is that you may need this. Since sink and tub drain hole sizes vary, the preferable type is a flat suction disc of three inch or so diameter commonly used for kitchen sinks.

Kleenex or other facial tissue. For a hundred different uses and it's not available in Russian stores.

Deodorant. No convenient-to-use deodorant is sold in the U.S.S.R.

Gifts. Russian youngsters often cluster around the front of tourist hotels eager to trade lapel pins of any sort. Bring along your old Willkie buttons, Rotary Club pins, or America First buttons. The kids will love you. Some children also are anxious to trade coins; a handful of shiny pennies will go a long way. For the more mature set—maids and others who serve you will usually gratefully accept nylon stockings, lipstick, perfume, or ballpoint pens. Don't be surprised if occasionally a gift of any sort is rejected as a kind of capitalist bribe.

Other gifts. If your baggage space permits, you may care to take along chewing gum for children and phonograph records of American jazz and popular vocalists. One tourist found that Russians he met in art galleries were delighted to receive post-card size reproductions of modern paintings which hang in U. S. galleries. He had purchased these at the Museum of Modern Art in New York.

Books and magazines. Carry your own reading material because you won't find any entertaining Western literature available in Russia. Books were the thing that tourists most often borrowed from us in Moscow. By the time you leave, you very likely will have found fellow tourists or Russians eager to relieve you of your books and magazines. Women interpreter-guides and chambermaids often are anxious to see copies of Western fashion magazines. You may bring in any book you wish, including this one.

A quick-developing camera such as a Polaroid. We don't own any stock in Polaroid (and, in fact, don't have such a camera ourselves), but it *is* a great conversation-starter. Russians are pleased and amazed to see a picture of themselves only seconds after they've posed. (There is a Soviet quick-print camera, but it is not in wide use yet.)

Medicines. Don't plan to have any prescriptions renewed in Russia. It's just too much trouble. Carry a sufficient supply of any pills, tonics, or other medicines that you take regularly. If you plan a prolonged stay in winter, bring along vitamin tablets to compensate for the lack of fresh vegetables. Aspirin, cold pills like Coricidin and Band-Aids can come in handy. If you wear glasses it is a good idea to take along an extra pair in case you break or lose yours. Sunglasses are useful in the summer.

Powdered coffee. Although Russian tea is wonderful, Russian coffee is generally awful. If you can't get along without that morning cup, carry your own and ask for hot water.

For men only. Razor blades and shaving cream. Don't plan to restock in Russia; Soviet steel is great for ballistics but hard on beards.

For women only. Kotex, Tampax, etc., not sold in Russia. Also plan to take along your own shampoo and nail polish for use in Soviet beauty parlors; you'll be more satisfied with your own things and the Soviet attendants won't mind using them. Bring a supply of perfume and cosmetics; don't plan to buy the Russian variety. And finally, more important than all of these, a pair of comfortable, rubber-soled sight-seeing shoes for trudging over pavements and cobblestones.

HOW TOUGH IS SOVIET CUSTOMS INSPECTION?

You can bring in just about everything you want to for your private use—assuming, of course, that this does not include firearms or opium! Soviet Customs officials are courteous; their inspection of baggage is erratic. Sometimes they will carefully inspect every corner of your luggage, but on other occasions they wave you through without so much as opening a bag. On a score of trips in and out of Russia I've had thorough inspections on four occasions, cursory look-throughs a half-dozen times, and a friendly wave-through the rest of the time.

On entering and leaving Russia you will be asked to fill out a declaration which is printed in three languages (Russian, English, and French). The single sheet declaration asks your name, nationality, destination (the answer is "U.S.S.R."), and the total number of hand-carried and checked-through luggage. The declaration then asks you to declare whether you have in your luggage any of these items:

1. Soviet currency and U.S.S.R. State Loan Bonds.
2. Foreign currency.
3. Precious metals, precious stones, pearls, and articles made from them.
4. Army weapons and ammunition.
5. Opium and hashish.
6. Curios and articles of art.
7. Articles intended for sale or deliverance to third parties.

As obscure as some of these articles may seem, they are more likely to be included in a traveler's luggage than would "elk's horn," an item until recently included in the list.

The arriving traveler is expected to declare whatever currency he has including bank notes and traveler's checks. The Customs agent may or may not ask that the money be counted in his presence. Usually this is not required. Whether the agent wants you to count your money or takes your word for it, he then gives you a printed form—a "foreign currency declaration"—on which he writes the various sums. This sheet of paper must be returned to the Customs man when you leave. (Not infrequently a tourist loses his "foreign currency declaration" and I've never known of any barriers being raised to his leaving because of this.)

Whenever you change any money—dollars or pounds or any other currency you have brought with you—into Russian rubles at your hotel money exchange counter you receive a memo of the transaction from the clerk. You are supposed to give these memos to the Customs agent when you leave together with your foreign currency declaration. The sum on the memos and the amount left in your pockets should equal the money originally declared when you arrived. This procedure is to discourage illegal purchase of rubles from business-minded Soviet citizens (who of course would not dare to give you a receipt for a transaction, and it would not be official if they did).

It's a good idea for women tourists to declare any gold or silver bracelets or other jewelry. This will be entered by the Customs official on the declaration form along with your money. This eliminates any question being raised when you leave that the jewelry was purchased in Russia. (It is against the law to carry out of the U.S.S.R. precious metals or art objects originating before 1917.)

HOW TO GET APPOINTMENTS WITH SOVIET OFFICIALS

It's best to take steps *before* setting out for Russia if you want to speak with someone in a particular field of interest. When there were fewer tourists to Russia than there are now Intourist would try to arrange appointments and visits that really had very little to do with tourism. Now Intourist officials say that as a travel agency it is their job only to help the visitor see tourist sights—museums, statues, theaters. In fact Intourist's services *do* extend beyond that. Tourists are taken to factories, schools, and churches. And occasionally Intourist will help a physician make arrangements to watch surgery performed at a Moscow hospital or an artist to meet with Soviet painters. Arrangements were made for a printing-plant manager to visit Moscow printing houses and to meet with experts in that field of work. However, for anything out of the ordinary it's advisable to take steps on your own.

It is best to write ahead of time to the Soviet Government agency or Ministry that might deal with your occupation or interest. Addresses can be obtained by writing to the Embassy of the U.S.S.R. in Washington, Toronto, or London, or to the Embassy of the United States,

Britain, or Canada in Moscow, U.S.S.R. Here is a list of
Soviet Ministries and organizations to write to for appointments with Russians in your own profession:

PROFESSION	MINISTRY	ADDRESS
Artist, movie pro-ducer or director, actor, dancer	Ministry of Cul-ture of U.S.S.R.	Kuibisheva Ulitsa 10, Moscow, U.S.S.R.
Businessman	Ministry of Trade of Russian Social-ist Federated Soviet Republic (R.S.F.S.R.)	Kirova Ulitsa 47, Moscow, U.S.S.R.
Lawyer, barris-ter, judge	Ministry of Jus-tice of R.S.F.S.R.	Kachalova Ulitsa 12 Moscow, U.S.S.R.
Farmer, botanist	Ministry of Agri-culture of U.S.S.R.	Orlikov Pereulok 1/11 Moscow, U.S.S.R.
Athlete, coach	Union of Sports Societies	Skatertny Pereu-lok 4, Moscow, U.S.S.R.
Military officer	Ministry of De-fense of U.S.S.R.	Minister's Recep-tion Room. So-fiiskaya Embank-ment 34, Moscow, U.S.S.R.

PROFESSION	MINISTRY	ADDRESS
Professor, diplomat	Ministry of Foreign Affairs	Smolenskaya 32/34 Moscow, U.S.S.R.
Physician, dentist, surgeon, nurse	Ministry of Health of U.S.S.R.	Rakmanovsky Pereulok 3 Moscow, U.S.S.R.
Scientist, technician, engineer	Academy of Science of U.S.S.R.	Leninsky Prospekt 14 Moscow, U.S.S.R.

In each case address your letter to the Director of the Foreign Department. Bear in mind that Soviet officials invariably are sticklers for reciprocity. Be sure to stress in your letter that you want to *exchange* ideas and to give your hosts the benefit of *your* experience as well as learning firsthand of *their* work. Also include a brief biography of yourself in your letter; don't be modest.

If you are interested in speaking with Russians in your field of work it is well to carry a few letters testifying of your authenticity as a doctor, lawyer, Indian chief, or whatever. Russians are impressed with documentation and the more official-looking seals on your letters of recommendation the better.

Even if you do not receive a reply to a letter to Moscow requesting appointments, do not despair. Show a copy of your letter to your Intourist guide and ask him or her to phone the Ministry renewing your request. Also some tourists have achieved results with a follow-up letter mailed from Moscow.

A "court of last appeal" (and also a good place to write to in advance regardless of the nature of your special request) is: *The Union of Societies of Friendship with Foreign Countries, Kalinin Ulitsa, Moscow, U.S.S.R.*

This organization has incorporated the role of several now eliminated agencies that used to be concerned with cultural relations with foreigners. This Union of Friendship Societies is more interested in delegations than in individuals. One of its main functions is to stimulate the creation and subsequent activity of so-called Soviet Friendship Societies in foreign lands. It arranges exchanges of delegations with foreign lands. However, if this organization will interest itself in your particular project, it has the power to open seemingly impenetrable official doors.

CHANGING YOUR INTERPRETER-GUIDE

Your interpreter-guide can make all the difference in the world between a successful and an only so-so visit. Some of the Intourist guides are excellent by any standards and not at all the parrots of propaganda that you might expect. Others do bubble over with the *Pravda* line but are none the less interesting for this and for their knowledge of the various sights. However, as in every organization, there are bound to be some duds, and Intourist is no exception in this regard. Then, too, there may always be personality differences, and a guide who may please one person may annoy another. What can you do about it if you don't like your guide?

We had a frank talk about this with Leonid Khodorkov, a deputy minister of the Intourist organization in Moscow. He said that it might hurt the career of an Intourist guide if a tourist complains and asks for someone new. Life in Russia can be difficult enough without contributing as a tourist to a Russian's problems. However, Mr. Khodorkov added, certainly there were cases when a tourist might prefer another guide because of some special interest. That is, a tourist might find that his guide did not know enough about architecture, or art, or history, any of which might be your special interest, and that a tourist requesting a different guide on that basis certainly would not be reflecting on the qualifications of the originally assigned guide. In other words, if you want to change your interpreter-guide do so with a bit of discretion and diplomacy.

Many tourists derive a considerable degree of enjoyment from engaging in polemical political discussions with their Intourist guides. It is not at all unusual for a tourist to return from a trip to Zagorsk, for example, more enthusiastic about having bested his guide in an ideological argument than about the sights of that old monastery settlement. More than one Intourist guide has told me that he finds such discussions fruitless and, in fact, irritating. However, other guides say that they enjoy this sort of exchange, and presumably more than one guide has gone home in triumph, believing that he has scored a victory over the visiting tourist in argument. So, if this sort of discussion appeals to you, Russia is certainly a good place for indulging in it.

HOW ABOUT PHOTOGRAPHY?

By all means take along your cameras—whether Baby Brownie or movie camera. Generally speaking you can take pictures of almost anything a tourist might want to, but there are some important exceptions.

A Soviet Ministry of Foreign Affairs' circular sent to all embassies, dated February 11, 1954, lists the rules. Boiled down they amount to this:

No picture-taking (or sketching) from airplane windows while in flight over Soviet territory.

No photography of military installations of any sort, of seaports, hydroelectric dams, bridges, factories, laboratories, radio beacons, telephone-telegraph stations, railroad junctions, and railroad tunnels (even *if* there were enough light in a tunnel!).

No photographs of anything within 25 kilometers (15½ miles) of any Soviet frontier.

Pictures and sketching are permitted of architectural monuments; buildings of cultural, educational and medical institutions; theaters; museums; parks; stadiums; streets; living quarters, and all landscapes where there are no forbidden objects in the background.

"With the permission of the administration of these institutions and organizations," photographs may be taken at factories manufacturing civilian products, on farms, railroad stations, airports, river ports, and government institutions. (It's difficult to conceive of a more general category than "government institutions" in Russia where everything is owned by the government one way or the other.)

In practice the exceptions to these rules would occupy much more space to list than the rules themselves. Here are a few:

Even though photography of hyroelectric installation is specifically forbidden, a delegation of American farmers was invited and, in fact, urged to take pictures of the important Volga-Don Canal. (On the other hand, a New York *Times* correspondent was expelled from Russia for taking pictures of a Dnieper River dam that had actually been built with the help of American engineers who had drawn up the blueprints!)

Even though photography of streets and living quarters *is* permitted, more than one tourist has found himself surrounded by indignant Soviet citizens as he was about to take a picture of a run-down dwelling. The Russians in such cases complain that the foreigner is trying to show their country in a "negative" way. Often a policeman intervenes, and on a few occasions the tourist has been escorted to a police station as much to get him away from the angry crowd as to lecture him on the desirability of photographing only the more "constructive" aspects of life in Russia. On one occasion when I had taken a picture of Russians standing in line at an outdoor fruit stand, two "vigilante-minded" Russians insisted that I accompany them to the nearest policeman. He listened to their complaint, sent them on their way, and once they were out of sight, the policeman waved me on too.

Such incidents, it must quickly be added, are rare. Most visitors to Russia photograph pretty much what they please without any interference and, in fact, with co-operative and enthusiastic posing by Russians.

A final word of advice on photography: make a gesture of asking Russians whether you can take their picture. If you do so with a friendly smile, the chances are they will nod agreement. Rather than argue with Russians who try to dictate what you should or should not take, it is better just to walk away, and return again another day.

TELEPHONE SYSTEM

There's a dial system in most Soviet cities. Surprisingly hotels do not usually charge for local telephone calls. Public telephones are most often glass-paneled booths built outdoors against the sides of buildings; a 15-kopeck coin is dropped into a slot to make a call.

The dial consists of ten numbers. Each number has a corresponding letter, like this:

1 2 3 4 5 6 7 8 9 0
А Б В Г Д Е Ж И К Л

Most telephone numbers consist of a letter followed by
five numbers. However, it's a good deal easier for the
visitor to write down telephone numbers all in numerals.
That's the system followed in this book; the corresponding numeral is given instead of any letter.

The number 01 is to call the fire department, 02 sum-
mons the police, 03 is for an ambulance, 06 is for the
sending of telegrams, and 09 is for information.

Wrong numbers, long waits, noise on the line, and in-
terruptions are commonplace, so have a supply of patience on hand when you tackle the Soviet telephone
system.

Calls to foreign countries can be made almost any time
of day or night. As in the case of any overseas call, reception varies. There are certain hours for direct calls
from Moscow to the U.S.A. or Canada. However, if you
specify that you want your call placed "via London"
you should be able to have it accepted at any hour.
Place a call one day in advance if you know beforehand
that you will be calling. The price of any call abroad is
$4 per minute with a minimum of three minutes.

MAIL FROM HOME

Count on airmail from home (whether home is in the
U.S.A., Canada, or Great Britain) taking at least seven
days to reach Moscow. As a rule it will take at least the
same number of days for your letters to reach home.
It's not unusual for it to take longer—eight to ten days
is quite normal. Most of the delay seems to be in Moscow where Russians familiar with their Cyrillic alphabet
are slowed down by English addresses. Although there's
good evidence that mail sent and received by diplomats

and other foreigners residing in Moscow is opened and read (or photostated), it's unlikely that this is the case for most tourists.

There are several ways in which mail can be addressed to you. Mail may be sent to your hotel. If you are expecting mail be sure to cable your office or home when you arrive in Russia telling them what hotel you have been assigned to.

A second address that may be used is: Your name, care of Intourist, 1 Gorky Street, Moscow, U.S.S.R. This is the Intourist head office where mail for tourists is received and sorted. It eventually finds its way to the hotel where the addressee is staying, but it is preferable to drop in every other day or so to check if there is any mail for you.

One tourist tells of going to the Intourist office and finding great piles of mail which had accumulated and were awaiting delivery. It seemed futile to try to thumb through to find any that might be addressed to him. The tourist went back to his hotel and sent a telegram in English from the hotel post-office counter. It simply said I AM STAYING AT THE BERLIN HOTEL. PLEASE SEND ME MY MAIL. He signed his name. Sure enough the next day several letters were delivered to him!

The third and best way to get mail is to have it addressed to you in care of your country's embassy in Moscow. The mail will be kept safely for you, and when you depart you can leave instructions for it to be forwarded to you. The only disadvantage to this address is that it will not, of course, be delivered to your hotel. You must call at your embassy to pick it up. The addresses of the U.S., British, and Canadian Embassies are:

American Embassy
Chaikovsky Ulitsa 19/21
Moscow, U.S.S.R
Telephone: 52 00 08

British Embassy
Sofiiskaya Naberezhnaya 14
Moscow, U.S.S.R
Telephone: 31 95 55

Canadian Embassy
Starokonyushenny Pereulok 23
Moscow, U.S.S.R
Telephone: 41 90 34

HOW MUCH HELP CAN AN EMBASSY BE?

Except for receiving mail at your embassy and in extreme emergencies, don't expect too much help from the embassy, and you won't be disappointed. Not a few tourists have left Moscow indignant because the ambassador could not receive them when they called for an appointment. A visitor who would not dream of calling his nation's ambassador in Paris or Rome sometimes is impelled to do so out of the feeling of strangeness and remoteness that may come from being in Russia. But an ambassador is a busy man, and, in most embassies in Moscow, has too small a staff for the work he must do. That leaves little time for receiving travelers.

However, if you have some interest other than seeing the sights, chances are that you can arrange an appointment with an embassy diplomat concerned with education, political affairs, economics, industry, cultural affairs, or whatever your special field may be. This may best be done by a letter to the embassy before you set out for Russia, but a telephone call to the embassy after you arrive ordinarily will get you an appointment.

The consular affairs section of the embassy is directly concerned with problems of citizens abroad. If you get arrested, whether in Moscow or Milan, it is the job of the consul to try to get you out. If you lose your passport go to the embassy consul office to report the loss. If a citizen-abroad falls ill or is in an accident the consular officer would be called.

Although it's not essential if your timetable doesn't leave a minute free, it is a good idea to register at the embassy consular office. If you expect to receive mail at the embassy this registration provides your return address in case anything comes in after you've left. Registration has proved helpful on more than one occasion when a family emergency occurred at home and the State Department was asked to find a traveling relative.

It takes just a few minutes to fill out a registration sheet. The sheet at the American Embassy asks for: name, hotel, occupation, members of family on the trip, passport number, date and place of birth, address in the United States, purpose of visit, duration of stay, and a list of the cities in the U.S.S.R. and in other Communist countries that you intend to visit.

MEDICAL CARE

There is a special clinic in Moscow where the ailing tourist can receive attention from knowledgeable, kindly Soviet doctors—most of them women. If necessary the doctor will come to the hotel. Tourists who require hospital care receive the very best accommodations, usually a private room, in hospitals which fall short of western standards in comfort and facilities. The cost is only a few dollars a day (usually less than a pound sterling). Advice: have your teeth checked before making a trip to Russia. Soviet dental techniques are years behind the West, and metal crowns are often used for front teeth.

There is a doctor at both the American and British Embassies. The man at the American Embassy is usually an Air Force officer; the British, a civilian. These physicians have their competent hands full treating the aches and pains of resident diplomats and their families, but if a traveler has a medical problem that he fears the Russians can't cope with because of language or other reasons, the young British or American doctor usually is generously willing to help.

INOCULATIONS

The Soviet Government does not require inoculations of any sort for a foreigner to enter the Soviet Union. However, the U.S. Public Health Service recommends typhus, typhoid, tetanus, and smallpox shots. Only the smallpox shot is necessary to get back into the United States. Be sure to receive a yellow card when you get your smallpox shot and this must be presented at the time of your return to the U.S. This inoculation is considered valid for a period of three years.

CLIMATE

The mildest weather in Moscow comes in April, May, and June. The winter months are extremely cold. The temperature range from November to March is usually from freezing (32 degrees Fahrenheit) to 15 degrees below zero. It gets down to 30 degrees below zero too. Obviously a warm coat (preferably lined with sheepskin, fur, or other insulating material) is essential as are lined boots that come over your ankles and a hat (earmuffs are useful too). Women should bring along a warm scarf to tie peasant-fashion over the head.

The summer months are hot (not uncommonly in the high 80s), but it cools off pleasantly at night. There are often thundershowers in the afternoons in July and August.

The average daily high temperature in Moscow during July is 71 degrees Fahrenheit. The average low in January is about five degrees Fahrenheit and the high temperature 14 degrees.

KEEPING UP WITH THE NEWS

If you enjoy getting away from it all, Russia will please you because it is so hard to keep up with what's going on in the world. However if you do want to know what is happening, there are several ways of doing it. The American Embassy issues a daily bulletin consisting of news items received by embassy radio. The British Embassy makes a daily transcript of a morning broadcast of the British Broadcasting Corporation. Tourists may receive copies of each simply by calling at the embassies.

The only English language newspaper published in Moscow is the *Moscow News* published on Wednesday and Saturday. It contains very little in the way of news but you may enjoy reading it anyway. It can be purchased at almost any hotel newsstand. The Communist *Daily Worker* of London also is sold.

May we suggest too that you have your interpreter-guide read you a few items from *Pravda, Izvestia,* or one of the other Soviet newspapers. You may find it instructive to hear the Soviet selection and slant of the news.

If you *must* have all the news even during a short stay in Russia, may we suggest that you subscribe to the Paris edition of the New York *Herald Tribune.* A subscription can be ordered from the Paris office of this newspaper, 21 Rue de Berri, Paris (8e), France. It takes about two days on the average for the airmail edition to reach

Moscow, but sometimes the paper arrives on the day after publication; it's not unusual for three or four days to elapse before you receive your copy. You may also bring in a short-wave radio receiver (the new portable transistor models are quite light).

MEETING RUSSIANS

It's easy to strike up conversations with Soviet citizens if you speak some Russian. In fact, it's likely that before your trip is over you will meet some Russians with whom you can converse in English. Conversations begin easily in theaters, stores, queues, art galleries, market places, and particularly on trains and ships. More and more frequently now tourists are getting invited to Russians' homes for a brief visit, but this still is rare.

E. J. Kahn, Jr., writing in *The New Yorker* magazine after a tourist trip to Russia related his experiences this way:

"It would be fairly safe, I think, to say that all English-speaking Russians are eager to chat with all English-speaking visitors. . . .

"Russians will accost a foreigner on any street. Recognition requires no special deductive skill; with our Western clothes, our cameras, and our gaping mouths, we can be detected half a block away. . . .

"Museums are a favorite hangout of Russians who want to practice their English."

QUESTIONS RUSSIANS WILL ASK YOU

Whenever you enter into a conversation with a Russian you are very likely to be asked a number of questions. The same questions turn up all the time. They are not necessarily asked out of animosity, but rather out of curiosity provoked by what the Russian reads in *Pravda*. You will do well to premeditate answers to questions like these:

Do Americans want war? Why do Americans want war? Why are Negroes mistreated in the United States? Why is the United States opposed to admitting the Chinese People's Republic to the United Nations? Why does the United States have military bases in countries along the Soviet Union's frontiers? What is your salary? Why don't most women work in the United States? Why is there so much unemployment in the United States? Why are there bread lines?

CARRYING OUT MAIL AND FILM FOR MOSCOW RESIDENTS

If you have made the acquaintance of any foreign correspondents or businessmen living in or visiting Moscow, the chances are that before you depart you will be asked to carry out letters or film. Since mail delivery takes so long and since the shipment of film and radio tapes is subject to complications, it has become normal routine for those who live and work in Moscow to seek the aid of travelers. Surely the Soviet authorities are aware of this. Only on very rare occasions have they taken away such items when inspecting the luggage of departing tourists. Of course each tourist must make his own choice on whether or not to help, but having sought the assistance of numerous tourists myself, I can only recommend that, if asked, you do agree.

Eugenia Sheppard, women's feature editor of the New York *Herald Tribune*, described her departure from Moscow in this amusing way:

"The day you leave Moscow is momentous. As you

go to the dining room for no breakfast, you are way-laid by a stranger who darts from behind a pillar and slips a little package into your hand. Even the electronic telephone gets through to you with urgent requests to carry out contraband.

"When I left my hotel room to catch the Paris plane, the inner soles of my shoes were papered with letters to home folks in Indiana. Thirty spools of film were con-cealed in the toes of my evening slippers. Half a dozen rolls of recorded tape nestled in the heart of my nylon nightie. Every woman has a secret longing to be a Mata Hari. For my country, where there are switchboard operators and stoppers in the washbasins, I was willing to languish in a Russian jail.

"I looked the customs inspector firmly in the face. His glance slid over me indifferently and he tossed my suitcase on a baggage cart. Not even martyrdom in Moscow. 'Nyet'."

Neither my remarks nor Miss Sheppard's should be taken as a suggestion that you carry out material for *Russians*. This would be dangerous for the Russian and perhaps for you.

TIPPING

Soviet newspapers and other publications try to dis-courage Soviet citizens from giving or accepting tips. As a matter of fact, tipping is considered bribery and bribery is illegal. Tipping is officially regarded as a "vestige of capitalistic degeneracy." From time to time a waitress or a porter will indignantly refuse a tip. But most often, particularly when circumspectly offered, tips are happily received. A ten per cent tip is con-sidered generous in a restaurant. Don't offer Intourist interpreter-guides money, but they will usually be glad to accept a token of appreciation such as perfume, stockings, phonograph records, neckties, or books.

MONEY

The ruble is the basic unit of Soviet money.
There are 100 kopecks in one ruble.
One American dollar is worth 10 rubles.
One Canadian dollar is worth 10 rubles and 30 kopecks.
One British pound is worth 28 rubles.
Kopecks come in coins of one, two, three, five, ten, fifteen, and twenty-kopeck denominations. As in the case of ruble paper bills, the value of coins is clearly marked. Ruble bills come in values of one, three, five, ten, twenty-five, fifty, and one hundred rubles.

CONVERSION DATA

The Soviet Union uses the metric system of measurement. Here are formulae for converting Soviet measurements into more familiar units:

1 centimeter = .4 inch. Multiply centimeters by .4 to convert to inches.

1 meter = 39. inches. Multiply meters by 39 to convert to inches.

1 kilometer = .62 mile. Multiply kilometers by .62 to convert to miles. Or, if it's any easier, take ⅝ of the number of kilometers to obtain the approximate number of miles.

1 liter = 1.06 quarts. Multiply liters by 1.06 to convert to quarts.

1 kilogram = 2.2 pounds. Multiply kilograms by 2.2 to convert to pounds. It may be more simple to multiply kilograms by 2 and add 10 per cent.

1 hectare = 2.471 acres. Multiply hectares by 2.471 to convert to acres. Or, for a close approximation, multiply hectares by $2\frac{1}{2}$.

To convert Centigrade to Fahrenheit, multiply by 9, divide by 5 and add 32 degrees.

To convert Fahrenheit to Centigrade, subtract 32 degrees, multiply by 5 and divide by 9.

REPETITION

Repetition in the pages of *Travel Guide to Russia* is intentional. The object is to make every section stand on its own feet. For example, *shashlik* is described in several places as pieces of lamb broiled on a spit. There are several references to tipping, to the cities open to tourists, and so on. In each case the repetitiveness is intended to save the reader the trouble of looking elsewhere in the book for additional information on any particular subject.

AN EXPLANATION

There are a variety of ways to transliterate Russian letters into English. The word for the pre-revolutionary Russian ruler may be written Czar or Tsar. The complicating fact of the matter is that there are letters in the Russian alphabet that have no equivalent in English and vice versa. For example, the Russian letter that looks exactly like the English X is not pronounced that way at all. The Russian X is pronounced gutturally as if clearing the throat. The usual way to render this in English is by the letters KH. Khrushchev's name starts with an X in Russian.

There are sounds in Russian which are best rendered by the English letters I or II or Y depending on the Russian letter. For simplicity's sake, II is practically ignored in this book and I and Y are used interchange-ably.

Helpfulness to the traveler is the object of this *Travel Guide to Russia*. Simplicity rather than scientific pre-cision is the rule in putting Russian into English or Eng-lish into Russian. I've been guided by the consideration of how the tourist can most easily get where he wants to go or buy or order what he wants rather than whether the rules of scholarship in transliteration are strictly ob-served.

STREETS AND ADDRESSES

Simplicity is also the rule in giving streets and ad-dresses. Thus, the words *Ulitsa* and Street, which mean the same thing, are used interchangeably. For instance, Moscow's main street is precisely transliterated as *Ulitsa Gorkogo*, but you will find it referred to as Gorky Street (which is what it is in English) or Gorky *Ulitsa*, which takes the liberty of mixing Russian and English. Either way the aim is to help the tourist find his way.

Similarly *Pereulok* and Alley are used interchangeably as are *Plochad* (which can also be transliterated as *Plo-shchad*) and Square. *Prospekt* means Avenue and *Chausee* means Drive. The word *Most* means Bridge.

Russian street numbers can be confusing. For ex-ample, it's not unusual for a building with several en-trances to have one street number for the entire build-ing with the entrances numbered separately—entrance number 1, entrance number 2, and so on. Sometimes a street address consists of two numbers divided by a slash mark such as 12/18. This is usually a building which has replaced several old buildings and retains the former structures' inclusive numbers. Oftentimes numbers are nowhere near an entrance, but rather are posted at one end of the edifice, usually inconveniently high.

LANGUAGE

You will enjoy your visit to Russia a great deal more if you learn even a few words of Russian. In each hotel's Service Bureau there are clerks and interpreters who speak English varying from fair to excellent. However, among the general population there are considerably fewer people than in Western European countries who speak English or any other foreign language. German is the most commonly spoken of foreign tongues. This is in part an inheritance of the German invasion of the last war. Also before the war French and German were the most commonly studied foreign languages.

Even without any knowledge of Russian you will be able to get along perfectly well in Russia with the help of Intourist interpreter-guides. The personnel in Intourist hotels such as waiters, waitresses, key desk clerks and chambermaids attend classes in fundamental English in anticipation of the growing influx of English-speaking tourists.

It's a self-satisfying experience to be able to read the signs on stores, restaurants, and other buildings even if you can't always understand what the signs say. Although the Russian Cyrillic alphabet is quite different from the Roman alphabet it is a delightful surprise that certain words are the same. For example, this word appears on certain shops:ФОТО. It is pronounced "Foto" in Russian, and, as you've probably guessed, it is the sign for a photo shop.

The uninitiated visitor will read the word, РЕСТОРАН, the way it looks to an English-speaking person. However the word is not "pectopah," but, as an elementary knowledge of the Russian alphabet indicates, it is pronounced "restoran," and means "restaurant."

Given below is the Russian alphabet with phonetic indication of how each letter is pronounced, and this is followed by a brief glossary of useful, basic words and phrases in Russian.

ALPHABET

А, а	pronounced	as	a	in	father
Б, б	"	"	b	"	book
В, в	"	"	v	"	vote
Г, г	"	"	g	"	good
Д, д	"	"	d	"	day
Е, е	"	"	ye	"	yes
Ж, ж	"	"	z [s]	"	pleasure
З, з	"	"	z	"	zone, please
И, и	"	"	ee	"	meet
Й, й	"	"	y	"	boy
К, к	"	"	k	"	kind
Л, л	"	"	l	"	full, gold
М, м	"	"	m	"	man
Н, н	"	"	n	"	no
О, о	"	"	a	"	law, all
П, п	"	"	p	"	pen
Р, р	"	"	r	"	burr
С, с	"	"	s	"	speak
Т, т	"	"	t	"	too
У, у	"	"	oo	"	something between oo in book and school
Ф, ф	"	"	f	"	fire
Х, х	"	"	kh [ch]	"	loch (Scottish)
Ц, ц	"	"	tz	"	quartz
Ч, ч	"	"	ch	"	lunch (softer)
Ш, ш	"	"	sh	"	short
Щ, щ	"	"	shch	"	(no sample word)
Ъ, ъ	"				(no sound but rather sign of separation between sounds)
Ы, ы	"	"	i	"	ill
Ь, ь	"				(no sound but rather sign of separation and to denote soft consonants)
Э, э	"	"	e	"	men
Ю, ю	"	"	yu	"	you
Я, я	"	"	ya	"	yard

USEFUL WORDS AND PHRASES

ENGLISH:	RUSSIAN (capital letters are stressed):
Hello	ZDRAHST-voo—tee
Good morning	DAW-broy OO-tra
Good afternoon	DAW-brih DAYN
Good evening	DAW-brih VECH-eer
Excuse me	eez-ve-NEE-tee
Please (or) You're Welcome	pa-ZHA-loo-sta
Yes	DA
No	NYET
Where	G-DEH
Where is the toilet?	G-DEH too-a-LET?
To the right	na-PRA-va
To the left	na-LEV-a
Straight ahead	PRYA-ma
What is this?	SHTAW ET-a?
How much?	SKAWL-ka?
What time is it?	ka-TAW-rih CHAHSS?
Five o'clock	PYAT chih-SAWF
When	kahg-DA
Yesterday	f-chee-RA
Today	see-VAWD-nya
Tomorrow	ZAHF-tra
Sunday	va-skree-SAYN-ya
Monday	pa-nee-DEL-neek
Tuesday	F-TAWR-neek
Wednesday	sree-DA
Thursday	cheet-VAYRK
Friday	PYAT-neet-sa
Saturday	soo-BAW-ta
What's your name?	KAHK VAHSS za-VOOT?
My name is ——	meen-YA za-VOOT ——
I am an American (Englishman, Canadian)	YA a-mee-ree-KA-neets (an-gli-CHA-nin, KA-NA-dets)
Good-by	da svee-DAHN-ya
Thank you	spa-SEE-ba
How far is it?	KAHK da-lee-KAW?

ENGLISH:	RUSSIAN (capital letters are stressed):
I want ———	YA ha-CHOO ———
I want water	YA ha-CHOO va-DIH
Doctor	DAWK-tur
A glass	sta-KAHN
A fork	VEEL-koo
A knife	NAWJ
A spoon	LAWSH-koo
A plate	ta-REL-koo
A blanket	a-dee-YA-la
A towel	pa-la-TEN-tsa
Paper	boo-MA-gee
A pencil	ka-rahn-DAHSH
Hot water	gar-YA-choy va-DIH
Soap	MIL-a
One	ah-DEEN
Two	DVA
Three	TREE
Four	chih-TIH-ree
Five	PYAT
Six	SHAYST
Seven	SEM
Eight	VAW-seem
Nine	DAY-veet
Ten	DAY-seet
A hundred	STAW

MISCELLANEOUS HINTS

If your trip is made in winter you should have a fur hat both for warmth and in order not to stick out in a crowd as a foreigner. However, Russia is *not* the best place to purchase such a hat. If you come through Copenhagen, Stockholm, or Helsinki you will find fur hats of better quality and at lower prices than in Russia.

The water is safe to drink in big cities like Moscow, Leningrad, Kiev, Odessa, Kharkov, Stalingrad, and Minsk and even in important smaller towns such as Sochi and Yalta. However, in out-of-the-way collective farm villages it is safer to drink bottled mineral water.

Milk is pasteurized but is neither tuberculin tested nor bottled in a sanitary manner. Most Western foreigners living in Moscow use powdered milk shipped in from abroad, especially for children. Inconsistent though it is, most of these same foreign residents do not hesitate to eat Russian ice cream which is made from this very milk. Advice: if you're in Russia for only a short trip and can get along without milk, you're better off doing so. Fresh vegetables and fruits in hotels and other big restaurants are safe to eat.

Be careful of Moscow traffic. Main streets are broad, often more than 13 lanes wide (the center lane provides an island of refuge). Cars travel at high speed, but drivers do obey traffic signals. Even when crossing with a green light, it's necessary to be cautious because turns are often permitted by cars coming from the other direction at crossroads.

Also on rainy or snowy days watch out for the slopes that lead from sidewalks to street at many intersections. These wedges of asphalt are intended to provide a sort of ramp for women pushing baby carriages and for the infirm who find difficulty stepping off and on a curb. Actually, though, they constitute a hazard for pedestrians.

Rest rooms, by a happy coincidence, are marked by the same symbol in Russian as in English—at least for the men's rest room. The letter M is used on the door. Ladies should enter the other door which will be marked with the first letter of the word "women" in the Russian alphabet—Ж.

Unfortunately in many places, including the Bolshoi Theatre, the men's and ladies' rooms are at opposite ends of the building so that you're on your own.

Rest rooms in some prominent theaters, restaurants, museums, hotels, and other public places are usually kept clean, but there are many unpleasant exceptions. Usually only a damp towel is suspended from the wall. The soap provided is incapable of producing a lather and has a sickly sweet disinfectant odor more suitable for scrubbing floors than for your hands. Toilet tissue is seldom available.

By the way, don't be startled, men, if you find a woman attendant at work cleaning the men's room. Ignore her; and she will you.

The time difference between New York and Moscow is eight hours. Thus when it is noon in New York it is 8 P.M. in Moscow. The Russians do not observe Daylight Saving Time; when summer time is in effect in the United States there is only seven hours difference between Moscow and New York. There is three hours difference between London and Moscow; when it is noon in London it is 3 P.M. in Moscow.

Although when you are in Moscow your sight-seeing and hotel arrangements as well as your travel arrangements are entirely in the hands of Intourist, it may interest you to know that American Express does have a representative in the Metropole Hotel. Most foreign airlines which fly into Moscow also maintain representatives in the capital. They can be useful in arranging continuing reservations for you once you leave Russia but your flights from Moscow or other Soviet cities must be arranged with Intourist even though you may be flying on a foreign airline. These are the addresses of several foreign airlines in Moscow:

Scandinavian Airlines System, National Hotel. Telephone: 29 99 17.

Air France, Metropole Hotel. Telephone: 94 20 00.

K.L.M. Royal Dutch Airlines, Leningradskaya Hotel. Telephone: 90 11 40.

If there are children with you, you may be worried about babysitters. Russians love children. A chambermaid or the key desk attendant on your floor will very likely be pleased to look in frequently on the sleeping children, but it is difficult to hire a babysitter. Ask your Service Bureau.

The Russian word for "Entrance" looks like this: ВХОД. "Exit" is ВЫХОД.

The Russian words for "Don't Smoke" look like this: НЕ КУРИТЬ.

The public holidays observed in Russia when some stores and most government offices are likely to be closed are: January 1, New Year's; May 1 and 2, International Labor Day; November 7 and 8, Revolution Anniversary, and December 5, Constitution Day.

There are no facilities for renting cars in Russia to drive yourself.

Don't be surprised: to see pictures and statues of Stalin (there used to be many more before Khrushchev's famous speech denouncing his predecessor); to see Russians spending money in high-priced restaurants despite the steep cost of necessities like clothing and shoes (although wages are low, many Russians can afford to splurge on a night out because rent is never more than five per cent of the head of a family's wages and there's no need to save for medical care or education because both are free); to hear Communists say "God bless you," or "God willing" (it's just a figure of speech, not a lack of atheistic conviction); to hear Russians ask you extremely personal questions (it's not rudeness but rather a naive, unsophisticated curiosity).

Don't be surprised either to hear a high-crowned fur hat referred to as a "Macmillan" (the name caught on as a result of the white fur hat the British Prime Minister wore on his visit to Russia); to see fenced-in pigeon-feeding areas (there are 70,000 amateur pigeon fanciers in Moscow and there's a fine for a motorist who runs one of the birds down); to hear your Intourist interpreter-guide complain about the long queues or the housing shortage (it's not that she's disloyal, but rather that certain shortcomings are considered fair game for criticism by *Izvestia* as well as Intourist).

PLEASE WRITE

After your trip to Russia please do write us any comments, suggestions or criticisms you may have on *Travel Guide to Russia*. We would warmly welcome your reactions to our recommendations of museums, stores, restaurants, and so on. This will help make future editions more useful to other travelers to Russia.

The address is: Irving R. Levene, c/o Doubleday and Co., Inc., 575 Madison Avenue, New York 22, New York.

CHAPTER THREE

A Quick History of Russia

There's one version of Nikita Khrushchev's famous speech denouncing Stalin that is not likely to find its way into history books. The denunciation was delivered in 1956 at a Kremlin session of the Twentieth Communist Party Congress. Khrushchev charged Stalin with brutality, cowardice, near-treason.

As Khrushchev was speaking—so this apocryphal story goes—a note was sent up to the rostrum. "Why didn't you do something about all of this while Stalin lived?" asked the note.

Khrushchev read the note, and then sternly demanded that the person who sent it rise.

Dead quiet reigned in the hall. There was no reply. Everyone was afraid to stir, to breathe, lest the movement betray him.

"Now," smirked Khrushchev, "you know why I said nothing while Stalin lived!"

(When this story was mentioned to Khrushchev at a luncheon at the National Press Club in Washington, the Soviet Premier became obviously angry, called the story a provocation, and refused to comment on it.)

In Russian history fact is even stranger than fiction, and much stranger things actually have happened and still do.

For example, a Russian dictator decided to send a group of university students to England to acquire knowledge that might be of use to Russia. The students went.

But not all came back. To the Russian ruler's rage, some of the group chose to stay in the Western world.

These defections occurred not under Communism but more than 350 years ago. The ruler was Boris Godunov who governed Russia from 1590 until 1605.

The moral of this story may be that nothing really is new in Russia: it has all happened before. Stated broadly, this is the claim of some historians and to a limited extent it's true.

This chapter is a quick history of Russia. It is intended to be easy reading, it makes no pretense at scholarship, and it touches only on the highlights of the past that will often be reflected in the sights a present-day visitor to Russia sees. Knowledge of even a little Russian history will make a week or a month or a year in the Soviet Union all the more meaningful and fascinating. Knowledge of history also is a great asset in an understanding of the Russian people—their national characteristics and prejudices.

However, if history even in capsule form bores you to death this chapter can be skipped. May I suggest, though, that if you choose to bypass history, you do glance at the section on "Basic Facts" which follows immediately and the section on "The Personality of the Soviet People" at the end of this chapter.

BASIC FACTS

Before wading into Russia's past, there are a few basic facts about the present that will be useful.

First of all, the country's name. It is the Union of Soviet Socialist Republics. More often it is referred to simply as the Soviet Union. The initials are U.S.S.R.

The U.S.S.R. consists of 15 republics.

These republics are: Russia, the Ukraine, Byelorussia,

Estonia, Lithuania, Latvia, Georgia, Armenia, Azerbaijan, Uzbekistan, Tadzhikistan, Kazakhstan, Turkmenistan, Kirghizia, and Moldavia.

The largest, most populous and most important republic is Russia. Its full name is the Russian Socialist Federated Soviet Republic.

It's common practice outside of the U.S.S.R. to refer to the whole country as Russia. This is not correct. Russia is only one part of the country. It sometimes confuses the tourist to hear a government-employed guide say, "I am not a Russian." The guide then explains that he or she is a Ukrainian or a Georgian, or perhaps a Jew or a Tartar. These and a number of other peoples in the U.S.S.R. are each considered separate "nationalities." The nationality of each Soviet citizen is inscribed in his identity papers (known as a "passport").

Each nationality has its language. There are more than sixty different languages spoken in the U.S.S.R., and numerous dialects besides. Nationalities have their own dances, costumes, customs, and in some cases are permitted by Moscow to have their own newspapers, literature, and theater. However, all of this exists under the ever dominant flag of the U.S.S.R., and divided loyalties are neither encouraged nor tolerated. First and foremost, in the eyes of the Soviet state a person is a citizen of the U.S.S.R. and nationalism (other than Soviet nationalism) in any form is forcefully discouraged.

The country is enormous. It covers one-sixth of the surface of the world. The U.S.S.R. is bigger than the United States, Canada, and the United Kingdom combined. In fact, Canada and China could fit into the Soviet Union's frontiers with a bit of space to spare.

The population of this vast land (at the latest count in January 1959) is 208,826,000. There are 12 marriages every year for each 1000 people. Twenty-five babies are born each year per 1000 people. Each year death claims

7.5 Soviet citizens of every 1000. This is the lowest death rate in the world. Thus, the population is increasing at the rate of 3,500,000 a year.

The birth rate for the United States with its 176,000,-000 people is 24.4 babies per 1000 of population. The death rate is 9.4 per 1000 people.

The birth rate for the United Kingdom with its population of 52,000,000 is 16.5 per 1000 people. The death rate is 11.5 per 1000.

There are three cities in the U.S.S.R. with populations of over one million people. According to the 1959 census Moscow is the largest with 5,032,000 people. Leningrad has 2,888,000. Kiev has over a million.

Because of dreadful losses during World War II there are now 20,000,000 more women than men in the Soviet Union. The gap exists among those members of the population who were over eighteen at the end of World War II, and there is an equal number of men and women under the age of thirty-two.

PREHISTORIC ORIGIN

There are several theories to explain the origin of the Russian people. The State Historical Museum, which you can visit in Moscow, devotes many of its halls to support the theory that the Russians originated from prehistoric tribes which dwelt hundreds of thousands of years ago on territory that now is part of the U.S.S.R. and whose arrowheads are on display. Another theory says that the Russians originated from tribes that migrated some 1500 years ago from what is now the Balkan area in the eastern Mediterranean. These people have been named "Slavs" and various migrations of Slavs, traced by language similarity, are believed to have been the forebears of not only the Russians but also of the Poles, the Czechs, the Slovaks, the Serbs, the Croats, the Slovenes, the Bulgarians, the Ukrainians, and the Byelorussians.

800–882: FIRST RUSSIAN STATE

By whatever means they got there, the people living in the vast regions of what is now Russia were in the beginning separate tribes, many of them nomadic.

In the ninth century the first organized semblance of a state was created. Here again the exact events by which it developed is lost in the past.

The version favored by chauvinistic Soviet authorities has it that certain Slavic tribes organized themselves into the first state. This was near the present city of Kiev on the Dnieper River. Kiev received its name from Prince Kiy, leader of a tribe of Slavs known as the Poliane (who are represented in exciting dances in several Soviet ballets you can see at the Bolshoi Theatre in Moscow). The Poliane were noted for their talents in administration, trade, and handicraft. As early as the eighth century they had maintained active trade ties with other Slavic tribes. Kiev was favorably situated on an important river trade route and was visited by merchants from Byzantium, Scandinavia, Arabia, and Armenia. The Kiev merchants traveled as far as India and China.

It was also in the ninth century that the state of Novgorod was organized. It is believed that Scandinavian warriors and traders known as Varangians found their way into this region because of its natural waterways to the trading center of Constantinople. They then dispatched one of their princes named Rurik into this region to form a state. However, some historians believe that the Varangians did not *impose* their organizing ability on the tribes around Novgorod—lying about one quarter of the way from Leningrad to Moscow. Rather the Slavic tribes themselves, having no experience in community organization of a higher level, actually sought the advice of the more advanced foreign traders who passed through their lands.

This would not be the last time that the Russians sought foreign help. Later in the 1700s Czar Peter I borrowed architects, engineers, designers, and other technicians from the Western world. The Communists repeated this in the 1930s when their all-out industrialization drive began. Later, under Khrushchev, the Soviet authorities uninhibitedly sought to borrow foreign experience.

It was in this period that the roots of the name "Russia" came into being. The native Slavs called the Varangians by the name of "Rus" or by some variation of that root. It was from the name "Rus" that the word Russia developed to eventually describe the country as a whole.

The name "Rus" probably comes from the word *Ruotsi* which was used by the Finns to describe the Varangians. The word *Ruotsi* was a corruption of the Swedish word *Rothsmenn*, or seafarers.

882–988: THE GROWTH OF KIEV

The Novgorod ruler Rurik was succeeded by a relative named Oleg, an aggressively expansionist prince, who conquered much of the region around Novgorod southward as far as the hilly banks of the Dnieper River. In 882 A.D. Oleg shifted his capital to the thriving walled city of Kiev.

Under Oleg, Kiev grew in prosperity and in military strength. If you visit Kiev it is interesting to recall that this was Russia's greatest city even before Moscow was settled. Oleg's successors, who followed his energetic policies, included a woman named Olga—a name still popular among Russian women. If one is looking for origins, it may be that the domineering attitude and role

of Russian women in everyday life stem from this Olga
herself.

988: RUSSIA BECOMES CHRISTIAN

The next important event in the history of the develop-
ing Russian State with its capital at Kiev occurred in
988 A.D. This is a date learned by Soviet school children
as assiduously as American school children learn the
date of the Declaration of Independence or British school
children the date of the Battle of Hastings. This is the
date that Christianity came to Russia.

This is the way it happened. Prince Vladimir I who
reigned from 980 to 1015 A.D. had helped the Emperor
of Constantinople put down a rebellion. In return, the
Kiev Prince asked the emperor for his daughter's hand in
marriage. The emperor was reluctant to grant her to a
pagan, and the condition was set that Vladimir must accept Christianity. Vladimir did so, and thus began the
introduction of Christianity into this vast land.

A charming but not completely reliable account has
found its way into Russian legend. Documents of the fourteenth century kept in Kiev, written by a monk, report
that when Prince Vladimir decided to bring religion to his
pagan realm, he sent envoys to capitals of the Moslem,
Christian, and Jewish faiths. Vladimir is said to have been
much attracted to the Moslem religion, but when he
learned that Moslems were forbidden to drink alcohol,
Vladimir quickly rejected any idea of accepting Islam
for his people. It would seem that then as now wine, if
not vodka, was very much a part of Russian life. This
ancient account says that the prince was much awed
by the accounts of his ambassadors about the pageantry
of the Greek Orthodox religion. The elaborate icons which
the emissaries brought back also greatly impressed Vladi-

mir. It was like being in heaven, Vladimir's envoys told him, to witness a Greek Orthodox service. Vladimir decided to adopt this colorful religion.

Although under Communism the influence of the Church has declined, the results of Vladimir's decision are still to be seen. Throughout Russia Byzantine influences in art and architecture are in evidence. The Communists themselves seem to have been influenced by the deep-rooted Church in their use of great spectacles as a means of satisfying the masses. Obviously it was not the Romans alone who believed in bread and circuses.

988–1169: DECLINE OF KIEV

Kiev grew in importance as a center of agriculture as well as of commerce. Furs, hides, honey wax, and slaves were Kiev's chief exports. However, jealousies among princes of other Russian cities led to frequent battles and in 1169 A.D. a rival Russian ruler from the city of Vladimir attacked Kiev, conquered it, and proclaimed the city of Vladimir, 500 miles to the northeast of Kiev, as the new capital. This Vladimir conqueror was Andrei Bogulubski. He was the son of Prince Yuri Dolgoruky who had founded Moscow in 1147. A statue of Prince Yuri stands in Moscow. At this time of the decline of Kiev and the ascendancy of Vladimir, Moscow was still only a small village at the juncture of two rivers.

1169–1328: INVASION OF THE TARTARS

Even a greater blow to Kiev's supremacy was struck a little more than a half century later when ferocious fighters from Central Asia spread into the Russian lands. These Tartars, the so-called Golden Horde, overran Kiev and other cities of Russia. Only distant Novgorod and some other northern areas escaped Tartar conquest. The Tartars completed their conquest in an amazingly short period of time between 1237 and 1240.

Despite persistent, periodic attempts by the Russians to free themselves from Tartar occupation and taxation, these invaders managed to hold sway over Russia for more than 250 years. This long occupation left its mark. There was a certain amount of intermarriage, and there is a saying that "if you scratch a Russian you find a Tartar." This is intended to indicate that the Russians acquired many of the Tartar characteristics of cruelty, Oriental slowness and suspicion in dealings of any sort whether political or commercial. What is more, the tide of the Tartar invasion from Asia, as well as subsequent invasions from Russia's western frontiers, instilled in the Soviet people a neurotic fear of encroachments on their land. This suspicion and chronic fear is reflected in Soviet diplomatic relations today.

The nature of the Tartar conquest varied from city to city. In the case of Moscow the Tartars did not occupy the city, although in their initial conquest they did burn it to the ground. This might be seen as a forerunner of the great Moscow fire which marked Napoleon's invasion some six centuries later. However, in subsequent years Moscow actually benefited from, and prospered under, the Tartars. These Mongol conquerors appointed Grand Dukes of Moscow as their collectors of tribute and taxes from the other cities of Russia. The prosperity that this role brought to the Grand Dukes of Muscovy (as the state around Moscow was called) enabled them eventually to outfit an army for conquest against their benefactors, the Tartars. The role of Moscow as the tax collector for the rest of the country is seen to have been born in this ancient era.

In 1380 a Muscovy Duke named Dmitri led his army against the Tartars well south of Moscow on the plains of the Don River at a place called Kulikovo. Dmitri won the battle but it was not a decisive encounter. It did not cause the Tartar Golden Horde to withdraw back to Asia but it did greatly encourage the Russians in their struggle against the foreign conquerors and did serve to reduce the aggressiveness of the Tartars.

In fact, the Muscovy rulers began conquests of their own against their brother Russians. Feeling secure against new oppression from the Tartars, the Muscovy rulers gradually absorbed the other Russian princely states including Novgorod which had escaped invasion by the Tartars.

1328–1359: IVAN I AND II

Actually the word "Czar" did not come into use until the mid-1500s. At that time a Grand Duke, Ivan IV, assumed the title, derived from the word "Caesar." The title of Grand Duke had been bestowed by the Tartars.

This brief history can only touch lightly on some of the more important Russian rulers whose imprints you will see in buildings and paintings during a visit to Russia.

There was Ivan I, who reigned from 1328 to 1340. He was known as Ivan Kalita (meaning "money bag"). He got the nickname because of his financial shrewdness, his able administration, and his acquisitive tendencies. Ivan Money Bag actually sent his troops to fight as allies of the Tartars. This was in a Tartar campaign to avenge a premature attempt at liberation by the Russian town of Tver.

Ivan I operated on the thesis that if he could enjoy

the approval of the Tartar Khan ("Prince") by prompt payment of levies, he could strengthen his domain for eventual liberation from the Tartar's bondage. Ivan I used resources to buy back Russian hostages from the Tartars and he put these hostages to work in agriculture. The Tartars entrusted Ivan with the collection of their tribute from the other Russian states. If he had difficulty in extracting the extremely heavy tributes, Tartar armies were at his disposal to enforce payments. Obviously this was a powerful stimulus and catalyst in the growth of Moscow's dominance and pre-eminence over the rest of the country.

Ivan Money Bag left his successors an economic and military base on which Moscow further developed. His great-grandson, Basil I, expanded Muscovy's territory.

1462–1505: IVAN III

By 1480 Ivan III felt strong enough to refuse to pay further taxes to the Tartars, camped at the edges of Russia.

Ivan III had married the niece of the last Byzantine Emperor Constantine XI, not long before Constantinople fell in 1453 to the Moslem Turks. Centuries earlier when the capital of Rome, overrun by barbarians from Northern Europe, had been transferred to Constantinople, this city became known as "the second Rome." Now with the defeat of Constantinople, Ivan III, claiming lineal descent through marriage, proclaimed Moscow as "the third Rome." He intended it to be the center of the Orthodox faith.

Ivan III enjoyed the fruit of the efforts of his predecessors. The long occupation and oppressive rule of the Tartars had unified the Russian people in their suffering if not in political organization. The time was ripe for such political unity. Even so strong, and until now independent, a state as Novgorod with its vast territories was absorbed with comparative ease in gradual stages by Ivan III between 1465 and 1488.

1533–1584: IVAN THE TERRIBLE

In 1533 Ivan IV succeeded to the throne. He is better known as Ivan the Terrible, a man of ferocious temper, enormous energy, and great accomplishments. Ivan the Terrible sent his armies against the Khans of the Tartar-occupied cities of Kazan, 450 miles east of Moscow, and against Astrakhan, more than double that distance to the southeast at the mouth of the Volga River on the Caspian Sea. Before setting out on their crucial campaign, Ivan's armies stopped at the monastery of Zagorsk, which tourists can visit some forty miles from Moscow. Ivan the Terrible's armies were victorious. The Tartars fled, their long rule over Russia was ended, and the pre-eminence of Moscow was assured.

During Ivan the Terrible's reign from 1533 to 1584, Russia established trade with England. Cossacks (Czarist border troops) conquered parts of Siberia beyond the Ural Mountains which separate Asiatic from European Russia. Ivan IV established a special police force responsible only to him. It terrorized the opposition.

Ivan built the magnificent St. Basil's Cathedral, which stands in Red Square, as an act of thanksgiving for his victory over the Tartars.

This ruthless, purposeful ruler killed his eldest son in a fit of temper, and this act is depicted in one of the most famous paintings in Moscow's Tretyakov Art Gallery.

1598–1613: BORIS GODUNOV AND
HIS SUCCESSORS

With his eldest son dead, Ivan the Terrible was succeeded by his son Feodor who ruled badly from 1584 until 1598; the actual power behind the throne was a boyar (a member of the nobleman class) named Boris Godunov whose reign inspired a famous opera you can see at the Bolshoi Theatre in Moscow.

Boris, elected by the boyars in the absence of an heir, ruled from 1598 to 1603. It is believed that Boris had Ivan the Terrible's only surviving son, a child named Dmitri, murdered, thus eliminating any successors to the throne. The official version was that Dmitri died as the result of injuring himself during a seizure. Whichever version is true, the fact is that a pretender representing himself as Dmitri, the rightful heir to the throne, appeared in Poland. With the help of Polish interests (who financed an army) and dissatisfied Russian boyars (who acted as a "fifth column"), Dmitri succeeded in establishing himself as Czar for a very brief period from 1605 to 1606. He was murdered by a boyar who proclaimed himself Czar Basil IV; his reign spanned the years 1606 to 1610.

But Basil IV was not unanimously accepted and there were rival claimants to the throne. A situation of near anarchy prevailed. And in 1609 Poland invaded Russia resulting in a war which lasted until 1612.

1613–1917: THE ROMANOV DYNASTY

Russian history has a way of repeating itself. The assassinations and intrigues already recounted have continued into Communist times. There is nothing new about the purges. They had their precedents under the Czars. There is nothing new about the terror of Stalin; it had its precedents under the Tartars and under such rulers as Ivan the Terrible.

It is also true, and has been true through Russian history, that the Russians unite in time of trouble. This they did in the face of the Polish conquest. The Poles were finally driven out and a new Czar was elected in 1613. He was Mikhail Romanov who ruled from 1613 to 1645. He was coronated in the same Kremlin Cathedral that tourists can visit today and he was buried in another Kremlin Cathedral where his tomb may be seen along with those of other Czars.

Romanov's election by the privileged few of Russia of that day came about because of lack of agreement on any other candidate. Romanov was a member of the landed gentry and he had the support of the Church. Perhaps most important in view of the Russian love for hereditary links, was Romanov's connection through marriage with Ivan the Terrible who was his great-uncle. The Romanov line of Czars ruled until the revolution in 1917.

1682–1725: PETER THE GREAT

Mikhail was followed by Alexei Mikhailovich who ruled from 1645 to 1676 and by Feodor II who ruled from 1676 to 1682. Their reigns were marked by wars with Poland, Sweden, and Turkey. These wars imposed a heavy burden on the country and resulted in much discontent. There were peasant uprisings which were omens of revolution to come. In 1682, Peter I, better known as Peter the Great, was the successor to the throne when Feodor II died. However because of his youth, his half-sister Sophia, appointed as regent, resisted relinquishing power but she was finally sent to a nunnery in 1689.

Peter the Great's period of power until 1725 was one of the most fruitful periods for Russia. Even the Communists who hold small love or respect for the Czars, regard Peter as a "progressive" and recount his achievements with an obvious measure of respect. Peter had spent part of his youth in Germany and his early contact with the advanced Western way of life left a deep mark on his future conduct. In 1697 and 1698, he toured Europe and returned to backward Russia with a determination to Europeanize and modernize it. Skilled craftsmen, artisans, engineers, architects, and people of every profession who might benefit Russia were attracted by Peter's offers of generous wages. They came from England, France, Germany, Holland, and other countries of Western Europe.

Among other things, Peter introduced tobacco and smoking into Russia. He learned fourteen trades.

Peter was not without opposition and he too resorted to mass extermination by purges of the more conservative boyars and the *streltsi*, the officers of the palace guard.

The Baltic Coast was at this time controlled by the Swedes and thus Russia's access to the sea was blocked. In a series of battles Peter secured a stretch of coastland of the Gulf of Finland which forms the eastern end of the Baltic, and began building St. Petersburg, named for St. Peter. The influence of London, Amsterdam, Copenhagen, Paris, and Vienna can be seen in St. Petersburg (since renamed Leningrad) even today. However, the building of St. Petersburg and Peter's other projects did not serve to improve the lot of the peasants who constituted the greatest portion of the population of this agricultural land.

With Peter's death in 1725, there was a dismal period

in Soviet history with a series of rulers each less deserving and less able than the other. That great historian Sir Bernard Pares in his definitive work, A *History of Russia*, dismissed Peter the Great's successors this way: "Of the six immediate successors of Peter I, three are women, one a boy of twelve, one a babe of one, and one an idiot. Through the barrack capital of St. Petersburg, situated outside Russian soil and cut off from the life of the Russian people, brainless or squalid adventurers succeed each other."

1741–1761: ELIZABETH

Elizabeth was the younger of Peter the Great's daughters. She seized the throne from her sister Anne by leading a company of soldiers into the Winter Palace one night. Anne had spent most of her brief reign as regent indoors, seldom completely dressed, usually gossiping with a friend or quarreling with her husband.

Elizabeth was far more effectual—but also extravagant. During her reign Russia's territory was expanded at the expense of Sweden and Finland. She gave full support to her principal adviser Count Ivan Shuvalov to carry out his enlightened educational program. The first Russian university was founded. This was Moscow University, opened in 1755. Elizabeth is described this way by Sir Bernard Pares: "With a large frame, an easygoing nature and a lively disposition, living in apartments which were always untidy, possessing as many as fifteen thousand dresses, seeking her pleasure in the simplest company such as old peasant women, very Russian and assiduously Orthodox, she at the same time left her mark on Russian history by an edict abolishing forever the death penalty, though it was retained later for military and sometimes for political offenses." Her floor is said to have been littered with unpaid bills and her French milliner refused her further credit.

1762–1796: CATHERINE THE GREAT

In 1762, Catherine II, better known as Catherine the Great, came to power through the intrigues of a group of noblemen and the army which succeeded in dethroning her husband, Peter III.

Unlike most of the other Russian rulers, Catherine traveled occasionally through her realm and thus had greater contact with her people. She had numerous lovers and there are mansions and palaces in Leningrad that she built for some of her favorites. However, her reign was highlighted with plots and uprisings against her. Catherine dealt with numerous pretenders to the throne usually by having them exiled to the mines of Siberia; sometimes they were publicly beaten or even branded. Sir Bernard Pares describes her this way: "Catherine rose at five, lit her own fire at six, and often worked fifteen hours a day; she was particularly considerate to her servants. Her methods of work were Russian, not German: great bouts at a given task, leaving many gaps —full of interest and enthusiasm while they lasted."

She was a brilliant woman, well read, and her letters reflect her intelligence.

Catherine tried to initiate some much needed reforms in Russia and she introduced pharmacies into the country.

1801–1825: CZAR ALEXANDER I

Catherine ruled until her death on November 17, 1796. Her son Paul was strangled by conspirators in 1801 in a plot involving his own son Alexander I who came to power and ruled from 1801 to 1825. It was during his reign that Napoleon of France invaded Russia and marched all the way to Moscow. He entered the Kremlin through the Borovitsky Gate now used by tourists on Kremlin tours. Moscow began burning soon after Napoleon had established himself in the Kremlin. One explanation is that the Russians, practicing a scorched earth policy, set the torch to the city; another is that Napoleon's army was responsible for the conflagration. In any event, Napoleon's victory was Pyrrhic. He failed to destroy the army of General Kutuzov (the hut where Kutuzov planned the defense of Moscow is preserved as a museum). The onslaught of winter forced Napoleon's retreat in 1812.

During the era of Alexander I and prior to his reign, Russia expanded. The new territory for the empire included the Crimea in the Black Sea region, the Kingdom of Georgia where Stalin was later born, sections of eastern Poland, and a part of Finland.

1825–1855: CZAR NICHOLAS I

Alexander I was succeeded by Nicholas I who ruled from 1825 to 1855. He built Russia's first railroad—the straight-as-an-arrow line between Moscow and Leningrad —which is now a favorite tourist route. His reign was marked by the two-year Crimean War with Britain and France. This was fought to block Russia's attempts to expand into the Mediterranean area by acquiring Turkish territory. Besides the war which weighed heavily on the backs of the people, there were repressive measures in an effort to stifle criticism of the Russian monarchy.

It was during the reign of Nicholas I that the famous battle at Balaklava was fought with the immortalized-inverse charge of the Light Brigade. In this charge an English Cavalry attack was repulsed by the Russians with great English losses. Nevertheless Russia was defeated. Pares sums up the war this way: "For the Russian nation the war was an object lesson in the corruption and incompetence of the bureaucracy and the fine courage of the private soldier . . ."

1855–1881: CZAR ALEXANDER II

As Russian Czars go, Alexander II who ruled from 1855 to 1881, was one of the most liberal. The abuses of the past had led to an incessant series of peasant revolts.

Alexander II also inherited the Crimean War from his father Nicholas I. The war was brought to a rather inconclusive end during Alexander II's reign. On March 30, 1856, a peace was signed at Paris in which Russia lost territory and some rights in the Black Sea.

With the war ended, Alexander II turned to much needed reforms. It was not so much that he was a liberal as that he was a realistic conservative who recognized the huge pressures that had built up, particularly during the war, and the need to do something about them. Alexander II began a program to free the serfs. Permission was given for travel abroad by Russians. More liberal curricula were introduced into the universities. Censorship of the press was lightened. The excesses of the bureaucracy were exposed and efforts were made to correct them. However, as was the case later in Soviet history (when, for example, at the death of Stalin an easing of restrictions resulted in intellectual ferment in Russia and revolt in Hungary), the reforms undertaken by Alexander II led to a growth in the already robust revolutionary movement. Alexander II himself became a victim of the revolutionaries. In 1866 a shot was fired at Alexander, but he escaped. He was not so lucky in 1881 when a revolutionary threw a bomb at his feet. A church in Leningrad marks the site of the assassination. The murder had the effect of putting the brakes on Alexander's reforms. Russia's last best hope for gradualism and moderation to correct abuses was lost. The authorities reapplied restrictive and repressive measures.

1881–1894: CZAR ALEXANDER III

Alexander II was succeeded by Alexander III who ruled from 1881 to 1894. During his brief reign a modest attempt was made at industrializing Russia. Industries were built around St. Petersburg and Moscow, as well as in some Ukrainian cities. Deposits of coal and iron were found in the south and mining operations expanded. The output of pig iron, always an index to a country's industrial growth, showed a great increase during this period. There was considerable foreign investment. The construction of the Trans-Siberian Railroad was begun.

In 1886, Alexander III narrowly escaped death when revolutionaries derailed his train. Twenty-one other persons were killed. Repression and more repression followed. Every element of dissent, including religious groups, were persecuted. It was during this period that the Dukhobors, a religious group whose members refused military service, escaped in large numbers to Canada. There was repression of newspapers and of schools. Student clubs were forbidden. Children of the lower class were excluded from secondary schools. There were student riots at various universities at St. Petersburg, Moscow, Kharkov, and Odessa. Soldiers were used to suppress the demonstrations. Political suspects were exiled to Siberia in large numbers. The law courts became more and more corrupt.

1894–1917: CZAR NICHOLAS II

When Alexander III died on November 1, 1894, he was succeeded by his son Nicholas II. Nicholas reigned from 1894 to 1917, the last of the Russian Czars. Nicholas II was ill-prepared for power. He grew up in the shadow of his autocratic father, a man of obstinacy, iron will, and autocracy. Nicholas II was brought up to fear his father, but was untrained to wield power himself. He was deplorably weak, almost feminine in nature. From the outset there was no great promise of originality or initiative. Nicholas declared upon his accession to the throne that he would follow his father in everything.

At home and abroad Nicholas II suffered defeats. Vast Russia lost to small Japan in the war for control of Manchuria and Korea, fought in 1904 and 1905. The fall of Port Arthur on January 1, 1905, was a humiliating defeat for Russia. The peace treaty for this Russo-Japanese War was signed in the United States at the Wentworth Hotel at Portsmouth, New Hampshire.

The impoverishment of the peasants grew. Repression in education, the press, and civil rights was increased. The revolutionary movement grew. There was a succession of industrial strikes.

The distasteful war with Japan, the oppressive economic conditions, and civil repressions caused the Czar's stock to drop even further. On January 19, 1905, a gun in the Peter and Paul Fortress, now a Leningrad museum, fired a shot toward the Winter Palace (now the famous Hermitage Art Gallery). Fearful for his life and that of his family, the Czar moved out of St. Petersburg to the Imperial Village of Czarskoye Selo. Assassination followed assassination. The Czar's First Minister Plehve was assassinated by a bomb. The Czar's uncle, the Grand

Duke Sergius, Governor General of Moscow, was killed in the Kremlin by a bomb. This was an act of revenge which enjoyed popular support in Moscow because the Governor General was equally distasteful to people in every walk of life.

In an obviously far too long delayed attempt to be responsive to the growing sentiments, the Czar instituted the Imperial Duma, a watered-down representative assembly. It had no real powers and was intended in part at least to smoke out the leaders of the revolutionary movement. In December of 1905, small-scaled revolution broke out in Moscow. Although it was abortive, it has since become an important event in Communist history, and museums and monuments and Intourist guides in Russia commemorate it. Lenin called it a rehearsal for the 1917 revolution. It began with wide-spread riots. The numbers actually involved in the fighting in Moscow from December 27, 1905, to January 1, 1906, were comparatively small. Troops rushed into Moscow to suppress the uprising. Places used by the revolutionaries for secret meetings and to print illegal pamphlets are now preserved as museums.

The Czar's downfall was hastened by an unusual circumstance. The happy birth of a son to the imperial couple soon became a source of great worry for them. The heir to the throne, Alexis, was the victim of hemophilia, a hereditary disease in his mother's family, which meant that even a small wound might cause internal bleeding which could not be stopped.

The Czarina grasped at any straw that she thought might preserve her son's life. Eventually she fell under the influence of one of the strangest characters in Russian history, Rasputin. Rasputin, a large, shaggy-bearded man, ill-kempt and dirty in appearance, who had a reputation as a religious mystic in a country village, won the confidence of the Czarina and became a power in court.

With a weak-willed Czar, influenced by a strong-willed Czarina who herself was almost hypnotically controlled by a man who came to be known as the "mad monk," it was only to be expected that the course of events would go steadily downhill to disaster. The process was hastened by Russia's involvement in World War I. It was an unpopular war. The drain on Russian resources was great. The loyalty of the armies steadily diminished. Political opposition to the ineffectual Czar mounted. Finally, in March 1917, under pressure from all sides, Czar Nicholas II abdicated. The Czar and his family were sent to Tobolsk in Siberia and then to Ekaterinburg in the Ural Mountains. Those who succeeded the Czars were not quite sure what to do with the imperial family. Finally on July 16, 1918, they were slain by their guards in the cellar of their refuge-home. The next day a number of other members of the Romanov family were hurled down a mine shaft to their death.

1917: THE REVOLUTION

The Czar was succeeded by a provisional government that lasted only eight months. It was headed by Alexander Kerensky, a member of the Socialist Revolutionary Party. A constituent Assembly to draw up a constitution was convened. Kerensky's coalition government was recognized by all of Russia's wartime allies. It was committed to staying in the war and to constitutional government. At the time of the Czar's overthrow V. I. Lenin was in exile in Switzerland. Leon Trotsky was in New York. They rushed home.

Led by Lenin, the Communists sought to upset the embryo provisional government and take over. Actually, it was not called the Communist Party. It did not take that name until somewhat later. At this time Lenin's party was known as the Bolsheviks. This means "men of the majority." This name derived from a split years previously within the Social Democratic Party over various issues. The two factions were the Bolsheviks and the Mensheviks ("men of the minority"). For simplicity's sake, the term Communists is used in this book to describe the revolutionaries even for the period when they still were called Bolsheviks.

Lenin's real name was Vladimir Ilich Ulyanov. His birthplace of Simbirsk on the Volga River is now called Ulyanovsk and may be visited by tourists. Like other revolutionaries of the time, he assumed another name, Lenin. Under Lenin's leadership, the Communists rallied military units to their side, distributed pamphlets and arms, plotted. Full-scale revolution broke out on October 25, 1917, with the storming of the Winter Palace in St. Petersburg where Kerensky's government had its headquarters. You will see numerous paintings of this event in museums and art galleries. Later the Communists changed from the Julian to the Gregorian Calendar, and that causes the anniversary of the October Revolution to fall on November 7.

Bloody civil war followed. Troops of various Russian allies, including the United States and Britain, landed briefly on Russian soil to try to force Russia to maintain its wartime obligation to the alliance. This intervention is a sore point even now with the Soviet authorities who describe it as typical of Western aggression and hostility to Communism.

Kerensky went into exile in England and later went to the U.S.A. He is now working at The Hoover Institute and Library on War, Revolution, and Peace at Stanford University in California.

Lenin lived until 1924 and you can visit the mansion near Moscow where he spent his last years and died.

1924–NOW: THE STALIN ERA
AND KHRUSHCHEV

After Lenin's death, Stalin took power. He fell out with Trotsky who was forced to flee. Trotsky was assassinated in Mexico.

Stalin, who once wrote that "you cannot make a revolution with silk gloves," set to work amalgamating land (briefly seized by peasants in the revolution) into "collective farms." Peasants resisted this pooling of their land and cattle into a communal effort. There was a huge slaughter of cattle and much farmland fell into disuse. There was famine. Eventually, though, collectivization was enforced, and the tourist can visit collective farms all over the U.S.S.R.

In 1928, a half century or more after the West, Russia began industrializing on a massive scale. Human needs and even human beings were sacrificed to create a modern, industrialized Russia. Only after Stalin's death in 1953, with industrialization achieved (even with the heart-rending human extermination and property destruction of World War II), has somewhat more attention been given to consumer needs. Stalin's successors tried a form of "collective leadership" for a while, but this turned out to be only a transitory stage until one of them could demonstrate his dominance over the others. This man proved to be Nikita Khrushchev.

THE PERSONALITY OF THE SOVIET PEOPLE

Russians you meet and speak with today are in part at least the product of this history.

If the Soviet citizen expresses a suspicion of the outside world and a fear of attack it is not only because he has been indoctrinated but also because he has suffered from German aggression.

If a Soviet official moves with annoying deliberateness and caution in deciding whether to extend your visa it is not only because he is enmeshed in a cumbersome red-tape bureaucracy but also because the U.S.S.R. is as much Asiatic as European in its pace as well as its geography.

You will find that years of anti-Western propaganda carried by the Soviet radio and in the newspapers has not caused Russians to hate Americans, British, Canadians, or Frenchmen. Quite the contrary. Most Russians display affection toward the non-Communist foreigner. The official explanation is that propaganda attacks are not directed against the ordinary American or Briton or Canadian but against war-mongering leaders. Part of the explanation is found too in the fact that not *all* Russians swallow *everything* they are told *all* the time. Many Russians, especially young people, are skeptical, cynical, discerning. They remember that Russians and Americans fought side by side in the war. They realize that if Nikita Khrushchev is so anxious to catch up with and surpass the United States there must be much worthy of emulation there.

Russians are curious. Crowds gather around any foreign automobile. Knots of people congregate around a foreigner engaged in a sidewalk seminar with a Soviet citizen. Russians stare with mild good humor and acute curiosity at a westerner's shoes and suit.

Russians are kindly, emotional, demonstrative, uninhibited. They will vie with each other to help a tourist who has lost his way. They readily yield their precedence in a queue for a visitor. Russians may cry, even after a short acquaintance, when you depart. Russians are also stubborn and self-righteous.

Russians laugh heartily at a pratfall in the circus ring, but don't take this as an indication that they share your sense of humor. For example, when the Harlem Globetrotters, a basketball team that combines skill with a zany style of play, performed in Moscow, Russians were befuddled. The government newspaper *Izvestia* (*News*) complained that "we in the Soviet Union take our sports seriously, and while we recognize the playing skill of the American team we do not much like seeing a basketball game turned into a vaudeville show." Fundamentally, the Russians are a serious people, serious about their goals, their way of life, about themselves.

RECOMMENDED READING

The traveler to Russia who wants to know more about the country before—or after—his trip will find a number of excellent books available. Some of them are listed here.

A History of Russia, by Sir Bernard Pares. If anything, this volume suffers from too much information. It's an able reference book that omits not a single pretender to the throne, not a single battle, not a single purge. It's available too in an abridged pocket-size edition which is easier reading for the casual historian.

Inside Russia Today, by John Gunther. This is a fine, detailed job by an experienced journalist. It examines many phases of Soviet life with particular emphasis on politics.

The Future Is Ours, Comrade, by Joseph Novak. In a most unusual book, the author relates his conversations with many Russians in an atmosphere of confidence rarely enjoyed by a foreigner. As a citizen of another Communist country, carrying letters of endorsement from highly placed Soviet authorities, Joseph Novak (a pseudonym) had opportunities to learn details about present police oppression and other facets of Soviet life.

Eastern Exposure, by Marvin Kalb. The travels, conversations and observations of a keen-minded American during a tour with the U. S. Embassy in Moscow.

Lost Splendor, by Prince Felix Youssoupoff. This book was published several years ago, but it's the most intimate account we've read of what life was like for the nobility in the dying days of the Czarist Empire. The author assassinated Rasputin and this is related in an exciting chapter.

(Publisher's note: Mr. Levine's own book *Main Street, U.S.S.R.* will prove especially useful. As the title implies it tells about the everyday life of the Russian—how he eats, drinks, shops, goes to school, votes, works, obtains medical care, plays, marries, gets divorced, buys insurance and so on.)

CHAPTER FOUR

Moscow: Hotels

One evening I had been ringing fully five minutes for the elevator in Moscow's National Hotel. Nothing happened. Then I noticed someone behind me reaching out to push the button too. It was the elevator operator herself, holding a glass of tea in her hand. After several imperious rings had produced nothing, she sighed in resignation, and began plodding up the stairs in search of her errant elevator. I followed, and we found the venerable conveyance abandoned three flights up by an impatient guest who had tired of waiting while the lady was leisurely brewing her tea.

The Russian elevator operator, a friendly, imperturbable woman in her fifties, chuckled as we rode up two more flights to my floor. "It happens all the time," she explained. "Whenever I take a little time off someone steals my machine."

An elevator trip can be anything but commonplace in Russia. For example, controls in the lifts (a word preferred in Russian translations) at the Moskva Hotel look as if they had been intended for a space ship. The elevators in the Ukraine Hotel are run by some of the most attractive girls in Moscow. The explanation offered by one visitor was that the pretty girls are provided to make the often interminable wait for the Ukraine's elevators worth while. A kind of reward for patience!

CHOICE OF HOTELS

Whatever the traveler's taste in elevators or anything else he usually has no choice of hotels. The traveler to Russia ordinarily stays where he is assigned.

All hotels in the Soviet Union are owned by agencies of the government.

If the tourist in Paris, for example, dislikes the Crillon, he may if he wishes (and has the money) move to the Ritz. By the same token the management of a hotel in Paris, or in any other city where there is competition among hotel owners, may be expected to try to satisfy customers. With only *one* management there is less incentive for this attitude in Russia. However, there are differences among people, and consequently, differences in the standards and services of the various government-run hotels in Moscow.

Sometimes a cable or letter written beforehand will get you a reservation at the hotel of your choice. Such a cable or letter should be sent by your travel agent to "Intourist Moscow." It does not hurt either if—besides a cable sent by the agent—you send another cable requesting a room to the hotel you have chosen a week or so before your arrival. Sometimes such requests are honored, but more often not.

A simple sample cable for a couple might read: INTOURIST MOSCOW PLEASE RESERVE DOUBLE ROOM BATH NATIONAL HOTEL FIVE DAYS ARRIVING JULY EIGHTH. STANLEY JONES 863 PARK AVENUE NEW YORK

The tourist frequently does not know until he actually arrives in Moscow where he will be staying. Upon your arrival at the airport or railroad station, you will be told by the Intourist representative who meets you where you are to stay. By that time it is usually too late to do

anything about it if you are dissatisfied with the hotel
assignment.

A few tourists, wishing to move to another hotel,
have complained so loudly and persistently that they
were finally moved. However, this does not convey the
best impression to the Russians, and very often a valuable period of the tourist's limited time is consumed in
arguing about the transfer.

Our advice is to accept with philosophical resignation
the hotel to which you are assigned. After all, you are
in Russia to see the sights and not the inside of a hotel
room. As a matter of fact, although there are considerable differences among the hotels in service, food, and
general atmosphere, each one offers *its* peculiar atmosphere and, more likely than not, its anecdotes for future
conversation.

THE SERVICE BUREAU

In whatever hotel you stay, its Service Bureau will
quickly become the most important place in Moscow
for you. Soon after you arrive, or the next morning if you
arrive at night, by all means go to the Service Bureau—
usually a large room or several rooms off the lobby or
up one flight of stairs—to plan your schedule. The Service Bureau provides all the services, and more, of the
concierge or porter's desk in most European hotels. It
combines the services in an American hotel of the
theater ticket agency, the car rental agency, guide services, and many other essentials.

You can count on spending a full hour or more on your
first visit to the Service Bureau, but it will be well worth
it in time saved during the rest of your stay if you make
your wishes known at the outset. The Service Bureau can
tell you what is playing in the various theaters and when.

You can learn what tours are available and what days the various museums which you may wish to visit are open. It is at the Service Bureau, too, that you will exchange your voucher for meal tickets, order cars, and meet your interpreter-guide.

This unique Soviet tourist facility also will make your reservations for travel both within Russia and for your trip out. Even if you are flying out of Russia on a *non-*Soviet airline only the Intourist bureau can obtain a seat for you. The foreign airlines, even those with offices in Moscow, are not authorized to make reservations on their own planes for flights out of Russia!

There are three hotels in Moscow operated by the Intourist organization. These are the National Hotel, the Metropole Hotel, and the Berlin Hotel. However, with the increasing influx of tourists, Soviet travel authorities have been providing rooms in other hotels which are controlled by other agencies of the government, usually the Mossoviet (the City Council).

When tourists are accommodated at one of these non-Intourist hotels, the same facilities, including the all-essential Service Bureau, are provided on the premises.

PASSPORTS

When you arrive at a Soviet hotel the administrator will ask you for your passport. You may not see the passport again for several days; in fact, sometimes not until a day or so before you depart. Don't worry about it. It's just normal bureaucracy and not a plot to deprive you of this valuable document. Everyone gets his passport back in due time. Just let nature take its course.

NAMES OF HOTELS

Here is a list of Moscow's main hotels and a bit about each:

National: Having lived in the National Hotel for almost four years, I quite naturally am prejudiced about it. Prejudiced in *favor* of it, I hasten to add. The National Hotel is Victorian in style and has a certain quality of genteel poverty about it. Its furnishings will remind you of your grandmother's parlor, if your grandmother lived in the late 1800s.

The large double windows (double protection against winter cold with about a foot between the sets of panes) are draped with velvet, usually in shades of deep green or maroon. Lampshades are the size of umbrellas with tassles. Push buttons on the walls depict figures of a waiter, a chambermaid, and a bellboy, but the buttons seldom summon the desired individual. Some rooms have valuable porcelain figurines on tables or in glass cases, and Room 115, which is the ambassadorial suite (guests have included Eleanor Roosevelt), has a number of splendid antiques and a ceiling fresco that might well adorn a Venetian palace.

The National Hotel is, in effect, a national monument. A stone plaque on the building relates that: "Here V. I. Lenin lived in March 1918 following the removal of the Soviet Government from Petrograd to Moscow." Lenin slept in Room 107 and occupied the suite of rooms leading from it, including the fabulous Room 115. The large balcony at the corner of the hotel was Lenin's platform for declaiming to the Moscow multitudes. This was Lenin's residence only for a short period; he soon moved across the square to the Kremlin. In more recent days the National Hotel has had a variety of distinguished visitors including Elizabeth Taylor, a Canadian ice hockey team, and Randolph Churchill, Sir Winston's son.

The National Hotel's location is ideal. Many of its rooms look out across Manege Square on the Kremlin's magnificent turrets and gold cupolas as well as on the multicolored domes of St. Basil's church in Red Square. The hotel, built just at the turn of this century, stands at the corner of Gorky Street, one of Moscow's main thoroughfares. It is easy walking distance to Red Square, the Kremlin, and the Bolshoi Theatre, and to many other sights of interest in the center of the city. The National Hotel also has a good restaurant and, as do most other hotels, offers a small post office counter where you may send telegrams, mail letters, or purchase stamps. There is a magazine stand in the lobby if you wish to purchase *Pravda* or one of the English-language Communist newspapers, a beauty shop and a barbershop.

The National Hotel has our unqualified recommendation—*if* you can manage to stay there. It gets more difficult to arrange this as more tourists come to Russia, especially during the summer season of peak travel. (In any season, there are instances of tourists being assigned to the National who have never heard of the place, and didn't ask to stay there.)

The staff at the National is wonderful. Larissa Fadeyeva in the Service Bureau seems able to cut red tape when others throw up their hands. Ask for Larissa's help on any troublesome problem if you stay at the National. The other girls in the Service Bureau—Tamara, Alla, Ilyena, Lena, Rita—all are equally kind and charming. The women at the administrator's desk—Vera, Nina, and Marina—are efficient and helpful in answering questions, arranging a change of rooms, calling restaurants for reservations, and finding lost mail, luggage, or children. These girls speak excellent English, French, or German. Among waiters few can match Mikhail Stepanovich for efficiency and dignity. There is a custodian at a desk on each floor of the National (and of every other Soviet hotel) who keeps the keys for each room on that floor. You leave the key when you go out of your room. These "house mothers" are cordial and even manage a few words of English. They attend regular classes.

Metropole: Centrally located, the Metropole is one of Moscow's older hotels, and has large rooms and comfortable suites but it is a cheerless place with gloomy, long corridors and tasteless furniture. Its restaurant boasts a dance orchestra and, of all things, a small dribbling fountain in the center with a goldfish pond. The furnishings at the Metropole are as old as those at the National Hotel but lack the character and, if you will, the warmth.

Near the Metropole Hotel stands a noble, old brick wall, remnants of which may be seen elsewhere in the city. It once surrounded the oldest part of the city known as *Kitaigorod* which literally translated means Chinatown. But more than likely the name comes from the Tartar word *Kitai* meaning "stronghold." This part of Moscow was a commercial center for several centuries from the 1300s.

Berlin: Formerly called the Savoy Hotel, this comparatively small building has a bit of Old World atmosphere, but many of its rooms are small and cluttered. Another disadvantage is that, although even a poor room at the National or Metropole Hotels may command a view of sorts, the Berlin Hotel is situated on a Moscow side street and looks out only on the walls of other buildings. However, because it is limited in its number of guests, the Berlin Hotel, and in particular its Service Bureau, may render more personal and efficient service than some of the larger hotels. Incidentally, the name was changed from Savoy to Berlin shortly after Nikita

Khrushchev issued his famous Thanksgiving Day 1958 ultimatum on Berlin. This led to negotiations with the Western Powers starting with the Geneva Foreign Ministers meeting in May 1959. It was probably only chance that the Berlin crisis coincided with the change in the hotel's name; the explanation of Russian friends was that Moscow has Budapest, Bucharest, Sofia, and Prague as the names of hotels or restaurants but somehow the Communist East German capital had been neglected.

Ukraine: This is one of Moscow's new skyscraper hotels, but don't expect Statler-Hilton rooms or service. The giant revolving doors may awe you, but beware! If you try to slip into a revolving door just as a determined, burly Russian is coming in the other direction you may well lose an arm! Comedian Bob Hope stayed at this hotel and when he drove up to its massive entrance, he quipped: "Now I believe that the Russians *are* eight feet tall."

The Ukraine's furniture is a kind of Moscow Grand Rapids, its service is slow and the general attitude of its staff sometimes seems to be that the guest is an inconvenience to be tolerated rather than to be served.

The Ukraine overlooks the Moscow River, and (although this may lengthen the often long wait for the elevator) try to get a room high up on one of its 26 floors to command a view of the city. The Ukraine is somewhat out of the center of things, and in traffic it can take twenty minutes or more to get to the theater in the evening.

The Russians pronounce this hotel's name as *Ukraina*, which means Ukraine and for simplicity's sake that's what we call it.

Leningradskaya: This is another of Russia's grandiosely impractical skyscraper hotels. It is 26 stories high, but only 19 floors have rooms for guests. Much of its

height is wasted on an ornate tower. When you enter
you find yourself in a marble lobby with huge gold-
colored chandeliers that lend it the appearance of a
mausoleum. Vast space has been squandered in the
Leningradskaya, as in the Ukraine Hotel, in broad corridors with small public sitting room alcoves. It's been
said with more truth than jest that "even the lobbies have
lobbies." Some suites are divided into a room-size hallway with refrigerator, a large living room, a study, bedroom and bath. There is usually also a smaller bathroom
off the hallway. All very spacious but neither necessary
nor comfortable. If you arrive by train from Leningrad,
the Leningradskaya Hotel is conveniently near the railroad station. However, as far as most other Moscow
attractions are concerned, the Leningradskaya Hotel is
out of the main stream.

Moscow: Known in Russian as the Moskva, this massive, 14-story hotel has a roof restaurant with a good
view of the Kremlin. The location is central. The rooms
are generally small, its lobby cavernous, but most people
who stay at the Moscow Hotel find it comfortable if im-
personal in its service.

Grand: This is one of Moscow's smaller hotels which,
like the National, Moscow, and Metropole Hotels, is
situated close to Red Square. The Grand Hotel has a
good restaurant up one flight, a beauty shop on the first
floor and rooms which are furnished in a baroque but
comfortable manner.

Sovietskaya: Russians are most proud of this hotel.
Visitors just below the rank of those entitled to an apartment at the Kremlin (heads of foreign countries) or a
government mansion (leaders of foreign governments)
are put up at the Sovietskaya. Its furnishings do not

differ greatly from the stark, shiny wood wardrobes (there are very few closets in Moscow hotels) and the stiffly stuffed chairs of the Ukraine and Leningradskaya Hotels, but everything, including the service, is of better quality. The hotel is situated rather far from the center of town. The distinguished names on the register at the Sovietskaya include Adlai Stevenson, Duncan Sandys, and General Nathan F. Twining. Occasionally, when all other hotels are full, Intourist rents a few rooms at the Sovietskaya for tourists, but this does not ordinarily happen.

Other Moscow hotels include the Europe (Evropa), the Budapest, the Bucharest, the Tourist, the Kiev, the Peking, the Tsentralnaya, and the Ostankino.

HOTEL RULES

A standard set of rules is posted (often under the glass top of a table or desk) in Intourist hotel rooms. The rules, printed in English, German, French, and Chinese, are these:

(1) The Intourist hotel provides service to foreign tourists, members of foreign delegations and other foreign visitors.

(2) Tourists are accommodated in accordance with the class paid for in advance, no cash payment being required at the hotel.

(3) Guests who have not purchased tours are requested to pay for accommodation in cash. Payment for a full day is required on the day of arrival. After the first 24 hours, payment is made per day, plus 50 per cent if the guest stays less than 12 hours on the last day. If the guest stays over 12 hours, payment is made for a full day's stay.

(4) Tourists will make use of the baths and showers free of charge; other guests are expected to pay.

(5) The hotel will accept orders for laundering, shoe cleaning, and shoe repair, as well as for medical, postal, long-distance telephone and transportation services.

(6) Guests are expected, upon leaving their rooms, to leave the key with the person in charge of the given floor or with the manager of the hotel.

(7) Guests are requested not to:

  (a) sing or play musical instruments between midnight and 10 A.M.;

  (b) receive other persons in the rooms between midnight and 8 A.M., except on special occasions when the permission of the management has been obtained;

  (c) allow other persons to remain in their rooms in their absence without the permission of the management;

  (d) keep bulky belongings and inflammable materials in their rooms;

  (e) use any heating device;

  (f) bring animals or birds to their rooms.

(8) Guests will be held responsible for damage of furnishings, appliances and other property of the hotel, caused by the guests themselves or by persons they had invited.

(9) The hotel will ensure the security of money, valuable papers and valuable things belonging to the guest only if they have been put in its safekeeping. Otherwise, the hotel accepts no responsibility.

(10) Belongings left behind by a departed guest will be kept for six months after the owner has been duly notified, after which they will be disposed of in the manner stipulated by law.

(11) Guests are expected to give the management an hour's notice of their departure.

TELEPHONE SERVICE

The magic word to remember in making a telephone call is *gorod*. This means "town" and is the Russian way of asking the telephone operator for an outside line.

In some hotels you dial a number, usually 8, to get the dial tone for an outside line. Other numbers are dialed to reach the Service Bureau or other offices or rooms within the building. This direct line system avoids the interminable delays often experienced at some hotels in reaching the operator. Each room at the Moscow and Ukraine Hotels has its own telephone number. There's no need to phone in through the switchboard from outside. Thus, if someone wants to call you at the Moscow Hotel he dials 922 and then your room number. The prefix number to dial in the case of the Ukraine is 432.

In the case of the Leningradskaya Hotel someone has managed to complicate hopelessly this simple system. Each Leningradskaya room has a telephone number which bears absolutely no relation to the room number. You have to learn *both* your room number *and* a completely unrelated telephone number!

ASSORTED ADVICE

Here are a variety of tips that may be helpful in hotels in Moscow and elsewhere in the U.S.S.R.:

Beware of using electric shavers and other appliances in Soviet hotels. Even within the same city there may be varying voltages. Check up before you plug in! Some Moscow hotels have 127 volts; other have 220 volts. All are 50 cycles. Although voltage peaks vary which, in extremes, can damage electrical gadgets, travelers do use

110 volt, 60 cycle equipment without complaint on the 127 volt, 50 cycle Soviet lines.

When ordering a car from the Service Bureau ask for a ZIM, especially when you are taking a long ride. This is the most comfortable Soviet car, especially on the open road. The Pobeda ("Victory") and the Volga are cramped for leg space. The ZIL (formerly called ZIS, named after the initials of the factory as is the ZIM) is a very roomy limousine, but riding in the back seat can feel like clinging to the end of a whip!

Especially in the case of the smaller cars make sure that doors are locked, and even then don't lean against them. The doors spring open easily.

Laundry service is fast and not overly expensive in Soviet hotels. It is often possible to get one-day service. The price of laundering a man's shirt is about 2.50 rubles (25 cents or 10 pence), a woman's blouse is the same price, and a pair of socks is 50 kopecks which is half a ruble (5 cents or 2 pence). Over a sustained period of time Soviet laundry service can be hard on clothes and shirts lose their whiteness. The quality of pressing leaves much to be desired.

Dry-cleaning service takes longer. The quickest I've ever managed to get a suit cleaned was six days, and that was "urgent."

The first floor is seldom the ground floor. In the National Hotel, for example, there is the street level floor, the restaurant floor, and only then the first floor.

An exit visa is necessary to leave Russia. If you decide to depart earlier than planned be sure to let the Service Bureau know so that they can have your passport properly stamped. In pocket-size folders published by Intourist and distributed at hotels guests are advised to apply for exit visas three days ahead of time. It *can* be done in one day.

If you want a transit visa for a stopover in Poland, Czechoslovakia, or one of the other Communist East European countries it is necessary to present your passport at that country's embassy in Moscow, often with the Soviet exit visa already stamped in.

Hotel baggage stickers lettered in Russian are available in the Service Bureau or at the administrator's desk at most hotels. Ask for several of them if you want a sure conversation-starter on your luggage.

CHAPTER FIVE

Moscow: Sight-seeing Highlights

As you drive the 18 miles into town from Moscow's airport your first view of the Soviet capital will be Moscow State University. During the course of your visit your Intourist guide will almost certainly take you through this towering skyscraper. The guide probably will not tell you about the girl who posted an anti-Communist paragraph from *Doctor Zhivago* on a bulletin board. The student boldly wrote the name of V. I. Lenin as the author of the quotation. It stayed up for several days, students glanced at it, but it did not register even on those who read it. Finally someone realized what he was reading, and called it to the attention of the university authorities. Somehow the prank was traced to the guilty student. She readily admitted that she had put up the quotation; it was intended as an object lesson, she said, to demonstrate how lax and unalert were the university's young Communists. This explanation confounded the authorities who did not know whether to praise or reprimand the girl. They did neither.

The university is one of the important places to see in Moscow. There are many others. This chapter deals with the standard sights, the not-to-be-missed landmarks, and the historical sites. There is a separate chapter that deals in detail with Moscow's museums. Another chapter describes places of off-the-beaten-track interest. First, though, a few basic facts about Moscow are in order.

BASIC FACTS ABOUT MOSCOW

Moscow is really three capitals in one.

It is the capital of the R.S.F.S.R.—the Russian Socialist Federated Soviet Republic, the largest of the 15 Soviet republics.

It is also the capital of the U.S.S.R.

And finally it is the capital of the entire Communist world.

Five million people live in Moscow.

The city covers an area of almost 128 square miles. It is moderately hilly, but with no really steep climbs.

It is not only the nation's political center.

It is also the scientific center (the Academy of Science has its headquarters here).

It is the industrial center with hundreds of factories in and around Moscow (only a few have signs identifying them by name and only an expert can guess by the smokestacks and other characteristics what is being manufactured inside).

It is the cultural center (with the Bolshoi Theatre, the Moscow Art Theatre, a score and more of museums, a university, and many institutes of higher education).

Moscow used to be the center of Russian religious life, too, before atheism became a matter of state policy. The Patriarch of the Russian Orthodox Church lives in Moscow. Before the revolution there were so many Russian Orthodox churches in Moscow that it was sometimes called the "city of 40 times 40 cupolas."

Moscow used to be known as the "Calico City" because the manufacture of textile goods was its principal industry in pre-revolutionary times. It's been called the "Holy City of the Russians." A reference book on Moscow which makes no claim to a lack of prejudice was published by the Soviet Government's Foreign Languages Publishing House in 1955. It described Moscow this way: "Moscow. . . . So many happy thoughts and bright hopes of millions of people are connected with Moscow, the cradle of Russian statehood, the capital of the world's first socialist country."

Moscow is an ancient city. In 1947 the city celebrated its 800th anniversary. In fact, though, archaeological finds indicate that there were settlements here on the banks of the Moscow River before the 1147 date mentioned in old chronicles.

Moscow is an amalgamation of many types of architecture. There is the wonderful Kremlin which shows the distinct influence of its Italian architects; the swallowtail crenelations of the Kremlin's walls are very similar to those seen on a building in Piazza Venezia in Rome and elsewhere in Italy. There are the baroque mansions of the 1800s, heroically proportioned, often overly elaborate structures of Stalin's era, and the utilitarian apartment houses of the Khrushchev administration.

Moscow's main avenues are unusually wide. There are many with 12 lanes for ordinary traffic and a center lane reserved for fire trucks, ambulances, and the cars of the leaders. The center lane also provides a haven for pedestrians caught in mid-stream by a change of traffic light.

For many Soviet citizens the city of Moscow is Washington, D.C., London, Ottawa, New York, and Paris all rolled into one. It is a kind of Mecca for the Communist faithful because here is the shrine that contains the bodies of the saints, Lenin and Stalin. The mention of Moscow fires the imagination of the Siberian sheep tender and the Kazakh cowboy.

Every day thousands of Soviet tourists stream into Moscow from Dzerzhinsk and Dnepropetrovsk and Drogobych—wide-eyed and eager. Many wear their country high boots on the city's streets. More than one Western tourist has had the feeling that someone is playing a practical joke when a peasant from Petropavlovsk strides up to him in the street to ask directions to Red Square. To the man from Petropavlovsk they're all city slickers whether from Moscow or Miami, and, having just arrived in the big city himself, he may not be able to tell them apart!

STATUE OF YURI DOLGORUKY
Sovietskaya Square

Usually statues are among the dullest of landmarks. However, this statue of an ancient prince (whose name translated means "George of the Long Arm") is a good place to start a tour of Moscow. Yuri Dolgoruky was the founder of Moscow. Yuri was a prince of Vladimir-Suzdal, one of the independent principalities (a state governed by a prince) that dotted this vast land in ancient times. The site of Vladimir-Suzdal was not far from the junction of two rivers which later became known as the Moscow River and the Neglinnaya River (the Neglinnaya River in modern times has been piped, and now flows below the ground near one branch of the Kremlin's wall). Prince Yuri had a country home at this river junction, but because it had a location of defensive importance it was soon transformed into a small wooden fortress covering about two and a half acres. During the twelfth and thirteenth centuries Moscow consisted of a fortress (frequently rebuilt because of fires) and a small settlement surrounding it. It began its growth into an important city in the thirteenth century.

The bronze statue, 46 feet high, shows Prince Yuri in a coat of mail and mounted on a horse. Its rectangular pedestal is of dark-gray polished granite. The monument was intended to commemorate Moscow's 800th anniversary in 1947, but was not unveiled until June 6, 1954. It stands in Sovietskaya Square which is opposite number 19 Gorky Ulitsa, the address of Moscow's City Hall.

MOSCOW CITY HALL
Gorky Ulitsa 19

The proper name of this institution is the "Moscow City Soviet of Working Peoples' Deputies." It is abbreviated in Russian to *Mossoviet*. The red-stone building has an architectural history as complex as its political history. It was built in 1782 by Matvei Kazakov, a talented architect who designed many late eighteenth-century and early nineteenth-century palaces, such as the home of Moscow's Governor-General. In 1946, when a number of Moscow streets were widened, engineers moved this building back 35 feet and added two more stories to it. The architects did their job skillfully and this city hall, with its classic columned façade, is one of the capital's most handsome buildings.

Here deputies elected by one-name-per-office ballots administer Moscow's municipal affairs.

THE KREMLIN

This is the center of Moscow. It is also the heart of the U.S.S.R. Probably nothing surprises more visitors than to find that the Kremlin is not a gloomy, foreboding building with prisonlike walls, but rather is a magnificent arrangement of palaces and churches surrounded by turreted walls of medieval majesty. The Kremlin is a sight of unforgettable beauty; it conjures many moods depending on whether it is seen with brilliant sunlight striking its burnished cupolas or when its red-brick walls are flecked with winter's snow.

The Kremlin is especially beautiful illuminated at night. The best vantage points are from the Bolshaya Kammeny Bridge and the Moskvoretsky Bridge which span the Moscow River at either end of the Kremlin.

The Kremlin's origins are almost as old as those of Moscow itself. An ancient historian, or chronicler, made the first known written reference to the Kremlin in 1156. In that year Prince Yuri Dolgoruky erected a wooden stockade around his hilltop estate at the junction of the Moscow and Neglinnaya Rivers. This small fortress expanded through the years and by the mid 1300s it covered almost as great an area as it does today. The Kremlin's walls now enclose an area of 64.2 acres.

The present day Kremlin's Cathedral Square with its cluster of splendid churches began to take shape under the ruler Ivan Kalita (Ivan Money Bag) between 1325 and 1340. By 1360, during the reign of Dmitri Donskoi, the Kremlin had been rebuilt in white stone. There are paintings of it as it looked in those days which hang in various Soviet museums including the Kremlin Museum, the Museum of the Reconstruction of Moscow, and in the Tretyakov Art Gallery.

The Kremlin was rebuilt again under Ivan III, the ruler who played such a significant role in amalgamating scattered princely states into a single Russian nation. A number of structures that stand today survive from that era— 1462–1505. These include the present walls, the turrets, the cathedrals which now are museums, and the Granovitaya Palace, one of the several Kremlin palaces. In 1505 the Ivan Bell Tower, perhaps the crowning achievement of Kremlin architecture, was begun, but it was not until 95 years later that it was completed. Until only recently it was the highest structure in Moscow. This marvellous tower with its gold cupola tipped by a Russian Orthodox cross is adjoined by a lower but more massive tower housing most of the bells. It is one of the most memorable structures in all Russia.

There is much to see in the Kremlin. There is the wall itself. A leisurely walk around the walls takes only an hour or so and provides an opportunity to inspect the towers and cupolas from a variety of arresting angles. A tour of the Kremlin grounds includes such landmarks as an immense cracked bell, the Czar's cannon, the gardens. The Kremlin Armory Museum, described in detail in the subsequent chapter on museums, can occupy a morning or more. Then there are the Kremlin churches and the palaces.

At the time of the 1917 revolution the Kremlin was the Czar's private and seldom used preserve. It was kept for coronations and for visits whenever the rulers tired temporarily of St. Petersburg. It was closed to common men. During the revolution the excluded masses broke into the Kremlin just as they did into the palaces of the Czar in the then capital St. Petersburg. They didn't stay long. The new rulers placed it off-limits, too. Under Stalin none but a comparatively few privileged Russians and foreigners ever saw the inside of the Kremlin walls. It was not until 1955, almost two years after Stalin's death, that this changed and the Kremlin was opened to the public. In the first year alone, from July 1955 to July 1956, 5,000,000 tourists trooped through the grounds. These were mostly Russians but there were also visitors from 50 foreign countries.

Although it's easy to get into the Kremlin's gates—usually not even a ticket is needed—it is less easy even now for Russians to get a ticket to visit the Kremlin Museum. A maid in our hotel had received various gifts from us—lipsticks, stockings, a dress, shoes—with appreciation but with no strong emotion. When we learned that she had never managed to see the museum and longed to do so, we ordered a pair of tickets from the Service Bureau and gave them to her. She cried with gratitude. (This is a gift to keep in mind for a Russian whom you want particularly to please.)

Now for some of the highlights to see in the Kremlin:

The Spasskaya Tower is one of five Kremlin towers that are crowned by stars of red glass, mounted on ball bearings, that face with the wind. The red stars replaced the imperial eagles of the Czars. The Spasskaya, or Savoir's, Tower was built in 1491—a year before Columbus discovered America! It is the most beautifully proportioned of the 20 towers that punctuate the Kremlin's walls. You may prefer the whimsically designed, canopy-shaped Czar's Tower or the history-steeped Borovitskaya Tower through which Napoleon entered the Kremlin's grounds, but you are likely to agree that for sheer grandeur the Spasskaya Tower is unmatched. It is the main portal to the Kremlin. An insistent modern bell clangs a warning to pedestrians when a car enters or leaves.

The Spasskaya Tower is 221 feet high. It is the tallest of the Kremlin's proud towers. In its top two stories are housed chimes, bells and the machinery of its huge clock. The chimes were installed in 1851 and when the Communists came to power the chimes were "taught" to play the strains of the Internationale's "Arise Ye Workers," but that has not been the case since World War II. The chimes now sound each quarter hour in a much more prosaic manner and introduce the giant bell whose clangorous chant counts each hour. This bell was cast in 1769 and weighs over two tons. All transmitters of Radio Moscow carry its notes striking midnight throughout the U.S.S.R. and abroad. It is an aural trade-mark much as are the notes of Big Ben.

The great clock of the Spasskaya Tower with golden

hands on its black face was damaged by artillery fire during fighting that brought the Communists to power, but Lenin had it quickly repaired.

The Spasskaya Tower got its name from an icon of Christ that stood in a rectangular niche just over the center of its archway. The niche still is there. The painting of Christ has been removed.

Cathedral (Sobornaya) Square retains a fifteenth-century atmosphere. As the name implies, this is the square around which are built the Kremlin's principal churches. The Czars also had small chapels adjoining their living chambers for their personal use. This cobbled square actually was first created in the early fourteenth century, with white stone churches situated there. However, the present cathedrals date from a century later. Seen in a winter's frosty morning mist, the church cupolas diffused against a leaden sky, Sobornaya Plochad transports the viewer back into another era.

The Assumption (Uspensky) Cathedral is the oldest (1475–79) and most elaborate of the ensemble of churches in Cathedral Square. This was the main church of the state of Muscovy. It was here that the coronations of the Czars were held, as well as other full-dress state services attended by the Czar. It was the Westminster Abbey of old Russia.

As is true of many Kremlin buildings and of the walls themselves, the Assumption Cathedral was designed by an Italian architect, Aristotle Fioravanti, from Venice. Unlike the walls, which borrowed heavily from the Italian style, the Assumption Cathedral is in the best early Russian tradition and more specifically is inspired by the twelfth-century cathedral in the town of Vladimir, originally one of the prince-ruled states (called Vladimir-Suzdal) that were combined to form Russia.

The cathedral, with its five bulbous domes, rises 115

feet from the ground, and its lofty interior contains a staggering collection of Russian religious art. The walls, columns, altar, and ceiling are covered with paintings of rich color. Skillful restoration work has brought much of the art work to life again. Through the ages they had become darkened by annual layers of varnish, by soot and by dirt. Starting with a square inch of a painting, specialists carefully remove layer by layer of these deposits, arriving at last after tedious labor at the original colors set down by the artist. Gradually the restoration artisan spreads out from his experimental square-inch, and after months of work, the religious work appears as it did centuries ago. Most of the Kremlin cathedrals' icons have already been thus restored. But you may still see old paintings, the figures blackened almost beyond recognition, in the process of being cleaned.

Be sure to see the tombs of patriarchs and metropolitans, the Russian Orthodox equivalent of popes and cardinals, who were buried here during an ancient era of Russian history. See too the magnificently carved walnut throne of Ivan the Terrible.

The Archangel (Arkhangelsky) Cathedral, like the other churches of this rare assemblage, was built in a remarkably short span of time. It took four years, from 1505 to 1509, to construct this formidable cathedral. Prior to the time of Peter the Great (1672–1725), who moved the Russian capital to St. Petersburg, Russian Czars and the Grand Dukes who ruled before them were buried in this Cathedral of the Archangel. You can see the burial vaults lining the cathedral walls. There are murals of Ivan Kalita, Ivan III, Ivan the Terrible, and others.

Here is a tomb, decorated with a carved white stone canopy, in which lie the remains of Czarevich Dmitri, the young son of Czar Ivan the Terrible. Dmitri died as a child, and years later a pretender claiming to be

Dmitri managed to seize the throne for a short period of time. It is the body of the ill-fated real Dmitri, who died in 1591, that is said to be in the tomb in the Cathedral of the Archangel.

The Annunciation (Blagoveshchensky) Cathedral was constructed in the period from 1484 to 1489 just at the time that Columbus was making plans for his voyage that discovered America. It started out as a rather modest chapel, but was destroyed in one of the periodic Kremlin fires. Ivan the Terrible had it rebuilt in a much more elaborate style with nine domes. It is the smallest of the three great churches in Cathedral Square, but in some respects the most remarkable. Its floor is laid with slabs of jasper from the Ural Mountains. The portals of the church are decorated with exquisite carvings in stone. Its magnificent icons were painted by some of the greatest names of that era—Andrei Rublyev, Feofan Grek, and Prokhor of Gorodets. Rublyov, perhaps the most talented of late fourteenth and early fifteenth-century painters, was a monk at the Moscow Andronikov (sometimes called Andronievsky) Monastery where he lived and worked as a monk, died and is buried. The monastery building has been converted into the Rublyev Art Museum.

One of the most intriguing of the Annunciation Cathedral's paintings is on the left-hand wall of the corridor which is entered after climbing the stairs from Cathedral Square. It is a primitive portrayal of the story of Jonah and the whale. It shows Jonah, in a series of paintings, falling off a ship, being swallowed by a whale, and finally being washed up on shore. The whale looks like a big trout!

The Bell Tower of Ivan the Great stands in Cathedral Square and served during Russian history as a watch and signal tower as well as a church. Guards kept a lookout for invaders. Signals could be seen for miles when displayed on its upper stories. The lower part of the tower was begun in 1505 and completed in 1508 during the reign of Ivan the Great. Then under Boris Godunov the belfry and the chapel next to it were added. Three lines of gold Cyrillic letters at the base of the belfry's gold cupola record the dates of the construction and the names of the two rulers who were responsible for it. In 1955 the cupola, including the cross atop it and the letters, were freshly gilded.

Twenty-two large bells and more than 30 small ones were hung in the belfry. It was an extraordinary feat of construction for Boris' era. The bell tower stands almost 250 feet high and its foundation below the ground is 120 feet deep. A deep foundation was necessary to support the weight of the bells. Like the Kremlin churches, the bell tower is built of heavy brick. White stone was used for the foundations, the ground floor, the balustrades, stairways, decorative ornaments, and as a covering material.

The Grand Kremlin (Bolshoi Kremlyovsky) Palace is a comparatively modern building, its construction in its present form having taken place from 1838 to 1849. The Russian architect K. A. Ton was successful in creating a structure that harmonizes with the rest of the Kremlin. The palace is a pumpkin yellow with white trim and a green roof. Rectangular and regular in shape, its windows give it a three-story appearance from the outside although there are only two floors through most of the large building.

Usually special permission is needed to go through the Grand Kremlin Palace. Brass plaques at the entrance announce the fact that the Supreme Soviet legislatures of the U.S.S.R. and of the Russian Republic meet here. The deputies convene in an assembly hall of monumental proportions which was built in 1939 by combining two Czarist-era halls—the Alexandrovsky and the Andre-yevsky Halls. The resulting assembly hall is more than a football field in length. At one end is a platform with places for Communist Party leaders. A more than double life-size statue of Lenin looks down from a pedestal. Deputies to the Supreme Soviet and to congresses of writers, architects, farmers, and other groups which are periodically held here sit at rows of polished walnut desks. Earphones are provided at each desk for simultaneous translations into several of the many languages spoken in the U.S.S.R. At the rear of the hall is a deep balcony that can seat more than 1000 spectators. The hall itself is able to hold twice that number. Smaller balconies provide places for members of the press and for diplomats.

Of the other chambers of imperial proportion and design in the Grand Kremlin Palace none is more regal than the St. George (Georgievsky) Hall. Six immense bronze chandeliers, each weighing more than a ton, light this gala hall in which the Czars and their Communist successors preside at affairs of state.

The leaders of foreign countries who have been entertained in the St. George Hall in recent years include British Prime Minister Harold Macmillan, Iran's Shah, the King of Afghanistan, President Nasser of the United Arab Republic, the ruler of Yemen, the President of Finland, and the Premiers of France, Sweden, Denmark, and Japan.

The hall is white with 18 spiral columns at regular intervals. Marble tablets on the walls are inscribed in gold letters with the names of military units and officers decorated in Russian campaigns with the Cross of St. George.

When the bronze chandeliers are ablaze, when members of the foreign diplomatic corps are present in their varied and colorful full-dress uniforms, when long tables are spread with caviar and other delicacies, the St. George Hall is a really imperial sight.

In contrast to these heroic proportions, the living apartments of the Czars were surprisingly small and intimate, with low ceilings that facilitated the task of the decorative tile stoves that heated the rooms.

The Hall of Facets (Granovitaya) Palace is entered through the Grand Kremlin Palace. Its brilliantly painted reception hall is all that remains of the main Kremlin palace of the fifteenth century. This served as the Czar's throne room for many years. It derives its name from the faceted blocks of its façade. From the floor to the vaulted ceiling the hall is decorated with paintings of religious scenes including Adam and Eve and other nudes—the only nudes adorning the Kremlin's artistically conservative walls. These paintings were done in 1880 by two peasant artists who followed seventeenth century descriptions of the hall. They are counted among the Kremlin's lesser treasures.

A system of air heating used in this hall was considered novel for its time. It was a kind of central heating instead of the tile stoves for each room used elsewhere in the Kremlin. A furnace was situated under the building with flues for heated air leading through the chambers.

In old Russia women of the Czar's family often were not admitted to court receptions. However, they were permitted to watch if not to participate. Just over the white carved portal that leads from the Grand Kremlin Palace into the Granovitaya Palace a secret room was located. Women of the royal family could peek through a cloth-draped grated window at the regal proceedings below.

More remarkable than the inside of the Granovitaya Palace is the cupolaed roof outside—and no special ticket is required to see *it*. A cluster of small, delicately proportioned cupolas with marvellously decorated bases point toward the sky. For a photographer with an interest in composition this is a highlight of a Kremlin tour.

The Czar Bell or King of the Bells (Czar Kolokol) has in part at least the same claim to fame as the American Liberty Bell—it is cracked. However, the Czar Bell never tolled for independence or anything else. It was cracked—a big piece of metal has broken away from the bell—before it ever had the opportunity to ring. The Czar Bell now stands on a stone base in the Kremlin grounds, but it was cast in 1737 to be hung in the Ivan Bell Tower. The bell was hung, preparatory to being raised to the belfry, on wooden scaffolding in a large construction pit dug in the ground. Several days before the bell was to be raised, one of Moscow's perennial conflagrations broke out and the wooden scaffolding caught fire. Fire fighters had filled the pit with water in an effort to prevent the fire from spreading to the scaffolding. Instead of saving the bell it ruined it. The burning scaffolding collapsed, the bell plunged into the water-filled pit, and the sudden change in temperature caused one of its sides to crack and a piece to break away. Disgusted, the Czars let the bell lay in the pit until 1836 when it was raised and placed on a stone pedestal.

It is a giant bell, weighing 197 tons, its walls are two feet thick and the bell is 19 feet high. Be sure to walk around the pedestal to look through a grating in order to see the bell's clapper on the ground.

The Czar's Cannon is a masterpiece of casting. This huge, decorative cannon standing in the Kremlin grounds near the King of Bells is aimed toward the office building where members of the Soviet Government have their offices. However the cannon is not loaded and in fact has never been fired. It is 17½ feet long, its barrel is three feet in diameter, and it weighs 38 tons which probably comes close to the weight of a modern atomic cannon. Each of the cannon balls which are displayed nearby weighs nearly 4000 pounds. To pursue these shooting statistics a bit further, the powder needed to fire one cannon ball weighs about half a ton. The proud piece was cast in 1586 by Andrei Chokhov, a noted foundry artist. The cannon was made for Czarist pleasure. There is a long line of smaller but equally elegant field pieces stationed nearby on the Kremlin's soil.

RED SQUARE

No public square in the world can equal Red Square for grandeur, vastness, and inherent atmosphere. Place de la Concorde in Paris may have greater beauty and more perfect proportions (but even this can be argued). Times Square in New York may inspire greater excitement (but Red Square generates an excitement twice a year on May Day and Revolution Day that is unparalleled). Piazza Navona in Rome has a unique unity and grace, but Red Square has elements even of these.

The cobblestone expanse of Red Square is rectangular in shape. At one of its shorter sides stands the severely-lined, spired Historical Museum and opposite it the Hänsel-und-Gretel-fairy-tale architecture of St. Basil's Cathedral. Along one of Red Square's longer sides is the massive GUM department store and across the square rises the wall of the Kremlin, spruce trees in the foreground and green domes and golden cupolas behind it.

There is no place in Russia, unless it be the Kremlin itself, which is associated with more significant events over a longer span than is Red Square. It is called Krasnaya Plochad in Russian; the word, *krasnaya*, means "beautiful" as well as "red" (although the former meaning has become archaic). Originally it received its name for the beauty of the buildings around it.

In the 1500s and 1600s Red Square was the main market place of Moscow where goods of all sorts were traded in the shade of the Kremlin's walls. Just as all roads of another empire led to Rome, so did highways from major towns of the primitive Russian state converge in Red Square.

In the sixteenth century the clamor of Krasnaya Plochad was separated from the Kremlin by a deep moat running alongside the Kremlin wall and bridges spanned the moat from Red Square to the Spasskaya and Nikolsky Gates (the Nikolsky Tower is no longer used as an access to the Kremlin).

On the south side of the square, where St. Basil's Cathedral stands, the terrain slopes steeply toward the Moscow River. *Lob* is the word for "slope" in Russian. Thus when a stone elevation was raised from which the Czar's edicts and sentences were to be read to the populace it became known as Lobnoye Mesto, roughly translated, "sloping place" or "place of the slope." Sometimes the Lobnoye Mesto is pointed out to tourists as the place where people were executed. It certainly *looks* like it might have been the site for gallows or a chopping block. There *were* executions carried out in Red Square. But not on the Lobnoye Mesto. A government-published Soviet *Short Guide to Moscow* by A. Kovalyov has this to say about Red Square:

"Whatever major political events unfolded in the city, they were inevitably consummated in Red Square. This is natural because it was in the immediate neighborhood of the Kremlin—the political, administrative, and ecclesiastical center of Moscow and the principality. Furthermore, the people sought safety from enemy raids behind the Kremlin's sturdy walls. Red Square has on several occasions been the site of popular vengeance against the hated feudalistic boyars. It has also been the site of public executions. In 1671, for instance, Stepan Razin, leader of a peasant uprising, was executed in Red Square, and in 1698 Peter I executed here the *streltsi*, a class of citizens and merchants who rendered hereditary military service to the Czars, and who opposed his progressive innovations."

(This event, by the way, is depicted in a canvas entitled, "The Execution of the Streltsi," by the renowned Russian painter of historical scenes, Vasily Ivanovich Surikov, 1848–1916. It hangs in Moscow's Tretyakov Gallery. After being replaced by regular troops, the *streltsi* tried to seize the throne from Peter I who then crushed them, staging a mass execution in Red Square.)

Red Square became a battlefield in 1917 when units of soldiers, who had defected to the revolutionaries, and armed workers stormed the Nikolsky Gate, guarded by military cadets and troops, and entered the Kremlin itself.

Nowadays Red Square is the scene of a gigantic spectacle twice a year. Portraits of Marx and Lenin in vivid colors cover the central section of the GUM department store. The rest of the store's façade is draped with great red banners with slogans of the Communist Party in huge gold letters. Opposite GUM, the wall of the Kremlin is festooned with tapestry-like flags of the 15 Soviet republics. The Lobnoye Mesto is tricked up in wedding-cake fashion with reams of red cloth covering the stone wall that surrounds this mound, and a flagpole is implanted in the center of it.

The leaders of the Soviet Union, often with heads of other Communist states by their sides, stand near the Kremlin's walls on an upper level of the mausoleum in which the bodies of Lenin and Stalin lie embalmed. A military parade of selected units of all branches of the armed forces, fifty and more abreast, marches past the Soviet leaders. After the men come the mechanical implements of war—armored carriers, tanks, artillery pieces, missiles. It is noisy, stirring, frightening. The earth quakes under the heavy-treaded vehicles. The air is filled with acrid exhaust smoke. Weather permitting, jet planes streak past, low over Red Square, coming from the direction of the State Historical Museum and disappearing over St. Basil's Cathedral. It is a sight and a sound and a sensation not soon submerged in memory.

Next come members of sports clubs, many units doing acrobatics as they march. Muscular, shapely girls perform on gymnastic bars carried by sturdy men. Jersey-clad women athletes manipulate ribbons of cloth in unison to form mass patterns above the surface of Red Square. Motorcycles, sports cars, bicycles go past in turn.

Finally, for several hours in unending wave after wave, emerging in broad serpentine streams from the tributary streets, humanity flows into the square. The people carry portraits of Lenin and of the present leaders, wreaths, balloons, placards, signs, banners proclaiming ambitious production goals for farm and factory.

Places in Red Square and on the approaches to it are jammed with diplomats, visiting delegations and tourists who receive tickets to see the spectacle. Russians at home can watch on television, but only a favored few are able to attend in person—unless they march. Streets in the center of the city are closed from early morning, and only ticket-holders are permitted to stand and watch. It is the most private of public affairs.

Even though it means standing on your feet for several hours, this is an event you will not want to miss if you are in Moscow on May 1—the annual Workers' Day—or on November 7—Revolution Day. Although it falls short of actually being in the midst of the activities in Red Square, a somewhat more comfortable way to watch the parade is from a front room in the National Hotel. If you know any other tourist in a room with a view at the National beg, borrow, or steal an invitation—even though it means arriving by 7 A.M. to avoid the roadblocks! The May Day and Revolution Day shows start at 10 A.M.

THE LENIN-STALIN MAUSOLEUM

Of all the sights that Moscow has to offer, if I could see only one, *this* is the one I would choose. Seldom has civilized man conceived of a more macabre monument. Here, deep in an underground chamber, air conditioned, dramatically lighted, lie the embalmed bodies of V. I. Lenin and Joseph Stalin in glass sarcophagi. It is a shrine of Communism. It is a testimony, too, to a highly developed Soviet science of preservation. Their eyes shut, their waxen faces wearing benign expressions, Lenin and Stalin are on display for thousands of reverent or simply curious people to see each week.

Russians wait for many months to get a ticket to enter the tomb, but a tourist is privileged in Russia. An Intourist guide shepherds the day's tourists into Red Square. They congregate at the Metropole Hotel or at the corner of the State Historical Museum. (Ask a clerk in the Service Bureau of your hotel for the meeting place and time.) The several thousand Russians holding tickets for any particular day crowd into the Alexander Gardens along one segment of the Kremlin's wall and wait patiently in line for several hours. But tourists go to the head of the line. Russians do not seem to resent this at all. They generously consider it appropriate hospitality.

With tourists leading the way (those from Communist countries sometimes bear wreaths to be placed at the entrance to the mausoleum), the long queue winds at funereal pace through Red Square and starts entering the

tomb precisely when the clock in the Spasskaya Tower
strikes the appointed hour. A soldier with bared bayonet
affixed to his rifle stands at rigid attention on each side
of the entrance. The "pilgrim" descends three dozen or
so steps and, as he turns to the right past another soldier
at the foot of the stairs, he finds himself in a lofty,
darkened, stone chamber with spotlights focusing slightly
pink shafts of light on two glass caskets lying side by
side—the resting places of Lenin and Stalin. Lenin wears
black, Stalin brown. Soldiers guard either end of each
sarcophagus. In hushed voices, officers keep the line moving along its course, past the two bodies, out the other
side of the chamber, and up another flight of stairs into
the daylight.

Be sure to take a moment to look at the faces of Russians, if you are lucky enough to be at the end of the
tourists' queue so that ordinary Soviet citizens are following after you. Here at arm's length lie the men whose
names were a part of every activity of every Soviet man,
woman, and child. In kindergarten, at school, at camp, in
the army, at work, on the radio, in the newspapers—the
names of Lenin and Stalin filled the Russians' eyes and
ears and minds. Lenin's name still does. Some Russians
may feel veneration. Others may experience a sense of
hatred. Others are awed.

A foreigner can not fail to wonder why there is an endless line of Russians waiting to see the occupants of the
tomb even though Lenin has been lying there for well
over a quarter century and Stalin for more than half
a decade. Part of the explanation is in the preceding
paragraph. Part may be found in the fact that Moscow
is *the* tourist center for the U.S.S.R.'s 210,000,000 people
and the Lenin-Stalin Mausoleum combines what the
Empire State Building, Madame Tussaud's Waxwork,
the pyramids, the Taj Mahal are to other tourist centers.

Although it comes as an anticlimax, tourists usually

are escorted from the Lenin-Stalin Tomb to the section of the Kremlin wall just behind it. Here various Communist greats are buried—either in graves in the grassy strip along the wall or their ashes in urns are placed in the wall itself. The remains of Andrei Vishinsky, the prosecutor at the purge trials of the 1930s and Soviet delegate to the United Nations, are here. So are those of John Reed, the author of *Ten Days that Shook the World*, a personal account of the revolution. There are also mass graves of revolutionary fighters.

The mausoleum, constructed of muted red Ukrainian granite, Karelian porphyry rock, and trimmed with black and gray labradorite, is shaped like the base of square-block pyramid without an apex. Its angular shape provides a ledgelike balcony from which the leaders review parades.

The trees along the Kremlin wall behind the tomb are often described as pines. However, Professor Scott S. Pauley, of the School of Forestry, Institute of Agriculture, University of Minnesota, wrote me after his trip to Russia to point out that these trees "are in fact spruces, and not spruces indigenous of the U.S.S.R. or the satellite countries, but one of our native American species: Colorado blue spruce (*Picea pungens* Engelmann)! This species is widely planted in the U.S.S.R. for ornamental purposes, as it is in the U.S.A. I had some amusement chiding Russian foresters about having our 'capitalistic spruces' guarding the tomb of Lenin and Stalin."

Try to witness the changing of the mausoleum guard. The tour of duty of the two soldiers posted at the entrance varies with the season—the colder the weather the shorter the tour. However, the brief ceremony takes place on the hour and, in any season, usually at noon. Your Intourist interpreter-guide can tell you the precise hour during your stay in Moscow.

The hours for viewing the bodies are: Tuesday, Wednesday, Thursday and Saturday: 1 P.M. to 5 P.M.; Sunday: 12 noon to 4 P.M. The tomb is closed on Monday and Friday.

THE SUBWAY

Moscow's extensive subway system is called the Metro. The word is borrowed from the French *Metropolitain,* the name of the Paris subway. A number of engineers who helped construct the Moscow subway were borrowed from the United States. The Metro is an astounding achievement of engineering. Exceptionally long escalators reach deep into clean, well-lighted, spacious stations. It is also, in the words of Soviet newspaper writers, a shocking example of overly elaborate, wasteful construction. Stations are adorned with mosaic work, with palatial chandeliers, with statues, with carvings and art work worthy of a cathedral.

The trains seem almost an afterthought, but they run quickly, smoothly, and on schedule. Many motormen as well as most platform workers are women. A subway ride costs 50 kopecks—half a ruble. Maps of the subway system are available at most newsstands in hotels and elsewhere. The Metro is a good way to get around inexpensively and quickly. Whether or not you use it for transportation, your tour of Moscow will not be complete without stops at several Metro stations. A small pamphlet put out by Intourist, entitled *Places of Interest In and Around Moscow,* states: "During an excursion the visitor will see the architecture, sculpture, and decoration of the Moscow underground and learn the history of its construction. Duration two or two and a half hours."

Unless subways are your business you may find two

MOSCOW UNIVERSITY

Moscow University's 32-story skyscraper is only one of 37 structures that comprise this outstanding educational institution. It was built after the war, and on September 1, 1953, its doors were first opened to students. Seven hundred twenty feet high (almost half the height of the 1472-foot tall Empire State Building), the main building is occupied by the office of the university rector (the European equivalent of a college president), the geological and geographical departments, an extensive library, an auditorium with a seating capacity of 1500 and a museum of the rocks and minerals of the Soviet Union, gymnasiums and a swimming pool as well as many of the student dormitories.

The students live in rooms of closet-size measuring about four feet by nine feet. Each unit of two rooms shares a common entrance hall, a toilet and shower. Girls and boys live on the same floor with to-be-expected consequences. Parties are often held late into the night.

The grounds are spread over 220 acres with many trees, bushes and flower beds.

The university is situated on a height overlooking Moscow. The area used to be called Swallow Hills, but the name has been changed to Lenin Hills. It is a favorite recreation area for the people of Moscow. In winter a ski jump is used for competitions. From a promontory there is an excellent view of the city of Moscow. There is an even finer view of Moscow from the university skyscraper observation tower. In the foreground is a sport complex with a huge stadium seating more than 100,000 people, tennis courts, basketball courts, swimming pools, and other athletic facilities. Soviet officials hope that this will be used as the site for a future Olympics.

Although a member of an Intourist tour has no difficulty getting into the university, it is quite a different story for a casual visitor. This is probably one of the few universities in the world requiring a special pass to enter the campus.

On a tour of the university be sure to see the basement stores and markets selling sausages, cheeses, and other foods to the students who may cook in kitchens provided on each floor of the dormitories. There are several categories of restaurants and cafeterias which offer menus of various quality and price. There is a bank for the convenience of students and, like other banks in the U.S.S.R., the university branch sells lottery tickets to those who wish to gamble in the government-sponsored drawings.

Book stands in the lobbies sell, besides such staples as paper and pencils, editions of Mark Twain in Russian and a pen copied from the "Parker 51," costing $8, and made in Communist China.

(The old campus with buildings for the faculties of literature and other humanities is situated across Manege Square from the Kremlin.)

OTHER MOSCOW SIGHTS

Gorky Park: This is Moscow's largest public park (or "Park of Culture and Rest" as it is called by Soviet authorities). Opened in 1928, Gorky Park lines a long stretch of the Moscow River. There is an amusements area which includes a giant Ferris wheel, "airplane" rides and a hall of distorted mirrors. There are a number of restaurants in the park, an area for chess and checker games, and pavilions where exhibitions of art work and machinery are held.

Sokolniki Park: This is another large recreation park. It gained its world-wide fame in the summer of 1959 as the site of the American National Exhibition. The Exhibition buildings, erected by the United States, were purchased by the Soviet Government. Although the U. S. exhibits no longer are there, you can visit the place where Richard Nixon and Nikita Khrushchev carried on their famous kitchen debate. Like Gorky Park, Sokolniki Park has an area devoted to various "rides" for children and adults. A visit to either Gorky Park or Sokolniki Park on a spring or summer Sunday, when Russians come out in droves, is a most worth while way of seeing how Russians enjoy themselves.

Zoo: The Moscow zoo is situated at Bolshaya Gruzinskaya Street 1. The animals here are much like those in any other zoo, but if there are children in your party they might be interested in spending an hour here.

Bolshoi Theatre: This is described more fully in the chapter devoted to theaters, but even if you do not attend a performance here you should see this renowned building to make your Moscow visit complete.

Moscow Conservatory of Music: The area in front of the building is graced by a statue of Chaikovsky, seated with arm raised as if writing down music. For those interested in music, this is the place to attend a concert; others should pass it on a tour of the city.

House of Trade Unions: Situated near the National, Moscow and Metropole Hotels this green-colored historic building stands on Okhotnogo Ryada ("Hunter's Row") Street. A former noblemen's club, it is now the property of the state's Trade Union Council. It's chandeliered Hall of Columns is the scene of funerals of famous men. If you happen to be in Moscow when a figure of importance in politics, literature, or science dies, you may be interested in walking through the hall to view the body which is placed in an open casket on a high bank of flowers while bands relieve each other in continuous rendition of the solemn funeral march. Long lines of Muscovites always participate in these peculiarly Soviet rituals. Andrei Vishinsky, who died while representing the Soviet Union in the United Nations, lay in state in this hall as did Lenin himself. The House of Unions is also used for meetings, concerts and convocations of various sorts.

Council of Ministers Building: On the same street as the House of Trade Unions and directly opposite the Moscow Hotel, this gray stone building houses the offices of the Council of Ministers, an important body of the Soviet Government.

Planetarium: It is at Sadovaya Kudrinskaya Street 5. There are lectures here for students and adults on astronomy and Soviet Sputniks and Luniks. If you understand Russian a visit here wculd be interesting.

Foreign Ministry: This is one of Moscow's most imposing skyscrapers. You won't get inside though unless you have an appointment because, as is the case in many government buildings, there are guards (polite but armed) at the door to keep all but the invited out.

Tass and **Radio Moscow:** Here again you need permission to visit either the Tass or Radio Moscow offices. It is possible to get an appointment if you have a professional interest in either of these enterprises. It is best to write ahead of time although a telephone call while in Moscow may secure you an invitation.

Railroad Stations: There are a number of railroad stations in Moscow. If you have the time a brief visit at night is interesting. The waiting room will very likely be filled with travelers waiting for trains. Often they sleep on benches and on the floor, great packages and parcels around them. Travelers from the provinces usually do not go to a hotel even if they have a 12-hour wait between trains but rather they camp out right at the station. The names of the most important railroad stations (named after the main terminal at the other end of the line) are: Byelorussia Station, Kazan Station, Kiev Station, Kursk Station, Leningrad Station, Paveletsk Station, Savyolovo Station, Yaroslavl Station, and Riga Station.

OTHER STATUES

In driving around Moscow you will see many statues, and a brief word or two about the most important may be helpful:

The statue of Minin and Prince Pozharsky was the first statue ever erected in Moscow. It stands in front of St. Basil's Cathedral in Red Square. Kuzma Minin, who died in 1616, was a merchant who rallied fellow Russians in 1611 to establish an army to drive out Polish invaders. Prince Dmitri Mikhailovich Pozharsky, was invited to head Minin's militia. With Minin and Pozharsky at their head the troops marched to Moscow from what is now the city of Gorky and fought a decisive battle on August 24, 1612, routing the Polish occupiers. The statue of bronze, resting on a polished granite pedestal, shows the two men, one seated, the other standing with his right arm upraised. On the pedestal the two bas-reliefs depict scenes of fund-raising for the army and scenes of the march on the capital.

The statue of Alexander Sergeyevich Pushkin, erected in 1880, stands in Pushkin Square off Gorky Street. The statue was financed by donations from people in all walks of life. Originally the site of the statue was the Strastnoi Monastery. In 1937, to commemorate the centennial of the poet's death, the Square was renamed Pushkin Square. It was at this time that the lines from Pushkin's poem "Monument" were engraved on the pedestal. They read:

The rumor of my fame will sweep through vasty Russia,
And all its people speak this name, whose light shall reign.
Alike for haughty Slav, and Finn and savage Tungus,
And Kalmick riders of the plain.
I shall be loved, and long the people will remember
The kindly thoughts I stirred—my music's brightest crown,
How in this cruel age I celebrated freedom,
And begged for truth for those cast down.

Pushkin, who lived from 1799 to 1837, is considered the founder of modern Russian literature. A number of Pushkin's poems inspired Russian composers in their creation of operas and ballets. Most noted perhaps are *Eugen Onegin, Boris Godunov* and *The Bronze Horseman.*

The Monument to the Battle of Plevna is one of the most unusual monuments in Moscow. It commemorated the battle fought in 1877 after Russian grenadiers had captured the Bulgarian city of Plevna from Turkish rule. Erected in 1887, the monument is in the form of a chapel with panels depicting the exploits of the Russian soldiers. The monument stands on the capital's boulevard ring. It is built of gray blocks of stone, and sometimes surprises visitors because of the fact that it is decorated with a cross.

Statues of V. I. Lenin are commonplace in Moscow as well as in every other Soviet city and hamlet. Lenin is shown in a variety of postures that have become classic. Sometimes he is standing with arm outstretched as if addressing a crowd. Sometimes he is seated on a bench with Stalin. Sometimes he is seated as if in inspired meditation. The latter is the pose of a statue of Lenin in Moscow's Sovietskaya Square.

A bronze statue on a black stone pedestal stands at Teatralny Proyezd. It depicts the first Russian printer, Ivan Fyodorov, a self-taught artisan. The inscription reads: *"The printer of books, till then unknown."*

Probably the most heroic staute in Moscow stands at the entrance to the Agricultural and Industrial Exhibition. Entitled "Worker and Collective Farm Woman," this enormous silver-colored statue shows a man and woman, each with an arm upraised holding a hammer and sickle.

A statue of the playwright Mayakovsky stands in the square which bears his name near the Chaikovsky Concert Hall.

A statue to the writer Maxim Gorky stands on Gorky Street near the Byelorussia Railroad Station.

INFORMATION BOOTHS

A particularly useful Soviet institution are the *Spravka* or "Inquiry" booths. These are situated on street corners, at railroad stations and at other convenient locations. Upon payment of a few rubles (and often only a few kopecks), the clerk will answer questions about railroad or airplane schedules, about what's playing in various theaters, the hours of museums, and will even find the

addresses of residents of Moscow. The clerk will also
tell you the shortest way to get from place to place
either by bus, subway or on foot.

By the way, the fare on Moscow buses is 45 kopecks
(4½ cents) anywhere in town. The fare for the Moscow
subway is 50 kopecks (5 cents) and you can ride all
day if you wish.

CHAPTER SIX

Moscow: Museums and Art Galleries

A slice of brown bread more than forty years old is proudly displayed under glass in one of Moscow's many museums. It is no ordinary piece of bread. It is the bread of a martyr and is preserved by those who inherited Russia's revolution in much the same spirit as are Peter's chains preserved in a Roman church.

One morning in 1917 a mother gave her son a piece of bread as he left home. For this poor family during the revolution period of food shortage this half-pound of bread was the boy's ration for the day. The lad was a sixteen-year-old Communist Party member named N. V. Khodyakov. After he had gone, his mother discovered that he had hidden the bread on the table for her. He was killed that day by a bullet while fighting with Czarist soldiers near the Metropole Hotel. His mother kept the bread in a small glass container for forty years as a precious memento of her son's bravery and generosity, and finally she gave it to a neighborhood museum where it is being preserved with chemicals.

This unique exhibit is characteristic of many Moscow museums. Just as Americans preserve houses in which George Washington slept so do the Russians under Communism preserve relics of their revolution, of the oppression which preceded it and of the accomplishment that followed. Of course, this omits many other aspects of Russian history. Museums ignore any material accomplishments *before* the revolution (although such ac-

147

complishments in literature and the other arts receives recognition).

Soviet citizens are earnest museum-goers. Groups of school children, led by condescending-voiced guides and shepherded by their teachers, troop through endless museum corridors. Adults from factories and offices are conducted through and dutifully record the guide's words in small notebooks. Seldom are the corridors of Moscow museums and art galleries empty. Sunday, the Soviet worker's day off, is a particularly crowded day, and it is good advice to stay away from these museums and art galleries on Sunday.

Tourists are often surprised that many Czarist treasures and art collections remain undamaged and are on display. The fact of the matter is that although a great many valuable pieces were carried out of the country (and, in fact, sold by the government to obtain foreign capital during difficult times), an astounding collection of jewels and treasures of all sorts remain in Soviet galleries.

At the entrance to many museums you will be asked to put awkward cloth scuffs on your shoes. These are tied around the ankles by strings but almost invariably fall off, particularly when you climb steps. These cloth shoe coverings are, of course, intended to protect the often valuable inlaid floors of the museums.

THE KREMLIN MUSEUM

Situated inside the Kremlin's walls, this richest of Moscow museums (built in 1851) is called Oruzhennaya Palata in Russian which means "Armory," and it contains fabulous Czarist treasures.

Be sure to see:

Precious jeweled Easter eggs given as gifts to members of the Czar's family. These exquisite objects were hand-made by artists of the Faberge firm whose work gained fame throughout the world. One delicately designed "egg" of gold, silver, colorful porcelain and diamonds has small portraits of members of the royal family around it.

Other Faberge work in the same glass display case includes a tiny and perfect model of the Czar's train including a chapel coach for worship. It has marvellous detail work and can be wound up and run.

Also in this case is an exquisite life-size pansy fashioned of gemmed enamel with the stem set in a small vase filled with glass to resemble water. Workmanship of infinite talent designed each jeweled petal of the pansy to spring open at a touch and reveal a perfect miniature of some member of the Czar's family.

A pair of boots that were worn by Czar Peter the Great. The boots come to the waist of an average man. Peter was a person of enormous height (more than seven feet tall) and of a variety of talents. In fact, he made these boots himself, having learned a number of trades on travels abroad—shipbuilding and bootmaking among them.

Magnificent long-trained gowns of Czarinas, wives of the pre-revolutionary rulers.

Ermine-fringed, jewel-encrusted crowns of various Czars comprise one of the museum's most valuable collections. There is the crown which Ivan III placed on the head of his grandson Dmitri in 1498. There are sceptres, golden balls surmounted by a cross with a crust of hundreds of diamonds, rubies, emeralds, and other stones.

Probably the biggest Bible in Russia is here, in a magnificent case of gold and diamonds.

Other outstanding pieces in the museum include Boris Godunov's throne and his begemmed ring; a set of

English Renaissance silverware which, it is said, can not be equalled in Britain itself; Church vestments encrusted with gold, pearls and other jewels, and a roomful of regal Czarist coaches standing behind full-sized model horses.

CENTRAL LENIN MUSEUM
Revolutionary Square 4

For a quick switch from treasures of Czarist days to a shrine to the Father of the Communist Revolution, visit this old red-brick building just off Red Square. Its nineteen exhibition halls are dedicated to V. I. Lenin as are so many smaller museums throughout the Soviet Union. His career is traced from a model of the appropriately humble home in which he was born to a death mask of his face. One glass case contains an overcoat which Lenin is seen to be wearing in many photographs. The coat has a bullet hole caused by an unsuccessful attempt on his life in 1918. (The woman assassin was seized, jailed and died only a few years ago.)

There are heroic paintings of every phase of Lenin's life, but it strikes many visitors that in not a single picture is Leon Trotsky shown although he was intimately associated with Lenin during the early years of the revolution. The answer, of course, is that Trotsky and Stalin disagreed after Lenin's death, Trotsky sought haven in Mexico where he was assassinated, and Stalin eliminated Trotsky's name from Soviet history except for references to him as an "enemy of the people."

The building of the Lenin Museum was constructed in 1892 and it housed the so-called "City Duma," or city council, before the revolution. There was bitter fighting between the revolutionaries and those who opposed the revolution in 1917 for control of this building.

STATE HISTORICAL MUSEUM
Red Square 1/2

Exhibits at this important Soviet museum trace the origin and history of people of the present Soviet territory from three hundred thousand years back until the last half of the nineteenth century. For the student of anthropology, this museum is a must. For the rest of us a more cursory tour through the halls of this spired brick building will do.

A large statue of Stalin stands in the entrance hall, as in many Soviet institutions, despite the de-emphasis in Stalin's importance by his successors. Display cases abound with archaeological finds of ancient civilizations including primitive mirrors, helmets, pottery, bells, beads, and horse bits. There is an ancient stone with inscriptions found in Yerevan and dating from 685–645 B.C. It's interesting to note that in this museum, as in others in the Soviet Union, the terms B.C. and A.D. are not used. Instead, in this state which does not recognize Christ or any other God, the terms "before our era" and "after our era" are used.

The development of society is explained in Marxist terms. For example, one chart showing a tribal movement in the first century A.D. bears an inscription which reads: "The process of disintegration of tribal relations [based on blood relations] continued and a class society and a union of tribes began to evolve."

The museum, across the street from the Lenin Museum, stands at one end of Red Square. A street running on either side of it leads into the square.

Until a decade or so ago the left-hand side of the building (as you face Red Square) bore an historic inscription. During the time of the revolution, Communists had painted in large letters on the red wall an inscription to the effect that "religion is the opiate of the people." However, with the passage of revolutionary fanaticism, this inscription was removed.

Treasures in this museum include: a painted clay vase used for storing grain in the second century B.C., unearthed in a Ukrainian village; a cobbler's wooden last inscribed with customers' names and found in Novgorod excavations, probably from the fourteenth century; coats of mail, helmets, and shields of Russian warriors of the fifteenth century; a robe worn by Ivan the Terrible; a map of Russia drawn by the son of Boris Godunov, and a model of a seventeenth-century printing press. A hall is devoted to the Tartars who overran Russia and dominated it for several centuries.

MUSEUM OF THE REVOLUTION
OF THE U.S.S.R.
Gorky Street 21
Telephone: 23 96 81

Just before the revolution this building was a noblemen's club. No women were admitted. The set-back, columned, central part was constructed in the mid-eighteenth century as a residence for a great Russian poet, named M. Kheraskov. The wings and the gates, guarded by statues of lions, were built in the nineteenth century. A six-inch gun inside the gate was used by revolutionary troops to fire on the Kremlin in October 1917.

The museum is the main repository of relics of the revolution. In the entrance hallway hangs a painting by V. Kuznetsov, "Storming the Winter Palace." Here are home-made bombs actually retrieved from hiding places where revolutionaries had deposited them. You can

even see bricks taken from a jail wall with initials
scratched out by prisoners. Diagrams show the disposition of forces in the abortive 1905 uprising against the
Czar.

Numerous paintings depict class struggle. One called
"Paying Off" is described in a useful English-language
booklet (which can be purchased at the museum) in
these words: "The artist shows a group of workers who
had come to their employer for a settlement. Separated
from them by sturdy banisters, he—their lord and
master—relaxes in an easy chair. His fat face expresses
self-satisfaction, his pose confidence; it seems that no
power on earth can dislodge his filthy, corpulent body.
However, suffice it to glance at the faces of the workers
to see how insecure is the position of the capitalist.
The people confronting him are not ignorant, humble
slaves, but enlightened workers insisting on their legitimate rights. The eyes of the workers burn with hatred.
They seem ready at any moment to tear down the
banister and wreak vengeance on their hated enemy."

We can recommend this museum only to those with a
special interest in the revolution or to tourists with
more than a week to spend in Moscow.

The museum is open on Monday, Wednesday and
Friday from 12 noon to 8 p.m.; Tuesday, Thursday, and
Sunday from 10 a.m. to 6 p.m. It is closed on Saturday.
There is no admission charge.

MUSEUM OF SECRET COMMUNIST MEETINGS
Bolshevistskaya Ulitsa 4

The proper complete name of this museum is "Museum
of Krasnaya Presnya, Branch of State Revolutionary
Museum." In the years between 1905 and 1917 this area
was the center of the workers' district of Moscow. In some

ways the section has changed little. Across the street from this museum is a sidewalk water pump which is a principal source of water for the immediate neighborhood. In both the unsuccessful 1905 uprising and in the 1917 revolution by which the Communists were brought to power, the leadership of the revolutionaries in this worker's district convened in this building which was erected as a dwelling in the early 1900s.

A plaque on the outside of this board building reads: *"Here in October 1917 the District Committee of the Russian Social Democratic Workers' Party of Bolsheviks and the Revolutionary Committee of the Presnyansky District were housed."*

The museum conveys something of the flavor of those times. Pictures of bearded revolutionaries of the era look for all the world like the caricaturist's concept of bomb-throwing Bolsheviks. A drawing of the sort which is popular in Soviet museums shows a "pyramid of the social order" existing before the revolution. It shows exploited workers at the base holding the entire pyramid on their shoulders. The rich, exploiting, capitalist and land-owner classes are shown indolently eating and drinking. On the next level of the pyramid are Czarist soldiers. Above them appears the Russian Orthodox Church clergy. At the apex is the Czar's family.

A photograph shows the desperate living conditions of workers in a factory in this area of Moscow. In a men's dormitory people are sleeping on shelf-like bunks.

Probably the most interesting part of the museum is a mock-up representing the disposition of the fighting forces in the last days—December 17 and 18, 1905—of the 1905 uprising with workers defending what a guide will proudly describe as the "biggest barricade in Moscow at that time." Small figures of Czarist cavalry are shown charging the barricade as workers fire from it. The barricade was 18 feet high. There were more than 1000

store still bears the sign in Russian: WHOLESALE DEALERS IN CAUCASIAN FRUITS. KALANDADZE. This was the "front" used by the plotters.

The old-fashioned windows are of small rectangular panes of glass. Behind them are displayed nuts and teas, a large mold of white cheese under glass, and dried prunes. When you enter the inner door a bell rings. This used to alert the shopkeeper as well as the revolutionaries downstairs. The simple furnishings of this fake store remain as they did in those days. There is a kerosene lamp. On the counter stands an abacus (a primitive adding machine consisting of beads on a wire frame, and still widely used in Russia). Display cases hold Caucasian nuts, raisins, and a large bag of rice.

In the back room of this small store the proprietor's wife used to live. It is now a museum which traces the shop's history. There is a picture of M. I. Kalandadze, a bearded, handsome man who rented his shop to the revolutionaries. There is another picture of S. Kabidze who was in charge of the shop. Be sure to look for the primitive duplicating or mimeographing apparatus. It bears the legend: *Made by Ellams Duplicator Company Ltd. 12 King Street, Cheapside, London E.C.*

At the time there were five underground printing shops of this sort in Moscow. A picture of a large cabin-type house where a similar press existed is shown in one of the old photographs on the museum's wall. Several of the illegal printing establishments were discovered by the authorities. This shop never was detected. However, after about one year of operation, the revolutionaries feared that they *might* be discovered, and the decision was made in September 1906 to move to a "grocery shop." There is a photograph also of this "phony" establishment.

After the successful 1917 revolution conspirators who

used to work here persuaded the authorities to establish
a museum. The store was rearranged in its original style,
and the "heart" of the establishment downstairs was restored. The restoration work was done in 1923–24 and
this museum was opened. Remnants of some of the original materials used were discovered in the restoration
work. A display case holds the lead type which was
used to print copies of the illegal newspaper *Rabochi*,
(*The Worker*). An article in this one-page revolutionary
newspaper on display reads:

"Old Russia is dying. A new Russia is being born. Old
Russia is darkness, oppression and the quiet of the grave.

"New Russia is life, freedom, the victorious struggle for
a better future for the people.

"Old Russia is illiteracy and ignorance of the people,
muddled-mindness and dullness of rulers.

"A worker helpless, a peasant docile—both exploited
without any limit by a capitalist, a kulak, a landlord,
officials shamelessly plundering peoples. . . ."

The newspaper called on workers to rally for the future
uprising. It said: "When peoples' masses are united no
one is able to oppose them. When they are conscious of
their interests, no one is able to deceive them. Then they
take what they need.

"Unity and consciousness are written on its banner by
our workers' party."

It is interesting to note that the idiom used in this early
document differs little from that used in Communist literature today.

Behind the counter of the main room is a trap door.
It leads down a steep plank staircase. *Be careful of your
head as you descend!* This leads to a damp cellar, musty
and dank. Just as in old days, barrels, boxes, and tools
are stored here. At the far end of this small cellar room
can be seen the opening of a well. At one time it was
much deeper, but it has been partially filled in. When

Kaladadze rented his shop, according to one version of the story, he did not know the real intentions of his tenants. They complained to Kaladadze of water gathering in the damp cellar, and asked that a well be dug for drainage. Kaladadze obliged his tenants. Part way down the shaft the revolutionaries dug a short horizontal tunnel into the wall of the well. It has now been lined with wood and a red, rough carpet put down for visitors, but it is still not recommended for overly corpulent people. You crawl through this tunnel into a room with floor dimensions five feet-square and its ceiling only slightly higher. It is dug out of the ground. Here by candlelight the revolutionaries printed their pamphlets and newspapers on a small hand press. A small electric lamp has been substituted for the candle, but otherwise all is as it was. There is the small printing press with the type set on it for a rabble-rousing sheet; in a niche in the wall there is a wooden box with compartments for the various letters of the old Russian alphabet.

It is uncomfortable to crawl through the tunnel, but the effort is highly recommended. In no other place in Moscow did we sense the flavor of the days that led to the Communists' coming to power.

Next door to this museum is a shoe-repair shop and there are apartments where people still reside in the other three stories of this building. A blue postal box at the entrance, and a sign reading MUSEUM are the only things that have changed since the days when Communist agents entered surreptitiously and tucked a package of pamphlets under their coats to be scattered suddenly in crowds or in factories.

The museum's hours are: Monday and Wednesday: 12 noon to 8 P.M.; Friday: 12 noon to 6 P.M.; Tuesday and Thursday: 10 A.M. to 6 P.M.; Sunday and Holidays: 10 A.M. to 6 P.M. There is no admission charge.

STATE LITERARY MUSEUM
Dimitrova Ulitsa 38

This museum can be recommended only to those with a special interest in Soviet literary figures. There is material on such famous Soviet writers as Maxim Gorky, Mikhail Sholokov, Alexei Tolstoy, Ilya Ehrenburg, V. V. Mayakovsky, and many others. Some of their original manuscripts are preserved. There are photographs and paintings of authors, playwrights, poets, and their families. One of the most interesting exhibits when I visited the museum (exhibits are changed from time to time) concerned the career of Mayakovsky, the great playwright and poet. Mayakovsky visited the United States in the early 1920s and an announcement card, printed in the United States, is displayed in one case. It reads:

"Unusual Event in Cleveland. December 29th. Lecture by well-known writer and poet Vladimir Mayakovsky, just arrived from the U.S.S.R. Admission 50 cents. Carpenter's Hall."

In 1926 Mayakovsky published a small volume entitled *My Discovery of America.* He wrote that he found America to be seven years behind the Soviet Union! He praised U.S. technology and production, but regretted the lack of human values. (Writings by Communist journalists and authors who visit Western countries today have changed little in this appraisal.) When Mayakovsky returned to the Soviet Union he gave a number of talks. A poster announcing a talk in the Ukraine reads:

"America as I see it. Ford As He Is. The Fables of Ford. Chicago—One Hundred Fifty Million Dollars and Slaughter Houses."

The rather cryptic titles of the lecture poster reflect something of the impressions that Mayakovsky brought back to his audiences.

Before the revolution the gracious building now housing the Literary Museum was a Moscow merchant's home and is typical of aristocratic residences of that era.

The hours of the State Literary Museum are: Sunday, Thursday, and Saturday: 10 A.M. to 6 P.M.; Wednesday and Friday: 12 noon to 8 P.M.; Monday: 10 A.M. to 4 P.M. The museum is closed on Tuesday and also on the last day of every month.

The admission charge is one ruble (ten cents or about ninepence). Although this is unlikely to affect you, Soviet soldiers are admitted free and students get in for half price.)

APARTMENT OF WRITER
NIKOLAI A. OSTROVSKY
Gorky Street 16, Entrance 1

Ostrovsky is one of the most famous and officially revered authors of the Soviet period. His was a tragic life. He died at the age of thirty-two in this Gorky Street apartment on September 22, 1936. As a young man he entered the Young Communist League and when he was fourteen years old he went to the front to fight in the civil war that secured power for the Communists. He was twenty, in 1924, when he entered the Communist party. His most famous novel, which dealt with the revolutionary period, was entitled *How the Steel Was Tempered.* It has sold more than twelve million copies, has been published more than three hundred times, including editions in eighteen languages in fifteen countries, making him one of the most successful authors of modern times.

An English language edition in 1937 was entitled *The Making of a Hero*. His relatives still collect the royalties.

After the revolution, in which he was wounded, Ostrovsky suffered from a form of polio. In 1927, he became partially blind, and in 1929 he was totally blind. *How the Steel Was Tempered* and another novel, *Born of the Tempest*, were dictated by Ostrovsky after his eyesight had failed.

He lived in this Moscow apartment for two years— from 1935 until his death in 1936. The apartment contains numerous mementos of his life including: his school report card which shows that he got all "5's" (the highest mark) except for a few "4's" in arithmetic, geography, and painting; a model of the village where he was born; and a map of the Soviet Union and Eastern Europe showing all of the various towns, schools, libraries, ships, collective farms, and other places, projects and enterprises named after this Soviet hero-author.

Ostrovsky's bedroom has been preserved very much as it was when he was bedridden there. As is true of national heroes in other countries there are now legends about Ostrovsky. For example, the eager guide at this museum will tell you that Ostrovsky, although blind, knew where every book in his large bedroom bookcase was placed. Ostrovsky dictated his books to willing volunteers and it is said that he could remember almost every word of long passages after he had dictated them. The guide will also play a phonograph recording of Ostrovsky broadcasting in April 1936 to a meeting of Soviet young people, telling them to lead upright, productive lives. He dictated *Born of the Tempest* often seven or eight hours at a stretch. When asked how it was possible to do this, Ostrovsky once replied that at night he concentrated on his characters and plots and had chapters all laid out in his mind when it came time to dictate.

A pitiful item in the bedroom is a long stick partially covered with cloth which rests near his bed. This was used by Ostrovsky, whose arms were partially paralyzed, for wiping his forehead or pushing his hair back. Buttons near his bed summoned various members of the family. He received from thirty to forty letters a day from admirers, and he dictated replies to each. Secretaries would read fourteen daily papers and many magazines to him, so the Ostrovsky legend goes. Many of the great of his era in literature, music, and the arts would frequently call on him and there are paintings to depict this.

Ostrovsky's wife, Ryissa, who often took dictation from him, is now director of this museum and if you wish, you may meet her. Although this is a museum to the memory of a literary figure, it is not without its political overtones. A cartoon recalls, with figures caricaturing the respective countries, that in 1936 *How the Steel Was Tempered* was confiscated by authorities in Japan, in 1940 it was banned in France, and 1957 the House Un-American Activities Committee of the U. S. Congress said it should not be read.

The museum's hours are: Sunday, Tuesday, Thursday, and Saturday: 10 A.M. to 6 P.M.; Wednesday and Friday: 12 noon to 8 P.M. Closed Mondays. There is no admission charge.

MUSEUM OF SAFETY AT WORK
Prospekt Lenina 10

This museum is a phenomenon of a state which claims to have eliminated all but the workers' (and peasants') class. It is intended to reflect the state's concern for the welfare and safety of its workers while at their jobs. Except for this "off-beat" aspect, the museum (run by the Soviet Trade Unions Council) has little to interest anyone who is not especially concerned with safety devices in factories.

Groups of Soviet factory workers go through this

dreary museum in a steady stream. Chairs are set up in each room and lecturers explain various factory safety methods. The exhibits include types of lightning rods, warning signals to protect workers from moving cranes, and various forms of ventilation. There are recommendations for workers including one that laborers in "hot shops" such as foundries shall drink salty water. The proper name of this museum: "The Soviet Trade Union Committee All-Union Permanent Exhibit on Labor Protection."

If after this description you still want to go, the museum is located within Gorky Park and a narrow road leads to it off the main avenue, Prospekt Lenina.

MUSEUM OF FOLK ART
Stanislavsky Ulitsa 7

Here in a one-room museum are displayed objects of Russian folk art. This museum is recommended to those who are especially interested in folk art or to the careful souvenir purchaser who wants to know more about the items he is buying. On display here are various small boxes of black lacquer work, carved wooden figures, gaily painted bowls of wood, and trays of metal. There is also embroidered work on tablecloths and shirts. Clay toys of vivid and imaginative designs and colors that are native to villages near Moscow are shown. Carved boxes, chests, pipes, and cigarette holders made from walrus bones by people of the far north are also displayed.

DONSKOY MONASTERY
Donskaya Square 1

As was true of many other ancient Russian monasteries, this gem of turreted walls and noteworthy churches was originally built as a fortification. This was the site of a Russian military encampment on the busy south-bound trade route to the Crimea, to Persia, and to Samarkand in central Asia. On this site the Russians won a battle against tribes from the south in 1591 and Russian ruler Ivan the Terrible built this monastery. It is now preserved as a state architectural museum.

Ancient red-brick walls, massive in girth and with ornamented towers surround the acres of this old monastery with its seventeenth-century church and cathedral. The church was begun in 1634 and finished in 1698. Its circular rotunda is newer, added during a remodeling in 1717. Services are still held here. It has been newly restored and its cupola is painted a rich royal blue. The cupola is set on a red tower made distinctive by scallops of three layers of green roofing. Implanted on the cupola is an elaborate gold Russian Orthodox cross.

An old graveyard of crowded, often elaborate but decaying tombstones lies at the foot of this small church. Many aristocratic old Russian families are buried here and among the famous Russians' graves are those of literary figure Alexander Dimitrivich Tolstoy and the mother of Ivan Sergeyevich Turgenev, the Russian writer who lived from 1818–1883.

The main cathedral was constructed between 1684 and 1693. It has five great onion-shaped cupolas of dull silver color on the surface of which gold stars are carefully scattered. Inside the lofty cathedral beneath the gray stone floor marked by metal plaques are the graves of a number of distinguished Russians including Patriarch Tikhon. He was head of the powerful Russian Orthodox Church when the Communists came to power. He died on March 25, 1925, having lived to see the decline of the church under Communism.

Although the entire monastery within the Moscow baroque-style walls is a museum, the cathedral houses

most of the exhibits. In the basement are old prints of
St. Petersburg in the 1700s. There are models of a number of Russian architectural wonders in their original
state. Thus a visit to this museum is preferable after you
have had a chance to visit some of the actual places,
such as the magnificent belfry of the Zagorsk Monastery,
about an hour and a half drive from Moscow. There are
also interesting paintings of Moscow as it appeared in
the 1800s. You will see what the original building of the
Lenin Library looked like when it was built between
1784 and 1786 as a private Moscow mansion. There is
also a model of Moscow's Kazan Railroad Station, built
in 1914, with its four-story square tower and its needle-
like spire, and its beautiful Zodiac sign clock. There is
a model of Leningrad's Kazan Cathedral built between
1801 and 1811 which is now History of Religion Museum
(*anti*-religious museum would be more accurate).

The grounds of the monastery are opened daily until
8 P.M. and it is a place of charm and beauty for photographs or simply for a walk.

The museum inside the old cathedral is open from 11
A.M. to 6 P.M. daily except Monday when the building
is closed. It is also closed on the last day of each month.

LEO TOLSTOY'S HOME
Ulitsa Lva Tolstogo 21

Tolstoy's most famous home is preserved at Yasnaya
Polyana, a full day's excursion from Moscow. However, Tolstoy lived in this spacious Moscow home with
its big fenced-in park during the winter months from
1882 to 1901. The museum is skipped by most tourists,
but it is well worth a visit especially for anyone who
has enjoyed the works of this remarkable author. Tolstoy was 53 years old and famous when he moved to

Moscow (to enable his children to attend proper schools), and great names of the era frequently congregated at the Tolstoy home. Stanislavsky came from the world of the theater. Repin gave one of Tolstoy's daughters painting lessons.

Tolstoy's irrepressible personality is reflected in items preserved here. There is a bicycle that he learned to ride when he has passed the age of 70 (he used to *walk* from Moscow to Yasnaya Polyana; it took the better part of a week).

A bearskin is spread on the floor of the second-story living room. Tolstoy wounded this bear while hunting in 1858. The bear charged and almost crushed him. He was rescued by a farmer. Years later Tolstoy shot a bear and a familiar bullet in the animal proved it was his old adversary. The incident is described in one of Tolstoy's stories for children.

A small English-language guidebook is available at the museum reception desk where you probably will be asked to sign the guest book.

OTHER MUSEUMS

Kutuzov's Cottage, Kutuzovsky Chausee 30, Telephone: 41 89 43. It was in this cottage that the Russian General Kutuzov planned the defense of Moscow against Napoleon. A room has been added to the original small building to hold an exhibit of maps and weapons. In the original room notice the old-fashioned stove with a shelf-like place where people used to sleep during the winter. For the military-minded this museum will prove valuable, but others will find it only mildly interesting.

Polytechnical Museum, Novaya Square 3/4, Telephone: 23 07 56. This is one of the largest museums in

Moscow. Platoons of school children are constantly marching through, taking notes as guides explain the workings of steam engines, coal mines and atomic piles. This is a museum of special interest to anyone with engineering or scientific background.

Museum of History and Reconstruction of Moscow, Novaya Square 12, Telephone: 94 84 90. For the visitor who is curious to learn what Moscow *used* to look like, the paintings and mock-ups in this museum will be rewarding. On the top floor there is a collection of gifts received by the city of Moscow from all over the world on its 800th anniversary in 1947.

Central Museum of the Soviet Army, Commune Square 2. You won't find any military secrets here, but the achievements of the Soviet Army are lauded in paintings, maps, and exhibits.

Moscow Art Theatre Museum, Proyezd Khudozhestvennogo Teatra 3-a, Telephone: 29 99 08 Extension 57. Except for the tourist with a knowledge and love of Russian theater, the rooms of this museum are as boring as a stranger's family album.

Chekhov Museum, Sadovaya Kudrinskaya Ulitsa 6. The great writer Anton Pavlovich Chekhov lived in this two-story house during the years 1886 through 1890. This is a museum for admirers of such Chekhov classics as *Uncle Vanya, The Cherry Orchard,* and *The Three Sisters.*

St. Basil's Cathedral, Red Square. The inside of this cathedral, now a museum, is disappointing compared to the imaginative exterior. Under each of the nine cupolas is a small chapel. Poorly lighted and of cramped dimensions, each of these chapels nevertheless houses unusual religious pieces and art works.

Novodevichy Monastery: This Kremlin-like monastery on Bolshaya Pirogovskaya Street was built at the end of the seventeenth century. Novodevichy has on its walled premises a five-domed cathedral and a museum of history. But what makes it an unusual place is the adjacent cemetery where many distinguished Russian artists, writers, and political figures are buried. Here is the Stalin family plot with a monument to Joseph Stalin's first wife. Elsewhere in the cemetery is the grave of former Premier Nikolai Bulganin's mother; the headstone bears a cross.

ART GALLERIES

There are a number of extremely interesting art galleries in Moscow. Even if you are not particularly interested in art you should plan to spend at least an hour in the Tretyakov Gallery, a treasure house of old Russian religious art (icons) and of paintings of historical interest.

The Tretyakov Gallery also contains examples of modern Soviet paintings which many Western critics dismiss as picture postcard or magazine cover art. Even so, these rooms are worth seeing as an example of the sort of art that has been encouraged and subsidized in the Soviet society. Other state-run galleries specialize in showings of contemporary Soviet artists. The character of these shows has changed in recent years. Until Stalin's death in March 1953, most of the pictures exhibited were complimentary paintings of Stalin, often depicting him simply standing in a greatcoat against a backdrop of the Kremlin's walls. In recent years Soviet art has come a long way from this sterility. However, Soviet art still is circumscribed by the rules, unwritten but clearly implicit, of Communist Party arbiters that art—whether painting, music, or literature—must play a role in the building of the Communist state. This rule is easier to apply to literature than to music or paintings. However, a basic yardstick is whether it can be easily understood by a simple working man. This has a tendency to reduce art to the lowest common denominator. It eliminates abstract and experimental forms of art.

In recent years, though, Soviet artists have had the chance to see Moscow exhibits of the works of Pablo Picasso and other nonconformist Western artists. Incidentally, Picasso once is said to have declared, "There is no art in Russia; just portraits of generals loaded with medals." The recent exposure to "revolutionary" art of the outside world has motivated some Soviet artists to paint in forms other than "socialist realism," and they are keeping these works at home until such time as the changing climate permits exhibition of such experimentation.

These are the principal art galleries in Moscow:

TRETYAKOV GALLERY
Lavrushinsky Pereulok 10
Telephone: 31 13 62

This not to be missed gallery is the result of the rivalry between two wealthy brothers who competed in the acquisition of masterpieces of art. Pavel and Sergei Tretyakov lived in the middle 1800s, and spent much of their lives and fortunes buying works of art, each trying to outdo the other in subsidizing talented artists. Sergei died first and left his collection (particularly rich in nineteenth-century sculpture) to his brother. Pavel, an industrialist and owner of numerous factories, bequeathed his collection of 4000 items and the building in which they were displayed to the city of Moscow in 1892. Shortly after the 1917 revolution the gallery was decreed to be the property of the national government.

The Tretyakov Gallery has its own workshops for restoration work, archives of more than 100,000 negatives and photographs of paintings and pieces of sculpture. The gallery is visited by one million people a year.

Since acquiring the gallery from Tretyakov, the administrators have added to its collection and it now consists of more than 50,000 paintings, statues, icons, and other art treasures. Within the Tretyakov's decorative walls the student of art can trace Russian art from the eleventh century up to the present time. I would suggest that the visitor with limited time to spend see at least these works:

Icons: Two large rooms are devoted to one of the world's most valuable collections of icons (religious mosaics or paintings on wooden panels) dating from the eleventh to fifteenth centuries. The four great schools of church art—Pskov, Kiev, Novgorod, and Moscow (independent states that were later united, together with others, to form Russia)—are represented. Since the Russian Orthodox faith came from Byzantium it is only natural that a strong Byzantine Greek influence is seen in the figures of saints, the Madonna and of Christ.

"Appearance of Christ to the People": The artist, Alexander Ivanov, spent twenty years of his life on this single, huge canvas. But for all his hard work he got only abuse. His father, Andrei Ivanov, was an artist, too, and when young Alexander Ivanov won a prize enabling him to go abroad to study, it was rumored in art circles that his father had helped him with his paintings which won the prize.

In 1825 Alexander Ivanov was commissioned by the Czarist-era Academy of Art to paint a major work. He went to Italy and started this daring canvas which, for the first time in Russian art at least, depicted the naked human body outside in the open air.

This painstaking, talented work shows a group of peasants and shepherds bathing in a stream just as Christ is walking toward them. There is lifelike detail in the figures and faces, and a three-dimensional depth to the rolling landscape in the background. Ivanov made over five hundred individual sketches and paintings of faces, eyes, noses, hands, feet, and every other detail before applying his brush to canvas. Each is an art treasure in itself.

On at least one occasion the entire collection of preliminary sketches and paintings were hung in the gallery with the finished work. Actually, it is not a *finished* work, because Ivanov never did complete the lower left-hand corner. You will notice that the reflection in the water in that corner is not the same color as the robe it mirrors.

Ivanov preferred women as models and most of the men's faces were drawn from females. The artist could not resist including himself as a figure in the center looking up toward the approaching Christ.

The final blow in Ivanov's execution of this life's work came when he showed it to representatives of the Academy that had commissioned him. Considering it too revolutionary, they refused to accept it.

"Ivan the Terrible and His Son, Ivan, November 16, 1581": This will very likely be the picture you will remember longest of all you see in the Tretyakov Gallery. The painting is by Ilya Yefimovich Repin, who lived from 1844 to 1930, and is considered one of Russia's all-time greats in historical subjects, everyday life, and lifelike portraits. This work shows the terrible-tempered

Czar Ivan IV holding in his arms his son whom he has just slain. The Tretyakov Gallery's excellent little English-language catalogue, which never is guilty of understatement, describes the painting this way:

"Repin chose the actual moment of the murder. Horrified by what he has done, Ivan IV raises the now lifeless body, presses it to his breast, kisses it and tries to cover the gaping wound with his hand.

"The tragic, well-nigh insane state to which he is reduced is conveyed with such power that it would be difficult to find the equivalent of this picture in the whole of world art. All the furnishings of the Czar's chamber are depicted with tremendous artistic skill; the disorder of the thick, brightly colored carpet, the discarded staff, the overturned armchair and the cushion that has fallen to the floor.

"The shrouds of time separate us from the event depicted by the artist, but it is depicted with such force that the visitor has the impression that the drama is being enacted before his eyes."

Although it would be difficult to conceive of any picture living up to *this* build-up, this one comes close. In fact, some years ago a Russian visitor to the gallery stood transfixed in front of the painting, then suddenly drew a knife from his pocket and lunged at Ivan the Terrible. The deranged visitor managed to gash the canvas slightly before being restrained.

The picture is now covered with glass which impairs viewing but protects it from overly affected sight-seers.

"Morning in a Pine Wood": You may think you've seen this before someplace. You probably have. It's one of the most popular paintings in Russia and reproductions hang in Soviet airport waiting rooms, in offices, and is even on the wrapper of a chocolate candy.

Ivan Ivanovich Shishkin, who painted in the mid 1800s,

specialized in landscapes. In fact, he is considered the father of Russian landscape painting. His other works in the Tretyakov Gallery are various landscapes, described by their titles: "Felling Trees," "Pines Illuminated by the Sun," "Rain in an Oak Woods," and "A Corn Field."

In "Morning in a Pine Wood" shafts of sun illuminate a stately pine forest where three bear cubs frolic on a felled tree under the mother bear's eye. Shishkin's talent for rendering animal forms was far inferior to his ability to convey landscapes, so he called on his friend Konstantin Apollonovich Savitsky to paint the bears into the forest. Neither man made a secret of this amiable arrangement, but only Shishkin's name appears on the canvas.

"Hunters at Rest": This work by Vasily Grigoryevich Perov (1833–1882) is also often reproduced in Russia. This is a gay, warm human study of three hunters resting in a field. With intense gestures an elder hunter is telling an enraptured young companion about his exploits while a skeptical third hunter scratches his head.

Unlike a number of Perov's other canvases, "Hunters at Rest" has no social significance. However, the works of Perov and of many other artists are hung in the Tretyakov Gallery because their creations do contribute to the concepts of the present-day Russian leaders that a painting should convey a social message. For example, Perov's "A Religious Procession in a Village at Easter" is described this way in the Tretyakov catalogue: "Perov depicts the cheerless spectacle of a religious feast in a feudal village. The priest, bloated with liquor, is seen staggering off the porch; the sexton, too drunk to stand, lies sprawling on the steps, and the groggy peasants are reeling past, down the muddy road. The Czar's government withdrew the picture from the exhibition for its bold and caustic exposure of the clergy, and prohibited its further reproduction."

Another brilliant work is entitled "Seeing Off the Dead Man." Done in 1865, the forlorn, bent figure of a peasant woman is shown holding the reins of a horse-drawn, crude sledge. Her two children huddle in back over the ill-made coffin of their father which is drawn over the bleak, snow-covered landscape to the grave. The Russian commentary on the painting states that the elements of the painting "all speak of the poverty-stricken, hapless existence of the (Czarist-time) Russian peasantry."

"Warriors": The artist, V. M. Vasnetsov (1848–1926), devoted much of his career to expressing the characters of Russian legend, folk tale, and epic poetry. The "Warriors" is his most famous work. Vasnetsov's biographer felt that this painting shows "a triumphant, calm and grand force, unafraid of anybody, and doing anything it pleases if it thinks it necessary for everybody, for the people."

The "Warriors" is a picture of three men in ancient armor on horseback against a mountainous landscape. They are guarding the borders of the Russian land (the fear of invasion reflects itself in Russian paintings as well as in politics). Each of the figures comes from Russian legend. In the middle is Ilya Muromets, the mighty son of a peasant, a kind of Paul Bunyan. On his right is Dobrinya Nikitich, the legendary fighter for truth. On the left is Alyosha Popovich, who combined strength with alertness and cunning.

In explaining his painting, the artist Vasnetsov wrote: "Warriors Dobrinya, Ilya, and Alyosha Popovich, on spirited chargers, scan the field for an enemy or a sign of injustice."

"Failure of a Bank": By Vladimir Georgiyevich Makovsky. This 1881 painting is more highly thought of today than it was at the time it was painted. It shows the consternation of depositors at a bank whose doors have closed. A smug banker is seen tucking securities into his pocket—the capitalistic banker who benefits at the expense of others.

"Boyarinya Morozova": Like many other of the great paintings in the Tretyakov Gallery, this big canvas by Vasily Ivanovich Surikov exudes the atmosphere of old Russia. Surikov devoted himself almost entirely to epic paintings of events in Russian history, often tragic. This painting shows a woman of the boyar class (the rich merchant class) being drawn on a sledge over the snow to the dungeon where she died in 1672. She was the victim of a movement in the Russian Orthodox Church that sought to change religious rituals that the people had been following for centuries. Boyarinya Morozova and many others refused to accept changes in either the liturgy or in the manner in which worshipers crossed themselves. Those who refused to accede were punished. Morozova goes to her death giving the sign of the cross in the old, traditional manner, defiant to the end.

Important note: Not all the paintings in the Tretyakov Gallery are on display. There is a large collection of paintings of so-called Russian moderns whose works do not conform with the tastes and ideological requirements of Soviet officialdom. However visitors, upon their request, are often admitted to this "closed fund." Piled one against the other and hanging without markings on the walls are works by Marc Chagall, Mashkov, Kandinsky, and many others. Perhaps the time will come when these modern masterpieces will be considered fit to be shown to the general public.

PUSHKIN GALLERY
Volkhonka Street 12
Telephone: 21 37 48

The Pushkin Gallery houses Moscow's fine collection of European art encompassing a spectrum of artists ranging all the way from Rembrandt, Vermeer, El Greco, Vandyke to an astounding collection of impressionists including Matisse, Toulouse-Lautrec, Degas, Picasso, Gauguin, Van Gogh, Renoir, Manet, and Monet. Many of these paintings had never been seen in the Western world until an American magazine, *Ladies' Home Journal*, received permission several years ago to reproduce a number of pages of these rare works.

The lighting in the Pushkin Gallery is far better than in the older Tretyakov Gallery, but even so it takes some squinting and maneuvering for a vantage point to get a clear view of some of the poorly hung masterpieces.

It is a truly remarkable collection, and a visitor to Moscow should not miss a visit to the Pushkin Gallery. If your time is short spend most of it in the two rooms where the impressionist paintings are hung.

Although I usually find Egyptian rooms in museums pretty hard going, the Pushkin has an unusually interesting collection of Egyptian antiquities—jewelry, mirrors, cosmetic instruments, and, of course, a mummy.

HOUSE OF ARTISTS
Kuznetsky Most 11
Telephone: 28 41 06

This gallery changes its exhibits frequently. Works of present-day Soviet artists usually are shown. It is a good place to buy postcards, catalogues and art books. It is open from 11 A.M. to 7 P.M., except Monday.

ACADEMY OF ART EXHIBITION ROOMS
Kropotkinskaya Ulitsa 19
Telephone: 46 66 42
46 16 02

Contemporary Soviet artists have their work shown here. Sometimes there are exhibitions of foreign artists, usually from other Communist countries. The hours are from noon to 8 P.M., except on Monday. There is an admission charge of two rubles.

MANEGE GALLERY
Manege Square

Sometimes the exhibits here are interesting, sometimes they are insufferably dull. For example, the vast hall has been devoted to hundreds of models of statues of Lenin submitted in a state-sponsored contest. Another exhibit here was of paintings by artists from other Communist countries (unexpectedly modern, abstract art by Polish painters caused considerable comment at the gallery and in Soviet newspapers).

The long building of pumpkin yellow was originally the stable for the famous Spanish Riding School of the Czars. After the revolution it became the Kremlin's garage, and in 1957 it was converted into an exhibition gallery.

OTHER GALLERIES

For the indefatigable art gallery addict, here are the addresses of several other places in Moscow where paintings and other art are exhibited:

House of Art Workers of the U.S.S.R., Pushechnaya Ulitsa 9, *Telephone: 23 77 75.*

Museum House of Russian Artist V. M. Vasnetsov, Vasnetsov Pereulok 14.

Exhibition Halls of Moscow League of Soviet Artists, Yermolaevsky Pereulok 17, *Telephone: 51 08 68.*

CHAPTER SEVEN

Moscow: Churches

The story is told of a Communist party member named
Georgi who came under suspicion. Neighbors reported
that every morning as Georgi set out for work he was
seen to cross himself with a sweeping gesture. Obviously
this manifestation of religious belief could not be tolerated in a trusted party member, who should be an atheist.
Georgi was summoned before a council of stern-faced
Communists and confronted with the damaging testimony.

At first Georgi was puzzled, but then he brightened
and offered his explanation. Exactly as he had been accused of doing, Georgi executed the sign of the cross on
his body, touching first his forehead, then just below
his waist, then the right side of his breast, and finally the
left.

"As a good party member," he explained, "whenever
I step out of my house I make a last-minute check. 'Let's
see now, Georgi,' I say to myself" (Georgi touched his
frowning forehead), " 'have you remembered everything?
Pants buttoned?' " (Hand from forehead to his belt)
" 'Party card?' " (Touching his right breast pocket)
" 'Lenin pin?' " (Checking the left lapel) "Only after I'm
sure everything is in place do I set out for the day."

Georgi was not only exonerated but was commended
by his comrades for his Communist caution.

Although Communist Party members such as Georgi
would lose their treasured Party cards by manifesting
religious tendencies, religion still *is* practiced in the
U.S.S.R. Atheism is taught in the schools. The young

people are brought up by all the powerful facilities of the state not to believe in God. Church services are attended mostly by older people. Although some young Russians, and even students, are seen attending church, the fact is that the greater part of any congregation is composed of worshipers past the age of fifty. The active suppression and oppression once practiced by the atheistic Soviet Government against the church and its ministers is now a thing of the past. Communist authorities are counting on religion dying out gradually as the old people die out. They may be right.

However, while time determines the fate of religion in Russia, there are today many churches that are open and can be visited. This chapter deals only with "working" churches rather than those that have been converted into state museums preserving architectural styles.

THE STATE OF RELIGION

At the time of the Communist revolution in 1917 there were 564 active Russian Orthodox Churches in Moscow alone. Today there are only about fifty. Many of them are run-down, although an increasing amount of restoration work is going on, usually financed by the church itself, but occasionally with state help if the building is of extraordinary artistic value. There is one Catholic church in the capital, one Moslem mosque, and one Jewish synagogue with two very small rooms elsewhere in town for prayer. Even with this paucity of places of worship, the atmosphere for worship has improved since Stalin's death. There are now small schools, operated by the respective congregations with government sanction, for training Russian Orthodox priests, Jewish rabbis, and Moslem mullahs.

However, attacks on religion are frequent in Soviet

newspapers. There are criticisms of young people who succumb to religious influences despite school indoctrination in atheism. Members of the clergy are often accused of engaging in begging, extortion or worse. Very frequently the Communist Party and the Young Communist League are upbraided for not being sufficiently active and militant in preaching atheism. A typical article was in the form of a letter written to the newspaper *Komsomolskaya Pravda* (roughly translated as "Youth Truth") by a truck driver named S. Dubinin. His letter reported what was going on in his native village of Atkilnya near the city of Riga. Whatever else it accomplished, it indicated that religion is far from dead in Atkilnya.

"About once a month or even more frequently," wrote Comrade Dubinin, "the village priest would rush into our house and start preaching, paying no regard to the fact that there might be no icons at all. If this were the case, a picture on the wall or even a wall clock would do for an altar. When through with his sermon he would briskly demand: 'Foodstuffs, fabrics, money. My cart is waiting at the window.' With those words he would make a bow and disappear quite abruptly in the same way that characterized his appearance; disappear, that is, in order to appear at your neighbour's place next."

The letter writer complained that the villagers never have the opportunity to hear an atheistic lecture. There are fifty households in the village, and "our people are good people. Doubtlessly, they don't believe in God, but nevertheless they wink at what is going on. In a way they even support the believers in as much as they would just as soon as not 'celebrate' with alcohol various holy occasions. This certainly plays into the hands of the clergy who do not confine themselves to church sermons, but rather come into our homes and all but thrust on us the rites of eucharist and fasting. Little by little the num-

ber of converts in our village is increasing. Uliana Ku-
prienko, who received a medal at the All-Union Agricultural Fair, has turned into a nun. She sees to it that her
nephew strictly observes all the rites and Lents."

Concludes the letter-writing truck driver: "I know that
our Constitution guarantees freedom of conscience.
Every citizen is free to choose any religion he likes or not
to practice any at all. Who then gives the clergy the right
to be unwelcome guest performers in our private quarters and to impose on me and on the others the rites
which we don't believe in and don't need?"

A SUNDAY MORNING TOUR

If you don't mind getting up early Sunday morning,
this is the opportune time to visit three of Moscow's
main houses of worship. Start out by attending part of a
mass at the Roman Catholic church, move on to a Russian Orthodox church, and end the morning by visiting
the Baptist church. You will be welcomed at each of
these. A visitor, whatever his religion if any, cannot help
but be moved by the indigent dignity of the Catholic
mass, by the fervently kneeling old women touching the
floor with their foreheads in the Russian Orthodox
church, and by the jammed-in-the-aisles reverence and
simplicity of the Baptist church. There are services every
evening at the Jewish synagogue; the main services of
the week are Friday evening and Saturday morning.

Here is information about houses of worship in Moscow where you can attend services:

RUSSIAN ORTHODOX CHURCHES

The main Moscow Russian Orthodox church is the
Yelokhovskaya Cathedral. This is the cathedral where

the Patriarch, the chief officer of the Orthodox church, officiates at religious ceremonies on special occasions such as Easter and Christmas Eve. By the way, the Orthodox church follows the old Julian Calendar; the dates of Christmas and Easter fall thirteen days later than on the calendar observed in the Western world.

The midnight mass is a moving experience on both of these holidays. The cathedral, with its high dome and numerous icons, is crowded with people. A few minutes before midnight members of the congregation start lighting small red tapers, purchased at the door. The income helps support the church. Suddenly at the stroke of midnight, lights illuminate the dim, domed edifice. Led by the Patriarch, a procession of priests dressed in jeweled, brocaded raiments and carrying enormous candles and paintings of Christ, parade slowly around the cathedral while chanting. The Patriarch swings an ornamented incense container slowly from side to side. Unable to force their way into the jammed cathedral, crowds, numbering as many as 5000 people, press against the iron bars of the fence to catch a glimpse of the procession. The crowd is predominantly old women, some shielding small candles from the wind, their faces almost wedged between the bars. Cordons of police, some on horseback, control the mob.

There are no pews in Yelokhovskaya Cathedral nor in any other Russian Orthodox church. Except for a few benches provided along a wall for the infirm, everyone stands. On Christmas Eve the service is five hours long, which can be tiring. (Tourists can come late and leave early.) Women should cover their heads; men's heads are bare.

If you are in Moscow on the Russian Christmas or Easter by all means attend a mass at the Yelokhovskaya Cathedral. The music will touch your heart as will the reverence of the Russians. Plan to visit this cathedral some time during your stay in Moscow, but on the Sunday morning tour one of the smaller churches is more typical of Soviet religious life. Liturgy in Russian Orthodox churches begins at 10 A.M. Evening services are at 6 P.M. Here are the addresses:

Yelokhovskaya Cathedral (Patriarchal Cathedral of the Manifestation of Christ), Spartakovskaya Ulitsa 15.

Church of the Resurrection, Rusakovskoye Highway 51.

Church of the Lamenters, Bolshaya Ordynka 40.

Church of Ivan the Warrior, Yakimanka 46.

Church of St. Nicholas, Teply Pereulok 1/2.

Church of St. Pimen, Novovorotnikovsky Pereulok 3.

CHURCH OF THE RESURRECTION
Bryusovsky Pereulok 15

Although you may find others among Moscow's Russian Orthodox churches which you prefer, this old (it was built in 1629), recently restored church with its golden dome is a gem of architecture. Members of the congregation receive visitors hospitably. On Sunday at noon mass baptisms take place. Babies are undressed, anointed by the priest and immersed three times in a brass fount. Then the fathers, carrying candles, march three times around the fount, led by the priest. It is fascinating to watch the infants being dressed for the cold outside air. Russian mothers wrap their babies so tightly that they resemble little woolly logs; mothers believe that the more layers of blankets used, the healthier the child will be. We once attended a Russian Orthodox wedding here. Church weddings are rare. Most Soviet citizens now get married simply by registering at the appropriate government office. There is no ceremony, no oaths exchanged. A church wedding is very elaborate, with jeweled crowns held for a long portion of the ceremony over the bride's and bridegroom's heads.

OLD BELIEVERS' CHURCH
(*Pokrovsky Cathedral*)
Rogozhsky Settlement 29

This is one of the most interesting of Moscow's churches because of its excellent religious paintings and its strange history. In 988 the ruler of the most important Russian principality, Prince Vladimir of Kiev, became a Christian in order to marry the sister of a Greek Emperor. This was the first step in Russia's adoption of the Christian faith. Unlike Roman Catholicism where the scriptures are read in Latin, the Orthodox faith permitted translation into the language of the country. Vladimir had the scriptures translated in the Slavonic tongue. The translation was poor and a number of errors crept in. These were perpetuated through practice.

In the 1600s when Alexei Mikhailovich, the son of the first Czar of the Romanov family, ruled Russia he was visited by the Patriarch of Jerusalem. The Patriarch was taken on an inspection tour of Moscow churches. He was shocked to find incorrect practices. For example, the Greek Orthodox manner of crossing oneself is to fold the little finger and the finger next to it and to rest the thumb against the extended middle and forefingers. Because of mistranslation, the Russians were holding the thumb against the two folded fingers and crossing themselves with only the forefinger and middle finger extended.

Czar Alexei Mikhailovich was interested in making reforms. It was a way of insinuating greater control over the increasingly independent and powerful church. The Czar undertook his program of changing these practices by organizing groups of eager young people into inspection squads. (It was a forerunner of modern day Komsomol, the Young Communist League, whose members are often the shock troops of Communist Party projects.) The reform gave the Czar an excuse for purging certain elements in the church hierarchy as well as many individuals who considered the old ways correct. Those who retained the "incorrect" rituals in the face of the Czar's reforms became known as Old Believers.

The Old Believers lived on despite persecution under the Czars and later under the Communists. Their church in Moscow has some of the finest icons in existence as well as an exquisite and mammoth brass chandelier. For the student of religious art, the Old Believers' Church provides an excellent opportunity to study icons of many centuries. Be sure to ask to see the Rublyevs and other outstanding icons, the church's best, behind the altar.

Services are held daily at 8 A.M.

CATHOLIC CHURCH
Malaya Lubyanka Ulitsa 12

Moscow's Catholic Church is just down the street from one of the iron gates that leads into the interior of infamous Lubyanka Prison. The church in no way resembles the traditional Roman Catholic Church in its exterior. The faded yellow building with six columns is surmounted by a pediment, and there is a small belfry at each end topped by a cross. The building looks like an Elks Lodge in any small town, set behind a small, grassy park where children play.

The interior of the church is equally unostentatious. There are wooden pews, many of them at rather alarming angles because of the unevenness of the floor. The hand-carved confessional stalls are along the side of the church. A chandelier of gold leaf is magnificent in its simplicity and design. The church, constructed in the middle of the nineteenth century, is more than one hundred years old. It was built by a French manufacturer, a resident in Moscow, for French Catholics and was named after Saint Louis. The priest in charge of this church also flies to Vilnyus on occasion to minister to a Catholic congregation there. There are also Catholic churches in Leningrad, Kiev, Odessa, and several other Soviet cities.

Mass is celebrated on Sunday mornings at this Moscow church at 8:30 A.M. and 11 A.M. There are also weekday services at 8:30 A.M. Evening mass is celebrated on Friday, Saturday, and Sunday at 6 P.M.

AMERICAN EMBASSY CATHOLIC MASS

There is a Roman Catholic priest attached to the American Embassy. He is Father Louis F. Dion. Father Dion conducts daily morning Mass as well as special Mass on holy days at his small apartment chapel at Sadovaya Samotetchnaya 12/24, apartment 23. He also hears confessions. Father Dion is always happy to receive those passing through Moscow as well as members of his own embassy parish.

BAPTIST CHURCH
Maly Vuzovsky Pereulok 3

This simple Baptist church resembles those known to Baptists in the Western world. Except for its shabby exterior, the Russian lettering inside, and the faces and clothing of the people, this could be a Baptist church anywhere. A foreigner arriving to attend a service is likely to be invited to sit on the platform, and he may even be asked to deliver to the congregation a few words which are then translated. Emotional Russians break into tears at greetings from abroad.

The Baptist church is a rectangular hall with a balcony on three sides. It is often so crowded with people standing in the aisles that when the congregation rises during portions of the service it is difficult to see where the pews end and the aisle begins.

JEWISH SYNAGOGUE
Bolshoi Spasoglinishchevsky Pereulok 8

This stone building with its façade of Greek columns was the scene of an emotional outburst of Moscow Jewry some years ago when Golda Meir, Israel's first ambassador to the U.S.S.R., attended services here. The synagogue was crowded and so was the street outside. Mrs. Meir was cheered. There was weeping, and Jews reached out to touch her. This was during Stalin's time, and there was retaliation against many of those who participated in this demonstration of affection for the Jewish state.

The synagogue is filled to capacity with hundreds of other worshipers in the street on Rosh Hashana and Yom Kippur, the high holy days. There are services every evening one hour before sunset as well as morning services at 10 A.M.

The interior of the synagogue is similar to synagogues elsewhere. A balcony for women worshipers overhangs three sides of the auditorium. There is an Ark where the holy Torahs are held. There is one distinct Soviet feature. On either side of the platform where the rabbi and cantor lead the service are signs in the shape of the tablets of the Ten Commandments with Hebrew script on one and Cyrillic on the other. However it is not the Ten Commandments which are inscribed on these tablets.

Rather, under the heading of "Prayer for Peace," are inscribed the words: "Our Father who art in Heaven, blessed be the government of the U.S.S.R., bulwark of peace."

OTHER ADDRESSES

Moslem Mosque, Vypolzov Pereulok 7. The namaz is recited five times daily and Friday at 1 P.M.

The Holy Synod and Moscow Patriarchy, headquarters for the Russian Patriarch, **Chisty Pereulok 5.**

CHAPTER EIGHT

Moscow: Surprises off the Beaten Track

It's only natural that Intourist guides should try to put the best possible face on all things Soviet, and that reminds me of this little story which requires an understanding of the word *agitpunkt*. An *agitpunkt* is a peculiarly Soviet institution. Translated it means "agitation point." And in the Soviet context of the word "agitation," these institutions have the purpose of educating, organizing, stimulating, and propagandizing Soviet citizens to vote and generally to be proud of their political system. "*Agitpunkt*" personnel promise great things and paint a glowing picture of life under Communism that does not always conform to reality.

The *agitpunkt* may be broadly described as the "sales organization" for Communism or the "Madison Avenue" for Marxism. Now for the story that Russians like to tell:

It seems that Ivan died and went to heaven. There he found life to be easy and comfortable enough, but insufferably dull. He just sat around all day napping and listening to harps. Finally, he was so bored that he thought that it might be interesting just to have a glimpse at hell. He got permission to go down and look around.

Ivan found hell a lively, delightful place. There were fine clubs, people playing cards, jazz music, vodka drinking, good conversation, and much gaiety. He liked it so much that he decided he'd like to stay. Ivan went back

191

to heaven and made application to go to hell. After visiting a half-dozen heavenly bureaus he received his passport and visa and the appropriate number of stamps on each, and he went happily off to hell.

When Ivan got there he found it quite a different place from what he had remembered. It was unbearably hot and ugly and full of unpleasant creatures. He was put into a dank, evil cell.

"But," howled Ivan, "I asked to go to hell."

"This *is* hell," replied the keeper.

"But what was the other place I visited before?" pleaded Ivan.

"Oh, that," said the keeper, "that was the *agitpunkt*."

Besides the *agitpunkt*, there are many sights that the Intourist guide usually skips because they are not of general interest or because they do not show the Soviet Union in the most complimentary light.

Not all of the places listed in this chapter will interest everyone. It all depends on the particular traveler's individual inclinations and tastes.

PAWNSHOP
Pushkinskaya Ulitsa 22

Russia, where Communist authorities frown on usury in any form, is the last place where you might expect to find a pawnshop. Certainly Intourist guides do not take tourists to see it. Surprisingly, too, the Moscow pawnshop derives its name from Lombard Street in London, which is the center of such establishments. The Moscow establishment is simply called "Lombard."

This Soviet version of a pawnshop, ironically enough, is across the street from the "Procurator's Office, U.S.S.R." If a private citizen were caught loaning money he would be apprehended by this state prosecutor's office but the "Lombard" pawnshop is entirely legal.

You enter through an open gate, at 22 Pushkinskaya Street, walk into a deep courtyard, and the doorway to the pawnshop is at the far left-hand side. Walk up three flights of stairs in this red-brick building to a large room with counters. The day I visited the unusual enterprise it was crowded with decrepit-looking people, with old clothes and other possessions in their arms. These were Soviet citizens short of cash, anxious to turn in their belongings for a loan, and having the intention to retrieve the items at a future date.

The Soviet pawnshop will accept clothing, fabrics, shoes, watches, jewelry, silver, and gold. These items, in a way, indicate what goods in the Soviet Union are to-day of special value. The pawned item is kept for four months and if not redeemed it is then sold to the public at a government Commission Store (a type of establishment described in the chapter on stores).

The client is charged 1.2 per cent on the sum given him for his item in order to retrieve it. A sign on the wall explains that .8 per cent is for the service and .4 per cent is a time charge. In other words, the Russian would pay 101.20 rubles to retrieve the pair of shoes he had turned in for a loan of 100 rubles.

The words PUSHKINSKY LOMBARD are lettered in gold on a sign of red glass at the entrance.

The hours of the proletariat pawnshop are: Daily: 8:30 A.M. to 4:30 P.M. The lunch hour is from 12:30 P.M. to 1:30 P.M. Wednesday is the day off. On Tuesdays and on the day before a holiday it closes early at 1:30 P.M.

LENIN LIBRARY
Mokhovaya Street 5, at corner of Kalinina Street

This is the largest of all Soviet libraries and is said by
the Russians to be the largest library in the world in
terms of numbers of books. As one enters the main entrance with its tall square columns, there is a small office
on the right carrying the legend in Russian letters reading INFORMATION BUREAU. The tourist will be provided
with an English-speaking guide to take him around. This
is recommended only for those who have a special interest in libraries, although it is an impressive place for anyone to see as an accomplishment of the Soviet society.

This is the Soviet Union's National Library—the equivalent of Washington's Library of Congress. A block from
the Kremlin, the massive, columned edifice of dark-gray
stone with several wings, contains twenty million items
including more than nine million volumes.

These books are stored in a most singular fashion—
not by subject, or author or even alphabetically, but
rather by *size!*

Books on any subject, say, anthropology, come in a
variety of sizes, of course. Cubic inches of precious stack
space are wasted when a twenty-inch-high book shares
a shelf with anthropological neighbors that are only nine
inches high. However, the conservation of space by putting only books of the same size on any shelf (regardless
of the subject matter) creates other problems. A student
doing research in anthropology has nothing to gain by
getting permission to go into the stacks. He might have to
wander through the eighteen stories of the library's book
stack building with its 170 miles of shelves to find all
the books he wants on the subject. Similarly, the task of
delivering to the student all the books he may desire from
his examination of the catalogues requires an enormous

amount of leg work by library assistants. It is no wonder that the Lenin Library employs 2000 librarians and assistants; and a total of 2500 persons including janitorial and other service staff.

Stopping at one shelf at random in the stacks of the Lenin Library, I found this incongruous array of books: A *Manual of French, Robinson Crusoe, Textbook of Russian Law, History of the Ancient World, Medical Dermatology, Physics, Social Crisis of the Roman Empire, History of Poland, Maternity and Child Care* (three volumes), *Volgini* (a Russian novel), and a pair of books in Chinese. The only thing each has in common is size—a neat 7¾ inches in height.

The minimum time for delivering a book to a reader at the Lenin Library is one hour. It usually takes a good deal longer and a person may choose to go off on errands after writing down the names and numbers of the books he wants and handing the slips to a desk attendant. Six to seven thousand people use the Lenin Library every day and, on an average day, 25,000 to 30,000 books are used.

The main reading room with walls paneled in dark wood part of the way to the lofty chandeliered ceiling is impressive and attractive. Chairs at individual, partitioned desks are provided for five hundred people. A map of the world covers the front wall. In front of the map stands the benign figure of Lenin, a statue several times life-size, gazing down on the scene.

Unlike most American libraries, the Lenin and most of other Soviet libraries are open on Sunday—the only day-off work for factory and office workers. In fact, the Lenin Library closes only one day a month—a *different* day each month. The day of closing is announced a week or so ahead of time simply by posting a notice in the reading rooms. A less than habitual patron of the library might thus be disappointed if he comes to the Lenin

Library on the particular day of the month that it is closed for general cleaning. In the context of complex, crowded, everyday Soviet life, this is not likely to be considered an unusual inconvenience by the Russian citizen.

LUBYANKA PRISON
Dzerzhinsky Square

This is the notorious Lubyanka Prison where countless numbers of political prisoners during Stalin's time were taken. The front part of the building facing on Dzerzhinsky Square houses the Ministry of Internal Security. The prison building itself is in the rear. It looks the role. The lower levels are of gray stone with shiny black marble trim. A sinister iron gate can be seen at the rear of the building. Because Lubyanka is on a hill the first story becomes the basement in the rear of building and it is in this section that many of the cells are said to be located. Executions are believed to take place here. In fact Lavrenti Beria, the head of the Secret Police under Stalin, is thought to have been done away with after a secret trial in this building. Execution in Russia, by the way, is accomplished like this: the doomed man is led without prior warning from his cell and shot in the back of the neck as he walks down a corridor, not knowing beforehand that it is to be his last walk. The Russians say it is more humane this way.

HOUSE OF JOURNALISTS
Suvorovsky Boulevard 8A
Telephone: 92 42 30

The "club" plays almost as important a role in the life of many Soviet citizens as it does in British society. But it is a different kind of club. People in the same profession in the U.S.S.R. are organized into a "union." This is not a union in the sense of a labor union. The Writers' Union, for example, supervises the ideological purity of authors' work, it chastises wanderers from the straight-and-narrow line, it acts as a "literary agent" between authors and government publishing houses. It also has a club, as do artists, scientists, and journalists among others.

The Dom Zhurnalistov ("House of Journalists") is typical of such clubs. It has a small garden restaurant which is cool on summer evenings, and the food is quite good. American, British, Canadian, French, and other foreign journalists from non-Communist publications are invited to the Dom Zhurnalistov only for very special occasions. Once they were invited, for example, to make the acquaintance of a quartet of unsmiling Soviet citizens. The Russians seated on the stage of the main hall recited in lengthy detail how "American imperialist spy organizations" had tried to recruit their services. These men were among the crew of a Soviet tanker captured by the Formosa Chinese. They told a lurid story replete with description of "tortures" to which the Russian sailors claimed to have been subjected. Sometimes such anti-Western propaganda shows are carried on Moscow television.

Once a year all foreign correspondents are invited to the House of Journalists for a more festive occasion. This is for the annual Soviet "Press Day," an occasion for editorials in *Pravda* and *Izvestia* on freedom of the press and sometimes for a few words of self-criticism.

There used to be a heroic-size statue of Stalin on the main staircase landing, but that disappeared immediately after Khrushchev's speech in February 1956 denouncing his predecessor. Many other Stalin portraits and statues around town disappeared too, but many have remained in their accustomed places.

For a full picture of Soviet life you should look in on one of the clubs, preferably in the evening when more members are around. The chances are you will be received cordially. Most of the clubs have fairly good restaurants. These are the addresses of the important ones:

Central House of Actors, Gorky Ulitsa 16/2, *Telephone: 29 03 43.*

Central House of Architects, Izeseva Ulitsa 7, *Telephone: 95 77 50.*

Central House of Art Workers, Pushechnaya Ulitsa 9, *Telephone: 23 77 75.*

Central House of Composers, 3rd Miusskaya Ulitsa 4/6, *Telephone: 51 63 47.*

Central House of Writers, Vorovskaya Ulitsa 50, *Telephone: 52 22 04.*

OTHER CLUBS

There are clubs for persons of similar avocations as well as for those in the same vocation. If you have a particular hobby and would like the chance to talk with fellow Russian enthusiasts, it would be a good idea to write to the director of the particular club. There's a club for almost every activity such as stamp collecting, radio ham operating and, of course, for chess. Here are the addresses of several:

Chess Club, Gogolevsky Boulevard 14, *Telephone: 28 95 84.*

Auto Drivers' Club, Novoryazanskaya Ulitsa 26, *Telephone: 61 39 76.*

Central Radio Club (ham operators), Sretenka 26/1, *Telephone: 94 54 66.*

City Service-Dog Club (an organization supervised by the military for training dogs), Morevsky Pereulok 11, *Telephone: 72 18 22.*

Baumansky District, Chernishevskaya Ulitsa 28
Dzerzhinsky District, Zhdanova Ulitsa 9
Zhdanovsky District, Taganskaya Ulitsa 34
Kalininsky District, Leningradskaya Ulitsa 11
Frunzensky District, Kropotkina Ulitsa 35
Kirovsky District, Osipenko Ulitsa 50

AMERICAN HOUSE CLUB
Kropotkinskaya Naberezhnaya 3
Telephone: 46 05 89

This club is mentioned in the chapter on Moscow night life too. The red-brick gabled building facing on the Moscow River looks like a gloomy residence in a Charles Addams cartoon. But inside it is a bit of home. When you get weary of hearing unintelligible Russian, English is spoken here.

The American House is the residence for most male bachelor members of the U. S. Embassy staff. A small library-lounge on the first floor and a larger hall one flight up constitute the club. Mimeographed notices of events point out: "The American House Club is a private club. Members of the American Embassy and members of foreign diplomatic missions in Moscow are welcome." In fact, though, a lonely tourist in search of a Coca-Cola or a Scotch-and-soda has always been received hospitably too. If you know someone at an embassy they might invite you to this club. Although the schedule changes from time to time, American movies are shown free of charge on Sunday, Tuesday, and Saturday starting at 9 P.M. After the Saturday movie there is dancing to juke-box music. Thursday is bingo night. On holidays such as Christmas, New Year's, St. Patrick's Day, and St. Valentine's Day there is usually a dance.

WHERE TO MEET THE SOVIET LEADERS

It's not our intention to endorse "gate-crashing," but if you can wangle an invitation to an embassy reception while you're in Moscow you stand a 50–50 chance of seeing one or more of the Kremlin leaders. Each of the some 60 embassies in Moscow celebrates its country's annual national holiday with a reception. For the United States it's the Fourth of July Independence Day, for Great Britain it's the Queen's birthday, for France it's Bastille Day on July 14. Citizens of a particular country are welcome at their embassy's party if they happen to be in Moscow on their national holiday.

Enterprizing tourists have devised ways to go to parties at embassies other than their own. Some have gone along with journalists (correspondents stationed in Moscow are invited to most national day receptions), others have had their embassy arrange for them to get an invitation, others have phoned the celebrating embassy themselves and asked for an invitation, and still others simply have walked right through the doors to the party as if they belonged. With several hundred or more persons present an uninvited guest may not be noticed. However, if invitation cards are checked at the door this "bull by the horns" approach can be embarrassing. Whether to try it or not depends on how much you want to see a Kremlin leader—if one *does* show up at the party.

Here is a recent calendar of national days celebrated by countries with embassies in Moscow, but be sure to confirm the date before setting out to a party because some, particularly Great Britain's, change from year to year.

January 1	Sudan
January 4	Burma
January 23	Luxembourg
January 26	India
February 4	Ceylon
February 22	United Arab Republic
March 5	Cambodia
March 23	Pakistan
March 25	Greece
April 4	Hungary
April 29	Japan
April 30	Netherlands
May 5	Ethiopia
May 9	Czechoslovakia
May 13	Israel
May 17	Norway
May 25	Argentina
May 27	Afghanistan
June 2	Italy
June 5	Denmark
June 6	Sweden
June 13	Great Britain
June 17	Iceland
June 24	Thailand
July 1	Canada
July 4	United States of America
July 9	Argentina
July 14	France
July 14	Iraq
July 21	Belgium
July 22	Poland
July 23	United Arab Republic

August 1	Switzerland
August 17	Indonesia
August 23	Romania
August 25	Uruguay
September 2	Democratic Republic of Vietnam
September 9	Bulgaria
October 1	China
October 15	Afghanistan
October 26	Iran
October 29	Turkey
November 15	Belgium
November 22	Lebanon
November 29	Yugoslavia
December 5	Thailand
December 6	Finland

MOSCOW RACE TRACK
Begovaya Ulitsa 22

There's no gambling casino in the Soviet Union, but horse racing and betting are permitted. In fact, the race track is run by the Ministry of Agriculture (its purpose is to improve horse breeds) and the pari-mutuel windows are operated by the Ministry of Finance. Trotting races are the most frequent. Even if you are not interested in horseflesh or gambling this is worth a quick visit. You will see the Soviet "race track crowd," men and some women earnestly studying forms with the horses' recent times, placing bets and casting anxious eyes toward the pari-mutuel board as the odds change.

In order not to provide a distraction to tempt workers away from their jobs, races are held only in the evening or on time off. Post time is 1 P.M. on Sunday; 6 P.M. on Wednesdays and Fridays, and 4 P.M. on Saturday. The hours may change so it's best to have the Service Bureau or your guide call before you drive out.

If your gambling streak runs deep you might want to buy a five-ruble ticket for the periodic lotteries that are run by Soviet republic governments to raise money. Prizes include cars, television sets, motor scooters, accordions, and cash—rubles, of course. Tickets are available at post offices, banks, and special sidewalk stands.

FASHION SHOWS
GUM, Red Square 3. *Telephone: 90 01 08*
Dom Modele, Kuznetsky Most 9. *Telephone: 28 61 09*

Even the men will enjoy this. I did. Any fashion-conscious woman—and what woman isn't—will find a visit to a Soviet fashion show instructive and perhaps amusing. Russian styles are improving each year—at least the styles displayed in the government-run fashion shows. The Dom Modele, "House of Fashions," is the Christian Dior, Jacques Fath, and Irene Galitzine of the Soviet fashion world all wrapped into one. Unfortunately the articles of clothing actually worn by Russians are many years behind those recommended by government designers at this institution.

The showings are quite western and even capitalistic. Both at the Dom Modele and at the GUM department store there is a runway on which attractive models (somewhat stocky by Western standards) parade the wares. In fact at the GUM show there is a band playing western popular tunes, even if they were popular in a much earlier era. There are male models, too, showing the latest styles in business suits and sportswear for Russian men.

An announcer recites the number of each garment and tells a bit about it. The customer may purchase a pattern for any of the items shown, and then either sew it herself or take it to a government dressmaker. The clothing shown is not sold ready-made.

The hours of the GUM shows, which change occasionally, are:

Sunday, Tuesday and Saturday: 1 P.M. and 3:30 P.M.; Monday and Friday: 1 P.M., 3:30 P.M. and 6:30 P.M.; Wednesday and Thursday are the days off.

The hours for the Dom Modele are:

Sunday at 12 noon and 2 P.M.; Weekdays at 2 P.M., 4 P.M. and 6 P.M.; Monday is the day off.

There is a small admission charge at both the GUM and Dom Modele shows.

HOUSING

Soviet authorities may hate me for this, but it is only fair that the visitor to Russia should see housing other than the showplaces on Intourist's escorted tours. Poor housing is partly the result of heavy war damage. The Communists inherited an enormous housing shortage from the pre-revolutionary regime. This has been compounded by the fact that the Communists have given priority to heavy industry rather than to consumer needs.

In order to provide housing quickly, certain things such as privacy are sacrificed. Many of the newer apartment houses are built in units of three rooms—one room to an entire family with a common bathroom, toilet and kitchen for the three families. Even this is a marked improvement, because it still is common in metropolitan areas for a half dozen families to share facilities.

Since speed is the major consideration in providing housing, quality sometimes suffers. This was the case in a group of apartment buildings recently constructed on Prospekt Mir. Foreign diplomats and their families moved in. Soon great cracks appeared in apartment walls. The explanation was that construction of a subway nearby had diverted the flow of an underground river and had caused the foundation of these buildings to sink. In any event, it was necessary to move about 80 families, mostly from Asian embassies, to other quarters. Several months later the apartment building in the same housing development in which many American Embassy families lived started to show the same signs of imminent collapse despite measures that had been taken to shore up these structures. It was necessary to evacuate these families too.

You can see these apartment buildings set back off Prospekt Mir. The address of the building which was occupied by the Americans is 118 Prospekt Mir.

You may notice a screening jutting out above the first floor of some recently constructed apartment houses. The purpose of this netting is to catch bricks from the newly constructed façade which might fall on the heads of passersby.

Even official Soviet newspapers have taken notice of poor Soviet construction. The newspaper *Evening Moscow* has criticised architects and construction workers for shortcomings of apartment buildings that line the road from the airport into Moscow. These are the very buildings that are pointed out to arriving visitors as examples of Moscow's fast, modern construction program. The *Evening Moscow* article was headlined "Fast Construction Should Not be Sloppy." It stated that although this work began in 1952 and people have been living in these eight- and ten-story brick structures for many months, there are many serious faults. For example, complained the article, there is water seepage through lavatory flooring, door and window frames are not properly installed, floors are warping, and elevators frequently do not work.

Evidences of the kind of slum housing the Russians are trying to eliminate are obvious to anyone who wanders down almost any Moscow sidestreet. An example at random is Trubnikovsky Pereulok. It is near the center of the city and leads to Spasso House, the pre-revolutionary mansion of a wealthy Moscow merchant and now the residence of the American ambassador. Many of the houses on Trubnikovsky Pereulok are crumbling. As in the case of other crowded sections in Russia, the number of television and radio aerials on the roofs is an indication of how many families share a small building.

HOMES OF THE LEADERS

The mansions where the Soviet leaders reside are set well back from the road and behind stone walls, but you can get a glimpse of them through the gates and over the wall. The top leaders—the members of the Communist Party's Presidium—live in almost identical big houses near Moscow University on a ridge overlooking the Moscow River and the city. After you have seen the Lenin Stadium and Moscow beyond it from the viewing area at the approach to Moscow University continue along the road with the Moscow River at your right hand. This is Vorob'yevskaya B. Street and as it gradually descends toward Berezhkovskaya Naberezhnaya you will see a dozen leaders' mansions at comfortable intervals facing toward the river. You can glimpse a greenhouse through one of the gates. That is where the Khrushchevs live, and the greenhouse is for Mrs. Khrushchev's flowers.

THE PALACE OF SOVIETS

There is a fenced-in, roughly triangular-shaped area enclosing a very large city block near the Kremlin bordered by Kropotkinskaya Naberezhnaya, Soymonovsky Pereulok and Volkhonka Ulitsa. This was to be the site of the world's tallest skyscraper. It was to be surmounted by a statue of Lenin. The project was started by Stalin, interrupted by the war, and dropped by Khrushchev as too expensive. All that remains now is a big hole in the ground intended for the foundations. There are plans now to build a more modest building to be called The Palace of Soviets and to house government offices. A local joke is that an anti-Communist is a person who can't tell The Palace of Soviets from a hole in the ground.

SPORTS

If you like sports and want to see this aspect of Soviet life there are ample opportunities in any season. Russians are great fans of soccer (called football), hockey, basketball, volley ball and track and field. There is no baseball or golf. Russian crowds are noisy and partisan. An exciting and unusual sport is motorcycle racing on a snow-packed track in winter. The Lenin Stadium, seating more than 100,000, is the largest in Moscow. The Dynamo Stadium, named after a sports club, seats about 80,000. The Stadium of Young Pioneers has an all-year skating rink as well as the usual sports grounds.

FACTORIES

Although sometimes reluctant to do so, Intourist can and does arrange tours of factories including the Likhatchov Auto Works (formerly named after Joseph Stalin), the Moscow Ball Bearing Plant (formerly named after Lazar Kaganovich) and the Mikoyan Ice Cream Factory (still bearing deputy Premier Anastas Mikoyan's name).

OTHER SUGGESTIONS

These are some other places which tourists have been able to arrange to visit through Intourist or by letter: Mosfilm Studio (this is the Moscow version of Hollywood where Russian movies are made); Moscow Television (the studios are small but busy); Bolshoi Ballet School (to see how future ballet stars are trained); Outdoor Swimming Pool (the water is heated, steam rises, and even in below-zero winter weather hearty Russians go swimming), and Skyscraper Apartment Houses (these are favored dwellings for ballerinas, high government officials, scientists, engineers, and other successful Soviet citizens).

CHAPTER NINE

Moscow: Theaters, Ballet, Opera, Circus, Movies

The story is told of a "Politeness Week" being decreed in Russia. All Soviet citizens are warned to be polite to one another.

The scene is a Moscow bus. Someone sneezes. The driver jams on the brakes.

"Who sneezed?" he demands authoritatively.

Inured by hard experience never to volunteer information to an official, everyone on the bus is silent.

The driver, standing in the aisle, repeats his question several times, but no one replies.

"This bus won't move," he shouts, "until the person who sneezed admits it."

Frightened half to death, an old woman in the back of the bus quavers, "I couldn't help it. It was me."

"*Gesundheit!*" says the law-abiding driver.

Russians tell this sort of "shaggy sneeze" story to each other, but you are not likely to hear jokes from the stage of Soviet theaters that rib or ridicule the Soviet system, even by innuendo. Variety show performers (the equivalent of vaudeville or music-hall entertainers) *do* crack jokes about poorly constructed housing (but then so does *Pravda*), about the difficulty of finding baby sitters, about bad telephone connections. The names of Soviet leaders are never mentioned in musical comedy jokes; the Communist party is never the butt of a joke. Performances of all sorts whether in theaters, circus ring, or on television come under government supervision. The Ministry of Culture is impresario, manager, talent agent, "angel," ticket-taker, and censor in the U.S.S.R. With enormous government funds at its disposal, the Soviet theater is active and ambitious. The visitor to Russia can spend many fruitful evenings attending performances of opera, ballet, plays, vaudeville, circus, and puppet shows.

There is an active theatrical life outside of Moscow too. Each of the republic capitals has a ballet and opera company as well as a fine theater. There are symphony orchestras in the major cities. There are more than 700 legitimate theaters in the U.S.S.R., and several hundred thousand theatrical groups in factories, offices, schools, and shops.

TIPS ON THEATERGOING

The autumn, winter, and spring are the choice seasons. Almost every theater has a permanent company of performers with a repertory of programs. Most companies go on vacation for the summer. Guest performers are usually from inferior provincial companies. The Bolshoi ballet and opera troupes can be seen in Moscow generally from September through mid-June. Even when a portion of the troupe goes abroad, some "name" stars remain behind.

A printed schedule of performances is posted in hotel Service Bureaus for the principal Moscow theaters. It comes in booklet form, too, and is useful if you read Russian.

Most shows begin at 7:30 P.M. Circus performances ordinarily start at 8:00 P.M., and puppet theaters at 8:30 or 9:00 P.M.

It's inconvenient to eat before a 7:30 P.M. curtain, and you may be starved by the time the show is over, especially in the case of some of the longer ballets, operas, and plays that end at 11:30 P.M. or midnight. One solution is to eat in "installments" in the theater buffet. Try a caviar (pronounced eek-rah) open sandwich during the first intermission, cold bologna on bread during the second, and cake or ice cream for dessert during the third. Beer and champagne (by the bottle or glass) are also sold, and of course hot tea.

Although it's commonplace to see men in shirt sleeves and without neckties at evening performances at the Bolshoi Theatre, it's considered the worst possible taste to take your overcoat or hat to your theater seat. In fact, you probably won't even get into the auditorium if you try wearing or carrying your coat. This applies to both men and women. Huge check rooms, often running the length of the theater's main lobby, are provided for hats, coats, boots, and umbrellas.

There's no charge for the coat-room checking service, but tips are expected and accepted. Unlike many European countries, though, the ushers who show you to your seats do not receive tips.

Opera glasses are rented at theater coat rooms. The charge is three rubles (about 30 cents or just under two shillings). It's worth twice as much even though the glasses may be of poor quality, because, by waving your opera glasses, you are entitled to go to the head of the formidable queue at the coat room after the show. It's a Russian custom.

If you hear a hissing sound when the ballerinas or bassos are taking curtain calls, don't interpret this as a manifestation of disapproval. It is simply cries of *bis* ("encore") from the enthusiastic audience.

Programs are sold by ticket-takers in the lobby. Prices range from 30 to 50 kopecks (a few pennies). Printed in Russian, these list the names of the performers, and, as a unique service, most programs give the time of the *end* as well as of the beginning of the performance. Some of the smaller theaters list the names of *several* people for each role. They are the actors in that theater's repertory company who *can* play that role. There is a check mark against the name of the person who *is* playing the role that particular evening.

Besides a program, you can also buy a "libretto." This is the story, act by act, scene by scene, of the ballet, opera, or play. It's very helpful *if* you read Russian.

There are titles after the names of prominent performers. "Honored Artist of the R.S.F.S.R." is such a title. "People's Artist" is a higher accolade, and the highest of all is to be labeled, "People's Artist of the U.S.S.R."

Sometimes you can pick up tickets you've ordered at the Service Bureau several days in advance, but that is unusual. Most often tickets are ready only a few hours before curtain time. Sometimes no tickets are available because the Ministry of Culture has requisitioned all seats for important delegations or for a government gala in honor of a visiting dignitary. This is rarely the case, though, and tourists usually get a high priority on seats.

Tickets for the Bolshoi Theatre range in price from 7 rubles (70 cents or five shillings) to 35 rubles ($3.50 or £1.5.–). Admission is less expensive to other theaters. For example, the range for matinees of the Branch Theatre of the Bolshoi is from 2 to 19 rubles and for evening performances, from 3 to 23 rubles.

The best (and most expensive) tickets in the orchestra (stalls, to our British readers) are almost automatically ordered for tourists unless they *insist* on cheaper seats.

Actually the balcony is preferable for some performances (such as *Romeo and Juliet* at the Bolshoi and *Swan Lake* at the Stanislavsky Theatre) because it commands an overhead view of the stage.

The show changes every night at most Soviet theaters. Since the company of performers is permanent, the actors are trained for a variety of roles in different productions, there are no "long runs" of a single show night after night as on Broadway, for example.

Russians are sticklers for punctuality. The curtain goes up on time. If you're late you will not be admitted to your seat if it means disturbing others. Late-comers are permitted to enter the rear of the theater or one of the balcony boxes, and it may mean standing during the first act.

Don't be surprised if you find someone in your seat. It's a Russian "game." As curtain time approaches, Russians feel free to appropriate empty seats more advantageously located than theirs. When the bona fide holder of that seat arrives, the interloper yields it with rarely a sign of embarrassment. No hard feelings are expected on either side.

There is a counter in the lobby of the Bolshoi and in some other theaters selling illustrated books about the theater. The Bolshoi book, printed in English, is particularly worth while and has photographs of the various stars. There is also a smaller, paper-bound book on the life of Galina Ulanova, the most prominent ballerina. Little packets of photographs of Soviet movie stars are sold for a couple of rubles at many newsstands.

A word of warning: Once in a while Intourist will present a couple with tickets for seats that are separated by an aisle! This detracts some of the "togetherness" from going to the theater. To be absolutely sure, ask the Intourist clerk to check the floor plan of the particular theater or circus ring to ascertain that your seats *are* together.

A word of advice: For added flavor of theatergoing in Russia stay after the curtain goes down rather than rushing for the exit. Especially at ballet performances, fans of particular stars applaud tirelessly for as long as a quarter of an hour to bring their favorites out for repeated bows. Little bouquets of flowers are hurled to the stage. The star's name is shouted rhythmically. It's an aspect of ballerina worship that shouldn't be missed.

BOLSHOI THEATRE
Sverdlov Square
Telephone: 29 17 51
23 35 06

This is a truly wonderful theater! Don't miss going to the Bolshoi (which means "grand" or "big") at least one evening during your stay in Moscow. The red-and-gold auditorium itself is worth seeing, even if the performance on the vast and versatile stage is not what you would have chosen.

The Bolshoi Theatre occupies an entire city block. A small park with a fountain and flower beds provides an attractive approach to the classic façade of the building with its eight Grecian columns. There are two pediments, the lower one surmounted by a Roman chariot drawn by four prancing horses. Custard-yellow, the Bolshoi building in its present form dates from 1856. The initial building for the Bolshoi company was constructed in 1824 but it was destroyed by fire nine years later. The Bolshoi company itself traces its history back to the time of the American Declaration of Independence in 1776 when a regular Russian professional musical theater group was founded in Moscow; it was the forerunner of the present company.

The Bolshoi Theatre consists of a famous opera company and an even more celebrated ballet troupe. Members of the ballet troupe have won acclaim since Stalin's death on trips abroad to England, the United States, France, Canada, Japan, and elsewhere. The acclaim is well deserved. Even the uninitiated can enjoy an evening of Russian ballet with its spectacular stage (which is as large as the auditorium itself) and its superlative dancing. The leaps of the males, the whirls of the ballerinas, the incredible "lifts" are the embodiment of grace; oftentimes athletic and acrobatic prowess of Olympic proportions is seen. The stage settings simulate storms and swans, fire and fairies.

The Bolshoi Theatre is an enormous organization. Dancers alone number 250. Five hundred people are employed in shops that manufacture wigs, ballet slippers, flowers, swords, costumes, and stage effects such as wind, fire, rain, and flood. There is also a school for training promising youngsters to become future ballet stars. Fortunately, ballet has suffered less from the strait jacket of ideological requirements than most other arts in the U.S.S.R. It has survived from Czarism to Communism as a classical art, and, although many modern developments have passed the Bolshoi by, it is theater matched by few in the world.

The auditorium, with its five gilt-edged tiers of red-upholstered seats, is perfectly proportioned. It is an opera house on the grand scale. A golden-colored chandelier of enormous proportions is suspended from a frescoed ceiling where the Muses are portrayed. The only traces of Communism in the theater are a small profile of Lenin over the stage and the letters *C.C.C.P.* (meaning "U.S.S.R.") woven into the stage's curtain. The audi-

torium holds 2000 spectators. There is a center box where
the Czars once sat; it is now occupied by the present
Kremlin leaders when they attend as hosts to foreign
heads of state.

The ballets we've enjoyed most at the Bolshoi, roughly
in order, are: *Swan Lake, Romeo and Juliet, Giselle, The
Fountain of Bakchisarai, The Bronze Horseman,* and
The Stone Flower.

Although a performance of the Bolshoi is a memorable
experience no matter *who* dances, it is well to see the
stars if you can. Galina Ulanova has been the prima
ballerina of the Bolshoi (and some say of the world)
for a number of years, but she dances more and more
rarely now as she approaches the age of 50. A dancer
of enormous talent who is even more exciting to watch
than Ulanova is Miya Plisetskaya. Other top ballerinas
of the Bolshoi are Raissa Strutchkova and Olga Lepe-
shinskaya. Sometimes it's impossible to find out beforehand who is dancing until you buy a program at that
evening's performance.

Recommended operas are: *Boris Godunov, Prince Igor,
Snow Maiden,* and *Eugen Onegin.*

BOLSHOI FILIAL THEATRE
(Branch Theatre of the Bolshoi)
Pushkinskaya Ulitsa 6
Telephone: 29 60 85

This is an annex of the Bolshoi Theatre. The same company performs at the Filial Theatre as at the Bolshoi itself just down the street, but the works chosen for presentation here are of smaller dimensions than such
"spectaculars" as *Romeo and Juliet* and *Prince Igor.* It
is an attractive theater, less formal and smaller than the
Bolshoi.

Some of the smaller-scale ballets presented at this theater are delightful. Try to see *Nutcracker, Coppélia* or *Fadetta*.

Russia is the place to see *Russian* operas. Operas of other national origins such as the Filial's *Madame Butterfly, The Barber of Seville, Rigoletto* and *La Traviata* just do not come off, and, in the case of *Madame Butterfly* can be slightly ludicrous with a hefty Russian female playing the role of a petite Japanese girl in a kimono. However, an exception is *Faust* which has a marvellous, sensuous ballet scene in the third act that most visitors unfortunately miss. Try to see at least this ballet scene of the opera.

STANISLAVSKY MUSICAL THEATRE
Pushkinskaya Ulitsa 17
Telephone: 29 96 68
29 42 50

This is another theater of opera and ballet. It is a completely different company of singers and dancers than that of the Bolshoi. About the only connection between the two is that the Bolshoi Theatre's ballet shoemakers also produce shoes for the Stanislavsky. The Stanislavsky's troupe is considered a niche below the Bolshoi's which is the Soviet Union's Metropolitan, Sadler's Wells, and Covent Gardens all in one non-economy-size package. However, there are those, myself included, who find the Stanislavsky's rendition of *Swan Lake* even more enjoyable than the Bolshoi's magnificent presentation. The Stanislavsky's *Swan Lake* is simpler, more literal, and with more imaginative choreography than the Bolshoi's version. See both if you can. Another fine ballet at the Stanislavsky is *Esmeralda*, a dance version of Victor Hugo's *The Hunchback of Notre Dame*.

MOSCOW ART THEATRE
Proyezd Khudozhestvennogo Teatra 3
Telephone: 29 99 08

This is one of the world's great theaters. It has a long tradition. It also has a long name. Its full title is: The Maxim Gorky State, Order of Lenin and Order of Red Banner, Academic Art Theatre. It is more commonly known as the Moscow Art Theatre or by its Russian initials, MKHAT which are pronounced "ma-khat."

The founder of this theater was K. S. Stanislavsky, the father of the "method" system of acting by which an actor playing the role of Napoleon is supposed to think of himself as really *being* Napoleon. Stanislavsky was born in Moscow (on a street now known as Bolshaya Kommunisticheskaya Ulitsa, at number 29). One night, June 21, 1898, he and V. I. Nemirovich-Danchenko, a playwright, started a discussion at a hotel which went on for twenty-four hours. During their talk they decided to found a new theater. This date has come to be considered the birthday of the famous Moscow Art Theatre.

Even if one does not understand Russian, an evening (or at least one act) of a play at the Moscow Art Theatre is a memorable experience. The productions are staged with tremendous care and with long rehearsals which privately financed theaters can not always afford. There is convincing realism not only in the acting but in the settings and costumes. Most rewarding of course are the renditions of Russian plays such as *Uncle Vanya* and *Three Sisters* by Chekhov and *The Fruits of Enlightenment* by Leo Tolstoy.

The theater's repertory also includes plays by Shakespeare. If you carry a volume of Shakespeare along to

Russia you can read up the night before going to see
the Russian rendition of *Twelfth Night* or *The Winter's
Tale*. Other theaters in town present Shakespeare too
and there's almost certain to be at least one production
of *Hamlet* (called *Gamlet* by the Russians whose alphabet has no sound similar to the English "h") or *Othello*
on the boards in Moscow.

We saw a production of George Bernard Shaw's *The
Devil's Disciple* at the Moscow Art Theatre which was
brilliantly performed even though Dick Dudgeon, the
hero, wore a fringed leather American frontiersman's
jacket instead of the garb of his early New England era.

MALY THEATRE
Sverdlov Square 1/6
Telephone: 23 26 21

The Russian word *maly* is the opposite of the word
bolshoi. *Maly* means "small." The auditorium of the Maly
Theatre, situated along one side of the same square on
which the Bolshoi Theatre faces, is a miniature version
of the Bolshoi. This is probably the most charming theater in Moscow. The low, light-yellow colored building
has a statue of Russian dramatist A. N. Ostrovsky in
front; a chain of heavy links separates the seated Ostrovsky from pedestrians on the broad sidewalk. (Almost all
of Ostrovsky's fifty plays have been performed at the
Maly.) Inside, like the Bolshoi Theatre, there is a "royal
box," but it is scaled down to the Maly Theatre's proportions as are the balconies, the stage, the decorations.
It seats 1086 people, just about half as many as the Bolshoi. If you go to the Maly Theatre after spending an
evening at the Bolshoi you may feel as if you have suddenly been shrunk to Lilliputian dimensions.

The Maly Theatre is the oldest of Moscow's dramatic theaters. It was opened on October 27, 1824. It presents a broad repertory, with emphasis on Russian classics by Tolstoy, Gogol, Ostrovsky, Turgenev. William Makepeace Thackeray's *Vanity Fair* is often played at the Maly, too. Of course *Anna Karenina* is a regular.

OTHER DRAMATIC THEATERS

For those who do not speak Russian, but do want to experience an evening at a Moscow legitimate theater, the best bet is to attend a performance of a play (translated into Russian) with which you are familiar. Besides those works already mentioned in connection with particular theaters, here, in no particular order, are some of the plays regularly presented in one or another of Moscow's dramatic theaters: *The Merry Wives of Windsor, Two Gentlemen from Verona, King Lear, Romeo and Juliet, Pygmalion, The Importance of Being Earnest, Lady Windermere's Fan*, A. J. Cronin's *Jupiter Laughs*, J. B. Priestley's *Dangerous Corner*, Graham Greene's *The Quiet American*, Lillian Hellman's *The Autumn Garden*, Hecht and MacArthur's *Ladies and Gentlemen*, Mark Twain's *Huckleberry Finn*, and John Galsworthy's *The Skin Game*.

If you read up on several of these plays before coming to Moscow you can be pretty sure that one or another will be playing during your visit.

Here are some other important dramatic theaters:

Vakhtangov Theatre, Arbatskaya Ulitsa 26, *Telephone: 41 07 28.*

A. S. Pushkin Drama Theatre, Tverskoi Boulevard, *Telephone: 95 44 18.*

Satirical Theatre, Bronnaya Ulitsa 2, *Telephone: 21 40 93.*

Mayakovsky Theatre, Gertsena Ulitsa 19, *Telephone:*
29 62 41.

Transport Theatre, Kazakova Ulitsa 8-a, *Telephone:*
61 55 28.

We have found the Moscow Gypsy Theatre disappointing. Its performances belie its name. Instead of gypsy
music and dancing as we expected, the theater presents
dull plays with "Communist-tamed" gypsy actors.

OBRAZTSOV PUPPET THEATRE
Gorky Ulitsa 32-a
Telephone: 51 33 61

This is one of Moscow's most unusual, delightful shows.
My friend John Gunther describes it as "by all odds the
finest puppet theater in the world," and says that "if I
had only one evening in Moscow, I would spend it at
the puppet theater." I would disagree with Gunther only
in one respect: If I had one evening I'd spend it at the
Bolshoi, but if I had two evenings the second would be
spent at the puppet theater.

The theater itself is small, perfectly scaled down for a
puppet performance. So much so, in fact, that the show
is not many minutes old before the small puppets, operated by a system of sticks manipulated from below the
puppet stage, begin to take on the appearance of normal-
size people. At the end of the performance the puppet-
eers step out and it is startling to suddenly see the in-
animate cast in comparison with life-size people. For a
moment the people look like giants.

The theater is the creation of a lively, imaginative man
who speaks English quite well; his name is Sergei Obraztsov. Russia had no puppet theater until he created this
one in 1931 with the consent and support of the Ministry
of Culture. There are more than one hundred people on

his staff and they have a repertory of forty plays—many of them exclusively for children. Saturday afternoon the Obraztsov Theatre is packed with classes of school children seeing Kipling classics such as *Mowgli* and other exciting works including *Aladdin and the Magic Lamp* translated into the world of puppets.

For grownups the most enchanting offering is *An Unusual Concert,* which requires no knowledge of Russian to be appreciated. It is a puppet variety show with a loquacious master of ceremonies introducing the acts. The hilarious acts include a child prodigy who plays the piano by reaching out of his carriage, an animal act which is broken up by a jealous dog chasing a singing hen off the stage, a parody version of an American jazz quartet, a chorus of thirty or so men and women whose lips move as they sing with hymnlike solemnity the praises of vitamin pills, and an overly vivacious gypsy group. It's good fun, universal in appeal.

During the height of the tourist season, *An Unusual Concert* is presented at least once a week. However, if you miss this Obraztsov masterpiece, try to see one of his other creations even though a knowledge of Russian is necessary for full enjoyment. *In the Flutter of Your Eyelashes* is a parody on Hollywood, *Mine, Only Mine* is a satire on detective and murder stories, and *Divorce Case* is a comedy about newlyweds caught in a series of coincidences that makes them decide to get divorced, but it has a happy ending.

There are several other puppet theaters in Moscow for children, but none approaches the Obraztsov show in magic of manipulation and make-believe. One such theater is the Moscow Puppet Theatre at October 25th Street 17; it has several performances a day.

CHAIKOVSKY HALL
Bolshaya Sadovaya Ulitsa 20
Telephone: 51 36 91

This is a hall of a most unusual and sensible shape. The stage juts deep into the hall with auditorium seats bending around the sides of the stage. Instead of balconies, the orchestra rises from stage level to what would be the height of a second balcony in most theaters. It has the shape of half an amphitheater.

The deep, open stage lends itself particularly to big choral groups and dance ensembles. The Moiseyev Folk Dance Troupe which scored such a remarkable success in the United States and England performs in this hall when in Moscow. They have to be seen to be believed. Wearing colorful national costumes, members of this cheerful, winning group jump so high that they seem to have springs instead of muscles. They whirl, twirl, gyrate, prance, and stamp. If you didn't see the Moiseyev dancers when they performed abroad, do try to see them in Moscow. The prices are a good deal less expensive than they were in New York or London.

The Soviet Army Chorus, consisting of several hundred voices booming like a miraculously tuned cannonade, performs in the Chaikovsky Hall too. This troupe—its full name is The Alexandrov Ensemble of Song and Dance of the Soviet Army—also includes some amazing dancers. Well worth seeing and hearing.

Also the Beryozka ("Birch") Dance Ensemble, which has toured the U.S.A., performs regularly on this stage.

MOSCOW CONSERVATORY
Gertsena Ulitsa 13
Telephone: 29 74 12

This old-fashioned, splendid hall is the scene of concerts by great Soviet artists such as pianist Emil Gilels and violinist David Oistakh. The hall itself is wonderful to look at but not very comfortable to sit in because of the straight-backed, lightly padded chairs. The stage has organ pipes as a backdrop, a balcony overhangs the main auditorium on three sides, and there are paintings of great Russian composers looking down.

There is also a smaller hall of no special distinction where concerts by lesser artists are held. Both halls are part of the Moscow Conservatory of Music where promising young Soviet students are prepared for careers in music.

MOSCOW CIRCUS
Tsvetnoy Boulevard 13
Telephone: 90 16 40
28 82 31

Whether in Moscow or in any other Soviet city, don't overlook the circus. As elsewhere in the U.S.S.R., the Moscow circus is a one-ring affair. This is in the European tradition of small intimate circuses rather than the three-ring-plus Ringling Brothers extravaganzas. I must say that I prefer the smaller shows; it's a good deal easier to keep track of what's going on.

I've seen some dull circus acts in Russia, but not many, and I can't think of any poorly prepared acts. Circus acts are pretty much of the same types the world over—

jugglers, trapeze artists, animal trainers, clowns, tumblers, and contortionists. The Soviet circus has all of these and a few acts that I've never seen elsewhere. For example, an animal act in which a tiger and his trainer wrestle and frolic in a pool of water. Another unique animal act includes trained yaks! One of the best magicians we've ever watched is a man named Kio. Be sure to see him if he's playing when you're in town. We were so intrigued that we went back twice before we divined his secret.

Two of Russia's clowns are exceptionally funny. Karand'ash is the older and more experienced. He wears a Charlie Chaplin-type costume and his routine of a bumbling bum who knocks over a statue in the park and then reassembles it with the parts of the anatomy hilariously jumbled is a circus classic. More versatile than Karand-'ash is young Oleg Popov, an astounding equilibrist and juggler. A very funny man.

All circus acts in the U.S.S.R. are controlled and assigned by a department of the Ministry of Culture. Thus, Popov may be playing for a three-month period in Moscow and then move on for a tour in the Leningrad or Irkutsk ring. He may play with an entirely different group of acts in Irkutsk than he did in Moscow.

There's a state circus school, by the way, where future Soviet circus performers are trained.

VARIETY THEATRE
Mayakovsky Square 1/29
Telephone: 50 31 51
51 36 72

The acts include musical numbers, dancers, comedians, and skits usually lampooning domestic situations.

The most famous comedian who often appears at this vaudeville theater is a Leningrad native named Raikin. But to understand Raikin or almost anyone else at this variety (*estradny*) theater, it is essential to understand Russian. A similar show is staged at the Hermitage Park where there are indoor and outdoor (for summer) theaters, a restaurant, a bandstand where an army band plays on warm evenings, and a pavilion for chess players.

DUROV'S CORNER
Durova Ulitsa 4
Telephone: 81 29 14

Very few tourists ever go to this delightsome little establishment. It is intended for children, but this is one adult who readily confesses to finding it a thoroughly wonderful place. The founder of this establishment in pre-Communist days was a famous trainer who believed that animals could be taught tricks by kindness and rewards rather than by punishment. This was a revolutionary concept at the time. Soviet authorities nationalized Durov's little theater and his zoo as they did all other theaters. Durov's children followed in his footsteps. His son—a man now well advanced in years—patiently puts animals through their clever paces in Soviet circus rings.

Not only dogs, monkeys, and equally familiar performing animals do tricks in the intimate, small hall of Durov's Corner. The cast includes such ordinarily untrained creatures as goats, possums, and crows. Feeding time at the little outdoor menagerie is a show in itself with the entire complement of Noah's ark from elephants to elk doing little tricks to earn their day's ration.

Durov's Corner is open every day except Friday. Performances on the weekend take place Saturday at 1:00

P.M. and 3:00 P.M. and on Sunday at 11:00 A.M., 1:00 P.M. and 3:00 P.M. You won't find Durov's Corner advertised on Intourist playbills, so be sure to ask your Intourist interpreter-guide to check the hours of the performances and to get you tickets. Go especially if there are children in your group!

MIR PANORAMA THEATRE
Tsvetnoy Boulevard 11

This is the Russian version of Cinerama. The movie house is one of the newest in Moscow, and although the lighting fixtures in the lobby are on the overly grandiose style of the Moscow subway, the circular hall itself is in excellent taste, almost Scandinavian in its wood-paneled simplicity. Super-wide-screen films include *How Broad Is My Country* and *Enchanted Mirror*. Both are travelogues of the U.S.S.R. This is the next best thing to actually visiting the Black Sea, Magnitogorsk, Sverdlovsk, Yakutia, and other far reaches of the Soviet Union, and there are the added Cinerama-type thrills of a ride on water skies, in an airplane and on logs shooting downstream from a Moldavian lumber camp.

If you want the experience of seeing a Russian film in a Moscow movie house, we recommend the Mir Panorama Theatre. *Mir* means both "world" and "peace."

There is also a circular (Circarama-type) movie theater on the grounds of the Agricultural and Industrial Exhibition.

Here are some other Moscow movie theaters:

Khudozhestvenny, wide screen, **Arbatskaya Plochad 14,** *Telephone: 21 76 21.*

Revival Movies, Gertsena Ulitsa 23, *Telephone: 29 72–28.*

Moskva, Mayakovskogo Square 2, *Telephone: 51 72 22.*

Avangard, Dmitrova Ulitsa 51.

OTHER HALLS

Many Soviet factories and trade union organizations have their own halls where interesting performances often are held. If you are in Moscow for only a brief period of time, the standard theaters will offer more than enough to keep you busy. However, for a longer stay, you may find it worthwhile to ask your Intourist Service Bureau what is playing in lesser known halls. For example, one of the most unusual performances we saw in Russia was held at the Central House of Culture of Railroad Workers. This was a performance by Mikhail Kuni who describes himself as a specialist in "psychological experiments." Kuni is able to memorize in a matter of seconds the arrangement of chess pieces on a board as well as a variety of numbers written on a blackboard and to add them up in an instant.

CHAPTER TEN

Moscow: Restaurants

The waiter brought the crepes suzette to our table at the Praga Restaurant in Moscow. With all eyes on him, he proudly lighted a match to the liqueur which he had poured over the dessert. Then he lighted another match, and another, and still the liqueur would not catch flame. A French waiter would have blown his brains out. The Russian waiter shrugged, and doled out a portion to each guest without worrying any more about it. Russian restaurants can be like that.

One journalist who visited Moscow wrote that it took only one meal in a restaurant to dissuade him of any illusions that he was in Paris. A British traveler wrote: "At the most expensive restaurant in Moscow, the Praga, where decorations are comparable with those in Mayfair and prices three times as high, the clientele looked like lorry drivers who had been on the road all night and were breaking their fast at a pull-up."

These comments accurately reflect the often plain quality of the food and the even plainer dress of Russian people when eating out.

However, it must be added that no one is going hungry in Russia, and least of all, the tourist. There is plenty to eat. There is considerable variety. Some of it is delicious. The caviar is relatively inexpensive and is often of unsurpassed quality. Although there is a shortage of fresh vegetables and fruits in winter, the tourist hotel restaurants get whatever is available, and this usually means oranges and apples.

231

ORDERING BREAKFAST

Service in hotel restaurants is often slow. It may be quicker to have some meals served in your room. At least, you will be able to write postcards or rest while waiting for the food to come. It's especially recommended to eat breakfast in your room if you don't want to waste time in the morning before setting out for the day's sight-seeing.

The best way to do it is this: Before you turn in for the night tell the attendant at the key desk on your floor what you will want for breakfast the next morning and what time you will want it. If she doesn't speak English you can indicate the time on your watch or by drawing a clock on a piece of paper.

Here with phonetic English spelling are some of the things you might care to order for breakfast:

Orange juice—*Apel-sin-ovy Sok*
Grape juice—*Vino-grad-ny Sok*
Bread—*Khleb*
Toast—*Tost*
Butter—*Maslo*
Jam—*Var-en-yeh*
Plain omelet—*Om-let Natur-al-ny*
Cheese omelet—*Om-let S Sir-om*
Jam omelet—*Om-let S'var-en-yem*
Two fried eggs—*Glaz-un-ya Na Dva Yai-tza*
Two fried eggs with ham—*Glaz-un-ya Na Dva Yai-tza S'vet-chin-oi*
Two four-minute eggs—*Dva Yai-tza Na Chet-ire Min-uti*
Two three-minute eggs—*Dva Yai-tza Na Tree Min-uti*
Coffee—*Ko-feh*

Milk—*Ma-la-ko*
Tea—*Chai*

USE OF FOOD COUPONS

Intourist food coupons can be used at any Intourist hotel restaurant, not only at the hotel at which you stay. Also several other restaurants, including the Praga, will accept these pre-paid coupons, but it is necessary to tell the waiter *before* you order that you want to pay in Intourist coupons.

Each food coupon has a definite ruble value. The breakfast coupon is worth 12 rubles ($1.20 or 4s 2d), the luncheon coupon is worth 20 rubles ($2.00 or 7s), and the dinner coupon will buy 30 rubles ($3. or 10s 6d) worth of food. (If there are tea coupons in your Intourist booklet each is worth 3 rubles which is 30 cents or 2s.) If you order more than your allotted amount at a meal, you will have to pay the waiter for the extra food or give him an extra coupon of the proper value.

You are entitled to a rebate for any full day of unused pre-purchased coupons for room and food. That is, if you stay fewer days than you have coupons for you will get money refunded. Turn in your unused coupons at the hotel Service Bureau and you will receive a receipt or voucher for them. This is redeemable for cash from your travel agent on your return home.

One note of caution: in doling out your coupons be sure to keep a full day's worth together whenever possible—that is, a coupon for breakfast, one for lunch, and one for dinner. If a tourist has coupons for the *same* meal rather than a complete set left over it has been known to cause difficulty in getting a voucher for a rebate.

Even if you stay the full length of time for which you have purchased coupons, you may not use all your coupons. If you ask the waiter on your floor or the restaurant manager, he usually will arrange to give you vacuum-packed jars of caviar, bottles of vodka, Russian cigarettes (you may not wish to smoke them, but they make appreciated souvenirs for friends), or chocolate bars in the amount of the coupons' value.

It is best to ask about this a day or so before you leave if you think that you will have some coupons left over, because the hotel may not always have caviar or vodka in stock.

Although prices vary, a small jar of vacuum-packed caviar costs 21 rubles ($2.10 or about 15s). You may also get fresh caviar which is somewhat better quality, but it is necessary to keep it refrigerated all the way home and eat it soon after arrival. Aboard airplanes this is more trouble than it's worth, and I don't recommend trying it after having had twenty-dollars' worth spoil shortly after I had tenderly cared for it for 5000 miles.

Chocolate is very expensive. A normal-size chocolate bar ranges in price from 1.60 rubles (16 cents or 1s) to 14 rubles ($1.40 or 10s), and even as high as 21 rubles ($2.10 or 15s).

Russian vodka (which surprisingly does not have as high an alcoholic content as many made-in-America brands) runs in price from 28.70 rubles ($2.87 or more than £1) for the government-brewed Moskovskaya brand to 30.70 rubles ($3.07 or £1.1.8) for the preferred Stolichnaya (meaning "Capital") label.

GENERAL INFORMATION ON RESTAURANTS

Before setting out for a restaurant in the evening it is important to make a reservation. Restaurants are often crowded. Ask your interpreter-guide, someone at the hotel Service Bureau, or a clerk at the hotel administrator's desk to phone for you.

It's customary in Russian restaurants to seat total strangers at the same table. Usually, though, foreign tourists—in general a privileged class in Russia—are given tables to themselves.

Intourist and other principal restaurants have menus available in English.

Menus (especially at Intourist restaurants) are often the same—identical items are offered and the identical red leather binding covers the menu. This is because restaurants are under one management—the government. In this case the agency of the government is Intourist or the Ministry of Trade. However each restaurant usually has its specialty either among the regularly printed items or listed separately.

A full course meal in Russia is hearty whatever the weather. If you are invited to lunch or dinner by Soviet officials (as you may well be if you are a member of a delegation) chances are your meal will begin with an assortment of cold dishes including salmon, cucumber salad, chicken salad, sardines, radishes, and of course caviar. Visitors have been known to assume mistakenly this to be the entire meal and to conserve no appetite for the courses that follow. Next will come a big bowl of soup, then a meat course, a dessert which probably will be ice cream, and finally tea or coffee and fruit. Sometimes there's a fish course before or after the soup. Russians may be offended, especially in provincial areas, if a guest does not eat all of his portion.

Restaurants can be fairly expensive. An abbreviated meal, by Russian standards—that is, an appetizer, a main course and dessert with wine and tea or coffee—will run from 30 to 120 rubles per person in restaurants like the Praga, the Aragvi, the Ararat, the Peking, the Metropole Hotel, the National Hotel, and the Grand Hotel. (That's from $3. to $12. or in pounds from about £1 to £4.)

Here are some sample prices from menus of average-priced restaurants for single portions: sturgeon—11.65 rubles ($1.17 or about 9s); hard-boiled eggs in mayonnaise—6.05 rubles (61 cents or almost 5s); assorted cold meats—7.55 rubles (76 cents or a bit over 5s); roast chicken—12.55 rubles ($1.26 or 11s 4d); steak—10.70 rubles ($1.07 or 7s); compote of fruit—3.85 rubles (39 cents or almost 3s); tea—50 kopecks (5 cents or 4d); tea with a slice of lemon—90 kopecks (9 cents or 7d).

Caviar (pronounced eek-rah) is less expensive than in most other countries, but it is certainly *not* a give-away item. A portion—and a generous portion it is—costs about 14 rubles ($1.40 or 10s). It would cost five times as much in New York or London. Although pressed caviar is usually more expensive and, for some reason, is preferred by some Russians, it is inferior—to my taste at least—to the real thing. Black caviar is superior to red caviar and is more expensive. The best black caviar is really not black, but a rich dark gray with eggs almost the size of buckshot.

Try caviar thick on black bread with or without butter spread on first.

One of the most delicious things we've ever eaten in Russia or anywhere else is a delicacy consisting of caviar spread on light, thin pancakes and covered with sour cream. Unfortunately the Russians make these pancakes, known as *blini,* only during certain months of the year, usually February and March, in connection with a Russian religious holiday. Be sure to ask for these *blini* with caviar and sour cream (*smetana*).

Tips: Waiters and waitresses increasingly expect tips as their contact with foreigners grows. Although officially denounced, tipping is practiced by Russians especially in the more "fashionable" restaurants. Ten per cent of the check is considered a very good tip; five per cent will be accepted gratefully. On occasion, particularly as you travel farther from Moscow, a tip from a foreigner will be refused by a waiter who is obeying the spirit as well as the letter of the law.

Tea is usually served in a glass with a handled holder. This is the Russian custom. However, sometimes waiters in Intourist hotels will serve tea in a glass to men but women get theirs in a cup. It is considered more elegant to serve foreigners that way.

If you feel so inclined, don't hesitate to "slurp" your tea. The best people in Russia do. Some say it makes the already tasty Russian tea taste better and one who has tried can testify that there may be something to this!

Don't be surprised if a woman with a broom sweeps under your very feet as you sit even in Moscow's better restaurants. Cleanliness is considered, if not next to god-liness, at least next to productiveness, and this sometimes includes nonstop sweeping of floors in eating establish-ments.

Each of the fourteen republics besides Russia that comprise the U.S.S.R. has a restaurant in Moscow serving dishes native to that region. If you can't travel all over the Soviet Union the next best thing is to eat at the various republic restaurants. For example, the Aragvi serves specialties from Georgia, the Ararat serves Arme-nian dishes, the Baku prepares Azerbaijan recipes. These and others are mentioned in the following pages of this chapter.

A WORD ON WINES AND OTHER DRINKS

The best wines in the U.S.S.R. come from the Georgian Republic. They are available at all Soviet restaurants.

Georgian wines are numbered. The even numbers are for red wine and the odd numbers are for white. Number 4 is an excellent, dry red wine. Numbers 1, 3, and 27 are the recommended white wines; 1 and 3 are dry and number 27 is rather sweet with a hint of apple taste. The lower numbers of wine are dry; the higher the number the sweeter the wine.

Soviet champagne is below the quality of French or even American domestic champagnes, but nevertheless quite good. It comes in various grades of sweet and dry. Ask for the kind you like. There are fairly good liqueurs and brandies too.

Vodka of course is the national drink. It is not only served before the meal as a sort of *apéritif* but during the meal as well—usually with the cold first course. Vodka is ordered by the gram and served in an open carafe. One hundred grams is enough for one drink each for four people.

The Russians are avid drinkers of mineral water. Various sections of the U.S.S.R. have local mineral water. Narzan and Borshom are the two most popular in Moscow and also are found in other cities. Both are carbonated. We prefer Narzan which is not as sharp-tasting as Borshom. Both are improved by a squirt of lemon juice in each glassful.

Russian beer has a tendency to fall flat. It seldom has a head. There are a number of government breweries. Leningradskaya beer is preferred by many. *Peevo* is the Russian word for beer.

Although Coca-Cola, Seven-Up, and Pepsi-Cola are

not available in Russia, there are various fruit flavors of soda water.

A favorite Russian summer drink is *Kvass*, usually made from fermented bread. It tastes a bit like unsweetened cider. *Kvass* is served not only in restaurants but from dispensers in the street which look like small water tank trailers, unhooked from their trucks.

Kefir is the Russian equivalent of yogurt.

NAMES OF RESTAURANTS

There are many hundreds of eating establishments in Moscow, counting stand-up snack bars and cafeterias. Quality of food, atmosphere, or some unique characteristic make these the most important:

PRAGA (Prague) RESTAURANT
Arbat Ulitsa 2
Telephone: 28 92 66
28 92 75

Some years ago when Nikita Khrushchev was in Yugoslavia he effusively invited a group of Western correspondents to come to Moscow. He told them that they would find restaurants better than those in Paris. A skeptical reporter asked Mr. Khrushchev for an example. The Soviet leader responded with the name of the Praga. It was recalled at the time by those present, and by some of them who later visited the Praga, that Khrushchev had never been in a Paris restaurant, or for that matter, in Paris.

The Praga is an elaborate four-floor establishment divided into many dining rooms. There is a so-called "café" on the ground floor which is the Praga's attempt at quick-lunch service. Few foreigners eat here. There is an outdoor roof garden which is pleasant. The floors in between hold a number of other public eating halls and small rooms where private parties can be held. The main dining room is V-shaped with high ceilings and wood-paneled walls. A dance orchestra plays at night, and this is the room we recommend for an evening out.

A sour note: Although it's been our experience that a foreigner is almost invariably treated honestly and courteously in a Soviet restaurant, it's with regret that I must report that this is not always the case at the Praga. Because of attempts at "petty larceny" it is a good idea to check your bill carefully.

To go from sour note to sweet, the food at the Praga can be excellent, not only by Russian standards but by those of other cities as well. A menu is available in English.

Here in phonetic Russian are some of the dishes worth trying:

Jul-i-en iz Krab-ov: this is a delicious hot crab dish topped with cheese and broiled. Served in doll-sized, metal saucepan-shaped containers, two to a portion, "Crab Julienne" can be ordered as an opening course if you plan a big meal or as a main course if you're eating lightly.

Kot-lyety iz Koor Po-Kiev-sky: The waiter will understand if you just say *"Kiev-sky"* cutlet." This is breast of chicken, boned, rolled, breaded and deep fried, with a finger of sweet butter in its center. Apply your knife tentatively because a decisive first cut can cause the butter to squirt out. Many a clean shirt or blouse has been soiled by an incautiously approached Kiev cutlet.

Bif-schteks Natoor-al-ny: This is steak. Sometimes it's excellent, other times it's inedibly tough. As is true in many other products in Russia there is a lack of standardization in meats. However, you stand a better chance of getting a good steak at the Praga and at the National Hotel than at other restaurants. Ask for it "with onions" (*S'loo-kum*) to try it the way the Russians prefer it, smothered in fried onions.

Ryab-chiki: Hazel grouse is a speciality of the Praga. However, it usually is small and lean, and scarcely a man-size meal.

Gribee V Smet-an-eh: This is a Praga specialty that shouldn't be missed. Broiled mushrooms are covered with sour cream sauce. It also comes with fried onions instead of the sour cream. Served hot, this is a delight either way. This may also be ordered by asking for *Cham-pin-yonee V Smet-an-eh.*

UZBEKISTAN RESTAURANT
Neglinnaya Ulitsa 29
Telephone: 21 31 77

This is the Uzbek national restaurant serving spicy dishes from the Uzbekistan Republic in the heart of the Asian section of the U.S.S.R. There are almost always a number of Uzbeks eating here. Dark-skinned with Oriental features, the men don't remove their *tubeteika*, black skullcaps with white embroidery, while they eat, and the women wear gypsylike rainbow-colored blouses and long skirts.

Unfortunately the atmosphere is often more memorable than the food. An orchestra plays at night. A garden restaurant is pleasantly cool in summer. There are paintings of Uzbekistan pastoral scenes. The ceiling is decorated in typically Uzbek mosaiclike patterns. A small counter in the lobby sells fresh and dried Uzbek fruits.

As is true of many Soviet restaurants, there is an annoying inconsistency in the quality of the Uzbekistan's food. Some days, for example, the *shashlik* is superb, but too often this lamb on a spit is tough and stringy.

These are characteristic Uzbek dishes to order:

Mas-ta-va: This is a soup only for those who aren't counting calories. If you think of soup as a liquid, abandon the concept when you order *mastava*. Its ingredients include rice, mutton, tomatoes, sour cream. Served in a deep bowl, it is eaten with chunks of bread dropped into this reddish-colored, rather greasy concoction.

Plov: We've found this to be the most dependably good item on the Uzbekistan's menu. It is Asian *pilaff,* a heaping portion of rice mixed with fried onions and pieces of meat, usually lamb. Flavor and color are added by the bits of prunes and carrots.

Manti: It takes practice to enjoy this dish. *Manti* are big dumplings of dough with meat centers. They are served in a bowl of broth.

Lu-la Ke-bab: Oval-shaped croquettes of chopped lamb cooked on a spit and served on a platter with pickles, onions, and other garnish. One of the best dishes at this restaurant.

Shash-lik: Lamb on a spit cooked Uzbek style. This is a staple dish in the entire Middle Eastern and central Asian region, and the spices and garnish vary from place to place.

Non: This is the native bread served in individual flat, round loaves. The way to eat it is simply to break off chunks with your hands. It's considered effete if not rude to use a knife.

ARAGVI RESTAURANT
Gorky Ulitsa 6
Telephone: 29 37 62

This is our favorite Russian restaurant. More accurately, I should say, "Georgian" restaurant because the Aragvi, named after a river in the Georgian section of the Soviet Union, specializes in food of that Caucasus mountain region. Among other things, Georgia is famous because Joseph Stalin was born in this land of historically fierce mountaineers that lies between the Black Sea and the Caspian Sea. Georgia is one of the fifteen republics that comprise the U.S.S.R.

The food served here is Georgian. A half-dozen typically swarthy Georgian musicians sit on a balcony overlooking one of the Aragvi's two main rooms. They play minor-key music native to that Middle East region on odd-looking flutes and stringed instruments. If you are lucky, there may be a number of Georgians (residing in or visiting Moscow) eating at the Aragvi. Chances are that before the evening is over they will burst into song accompanied by rhythmic hand-clapping, and perhaps even dance graceful Georgian folk dances (which employ the arms and hands as much as the feet) in the narrow spaces between tables. Russian couples at the restaurant dance between tables, too, but theirs are the more conventional "ballroom" steps.

Not long ago the director of the Aragvi and two assistant directors were taken into custody by police on charges of pocketing nearly 8500 rubles ($850 or more than £300) in tips per month. According to a report in the government newspaper *Izvestia* (*News*), customers had to tip the director or his assistants to get a good table, and then had to tip the waiters to get polite service. There's no

doubt that they did accept tips, but there are few waiters in Moscow who don't.

The famous who have eaten at the Aragvi include Sir
Winston Churchill, Field-Marshal Lord Alanbrooke,
Averell Harriman, Eric Johnston, and Bob Hope.

The setting is simple. The restaurant's two main rooms
are in a cellar. The walls of the larger room are lined a
third of the way to the high ceiling with a light shade of
marble and above it are panels of scenes from ancient
folklore of the pre-Soviet Georgian kingdom which gave
Europe more princes per capita of population than any
other monarchy. You won't be able to hear your companion's shouts when the orchestra plays, but for the first
visit it's worth the din to sit in this more interesting if
less quiet room. (There are small rooms above for private parties.)

Our suggestion for a meal at the Aragvi is to start with
a variety of cold dishes including caviar, salmon, cucumbers in sour cream, a Georgian bean dish that is supposed
to have fertility-inducing powers and one of the Aragvi's
most unusual specialities, cold turkey (or chicken) covered with a marvelous walnut cream sauce. Be sure to
ask for warm Georgian bread. For the main course the
recommended Georgian dish is plump young chicken
pressed and weighted quite flat as it fries to a crisp
brown. It is well seasoned before cooking but is served
with supplementary seasoning—pure garlic sauce and a
spicy reddish sauce. For dessert try the Aragvi's ice
cream with fruit and then Turkish coffee. A word of
warning: don't stir or you'll get a mouthful of grounds.
It comes sugared. Here is this suggested menu in phonetic spelling:

Black caviar—*Eek-rah Chor-na-yah*
Salmon—*Sy-om-ga*

Cucumbers in sour cream—*Ogur-tzi Sa S'met-ah-noy*

Georgian cold beans in spicy sauce—*Khal-od-nye Lo-bi*

Cold turkey in walnut sauce—*Sat-zivy iz Ind-yay-kee*

Warm Georgian bread—*Khleb Gary-ah-chy*

Butter—*Maslo*

Georgian chicken—*Tzi-plya-tah Ta-ba-kah*

Ice cream with fruit—*Plom-birs Fruk-tomi*

Turkish coffee—*Ko-feh Pa Tur-etz-key*

ARARAT
Neglinnaya Ulitsa 4
Telephone: 95 92 12

Although the Old Testament's books of Genesis, Jeremiah, Kings, and Isaiah mention Ararat (either the area or the 16,946-foot mountain) as the landing place of Noah's ark, there's not a single painting of the Biblical event in *this* restaurant. Actually it's two restaurants. One is entered through the Yevropa (Europe) Hotel, and the other (known as the Ararat Café) is next door.

The café is smaller and comes about as close to anything in Moscow to an *intime* atmosphere. (For the bachelor tourist: if you *do* get that attractive Intourist guide to go out with you, this would be a good place to take her.) There are only about fifteen tables and you can sit in a fairly quiet corner away from the glare of chandeliers—which is not an easy achievement in Moscow night spots. One wall is covered with a mural of snow-covered Mount Ararat.

The larger Ararat restaurant has attractive, vaulted arches and indirect ceiling lighting that is intended to give the impression of open sky—an illusion that is enhanced by clusters of artificial grapes trellised along the borders of the ceiling. Mirrored walls make the restaurant look bigger than it is. There's a small dance floor and an orchestra plays in the evening. For lunch, music is piped in—"Middle East Muzak," I suppose. The music is an Armenian-Russian-American hash that is likely to include minor-key melodies from the Ararat region as well as the "Beer Barrel Polka."

Service is slow. On one occasion we heard a Russian complain, "Every time I tell that waiter to bring something he goes to Yerevan for instructions." (Yerevan is the capital of distant Armenia.)

If you like Armenian food the Ararat is your dish. If you don't know anything about Armenian food here's your chance to try it:

Start with *lo-bi* (cold kidney beans with chopped scallions) and *ogurtzi so smetanoi* (cucumbers with sour cream dressing) as an appetizer.

Soup is a must in a hearty Armenian meal. *Piti* is a spicy, red soup with great chunks of potatoes, meat, bones, dried peas, and plenty of onions. It's a meal in itself, especially when eaten with wedges of the bread served.

An unusual main dish is *chebureki,* juicy meat covered by baked dough.

We prefer *lula kebab,* small oval-shaped croquettes of chopped lamb cooked on a spit. It's served on a big platter with sour pickles garnishing the edges and large thin slabs of *lavash,* an unleavened flat, tasteless bread.

The local mineral water, called *arzni* will taste a good deal better if you order a lemon to squeeze in it. Armenian cognacs are quite good.

NATIONAL HOTEL RESTAURANT
Manege Square at corner of Gorky Street
Telephone: 29 99 17

This restaurant on the second floor of the National Hotel has a wonderful view of the Kremlin and of St. Basil's Cathedral in Red Square. An orchestra plays almost every night. Be sure to sit in the main dining room for either orchestra or view; there is an annex room across the hall that has only a rather ugly stained-glass window to recommend it.

Saturday night is an especially good time for dining at the National, because it affords a glimpse of a set of Moscow young people who deliberately try to copy Western ways. The girls are smartly dressed by Russian standards and wear heavy eye make-up. The young men's suits are cut with narrower pants than the customary Soviet bell-bottom. They dance the tango, rhumba, and cha-cha with enthusiasm if not always with great grace. The National on Saturday night is favored by this Moscow "smart set."

Besides these attractions, the National Hotel restaurant, which caters mostly to tourists, offers good and sometimes very good food.

These are some of the dishes we've eaten and liked at the National:

Borsch pa Mos-kov-sky: This is the characteristic Russian *borsch* that is as much a cliché of a Russian menu as are caviar and vodka. Cabbage is just one of the ingredients of this robust soup; potatoes and large chunks of meat add flavor and body. Almost every restaurant serves *borsch* in one form or another and no visit to the U.S.S.R. is complete until you try it.

Kasha: These are groats, a staple of the Russian diet, served like potatoes. Like *borsch, kasha* should be tried to round out your Soviet gastronomical experiences.

Sue-dack Tes-teh: These are finger-length filets of a delicate, white fish covered with a light batter and deep fried. When the batter is flaky and crisp it's one of the best Russian fish dishes.

Bif-stro-gan-ov: Beef stroganoff is almost always a safe item to order when you can't think of what else to eat. A lot depends on the quality of the beef, but the sauce is usually excellent.

Oot-ka S Yab-lak-ami: Roast duck with apples.

Es-kal-op iz Tel-yat-inee: Veal scallopine, Russian-style.

Tzip-len-ok Zha-re-ny: Roast chicken.

RIVER BOAT RESTAURANTS

There are a number of river boats tied up at the banks of the Moscow River which serve meals while giving the patron the sensation of being aboard ship. Personally, the gently rocking motion makes me just seasick enough to spoil my appetite, but you may find these river restaurants pleasant on a summer's evening. Two of the most popular are the *Lastochka* (which means "Swallow") near the Krimsky Bridge and the *Chaika* (which means "Sea Gull") near the Navoarbatski Bridge.

QUICK EATING

A main tourist complaint is that so much time is wasted in trying to get something to eat. Service in most restaurants is agonizingly slow. There are several places where a comparatively quick meal can be ordered. As already mentioned, if sustaining life rather than gourmet-eating is your aim, you can save time when you go to the theater by eating in the theater buffet during the intermissions. There is an automat (called *avtomat* in Russian) near Dzerzhinsky Square where a quick (although uncomfortable) meal can be obtained. You eat standing up at chest-high, round marble tables with a half dozen other people. As in other *Stolovaya* ("Snack Bars") of this sort around town, you choose the food you want from a menu posted at the cashier's booth, pay for what you order, and present your receipt at a counter where you are given your food.

There is also a clean, quick cafeteria in the building of the Moscow Art Theatre at Proyezd Khudozhestvennogo Teatra 3.

Other Moscow restaurants worth noting are:

Astoria, Gorky Ulitsa 10, *Telephone: 29 02 41.* (Average.)

Baku, Gorky Ulitsa 24, *Telephone: 21 80 94.* (Serves Azerbaijan style food which is rather similar to that offered at the Ararat.)

Grand Hotel, Revolution Square 1/2, *Telephone: 95 89 01.* (Average food, slow service, old-fashioned dining room which is smaller than most with a dance floor that is larger than many.)

Metropole Hotel, Sverdlov Square 2/4, *Telephone: 28 40 60.* (Somewhat below the standard of the National Hotel restaurant, but worth trying. Pretty good orchestra for dancing.)

Krisha, Moscow Hotel, Okhotny Ryad 2, *Telephone: 92 12 56.* (The food could be better, but the view from this roof restaurant recommends it. The skyscraper Ukraine Hotel has a roof restaurant which commands a view of Moscow, including slums, in all directions.)

Berlin Hotel, Pushechnaya Ulitsa 6, *Telephone: 28 25 88.* (Plain but pleasant.)

Sovietskaya Hotel, Leningradskaya Ulitsa 44/2, *Telephone: 53 15 87.* (Often well-prepared food with less often good service.)

Peking, Bolshaya Sadovaya 1/7, *Telephone: 50 19 23.* By all means try Moscow's Chinese restaurant, a Chinese restaurant without Chinese waiters. Some of the dishes are not at all what you'd expect from the menu, but if you order a half-dozen for your party half of the dishes will likely prove to be delicious.

Sofiya, Gorky Ulitsa 32, *Telephone: 51 08 84.* (Small, noisy, but good food.)

Central House of Art Workers, Pushechnaya Ulitsa 9. (If, for some reason, you just can't get along without American apple pie, a reasonable facsimile is sold in the third-floor restaurant of this club.)

CHAPTER ELEVEN

Moscow: Night Life

It's been said that in Russia a hangover is more a matter of sore feet than of throbbing temples.

The reason is a suggestion (not always enforced) of one drink of vodka per customer in any restaurant. This idea, set down by Nikita Khrushchev, was intended to discourage alcoholism and drunkenness. However, the rule falls short on two counts: first of all, it does not apply to wines and a Russian can drink all the wine he wants; and secondly, there's nothing to prevent a thirsty Russian from walking from restaurant to restaurant for his "one" drink. Nothing, that is, except sore feet.

This chapter on drinking, dancing, and dating—the elements of what may loosely be called "night life"—is the shortest in this travel guide. The reason? There's less to write about on this subject than on any other. Plain and simple, Soviet night life is not very lively.

The visitor in Moscow can be kept busy every night for several months attending different performances of excellent opera, ballet, and theater, and eating out, as has already been described. But if the tourist seeks the night life of Paris from Les Girls to Les Halles or the all-hours imbibing of New York he will be disappointed.

DANCING

There is dancing, usually until midnight or 1 A.M., at a number of Moscow restaurants including the National

Hotel, the Metropole Hotel, the Grand Hotel, the Berlin Hotel, the Sovietskaya Hotel and the Praga Restaurant. It's best to telephone beforehand because the orchestra's night off varies from place to place.

It's considered quite proper in Russia for a man to ask a woman who is a perfect stranger to dance. In fact, it's a compliment to the lady. The Russian will approach a table and, with a nod toward the lady's escort, politely ask her to dance. If you'd like to dance, why not? In fact, it can be a most interesting way to meet a Russian in completely acceptable social surroundings—an accomplishment that is often difficult for a tourist.

By the way, don't be surprised to see two men dancing together. It's an outgrowth of country folk dancing, but is becoming less frequent in cities. Of course, women often dance together.

NIGHT CLUBS

There aren't any. For a short while, the Sovietskaya Restaurant changed its name to Noviy Yar, meaning "New Yar." Yar was the name of the owner of a famous pre-revolutionary night club which featured gypsy singing. It did business in the very room that is now occupied by the Sovietskaya Restaurant. The Noviy Yar featured blues and jazz singers, a floor show, lights-low dancing, a cover charge and even an occasional B-girl. However, the Noviy Yar was ahead of its time; it became the hangout of the officially denounced *stilagyi* (which comes from the Russian word for style), a genus of Soviet young man whose interests in jazz, loud clothes, Western ways, and making an easy ruble combine in him some of the qualities of the "Teddy boy," the "zoot-suiter," "the jazz set," and the "beat generation." In short order the Noviy Yar was shut down. However, the Sovietskaya Restaurant features one of the best orchestras in town, entertainment that may include a hefty vocalist in evening dress rendering Soviet songs of the soil or a hale-and-hearty team of acrobats. The dance floor is larger than most.

BARS

Once again, *nyet,* if you're thinking of an *intime* cocktail bar with soft lighting and pretty waitresses. With the de-emphasis on drink there's even been a move to close down *pivnye zaly,* beer halls. There is a Western-looking bar in the Sovietskaya Hotel, but with one peculiarly Soviet feature. Russians like things big, and the bar stools here almost require a rope ladder for an average-size man to get his perch.

At any bar, restaurant or café, scotch, rye, bourbon, gin or other liquors familiar to Western palates are rarely if ever available. Russian-brewed whiskey is considered awful by connoisseurs. Soviet vodka is excellent. Try the amber-colored and delicate "pepper vodka" for a good and different variation.

DATING

Contrary to what is often reported, it *is* possible to get a date in Russia. More than one bachelor tourist has succeeded in dating his pretty Intourist guide. As a matter of fact, a few have married their guides! However, it's not easy, because Intourist guides know that not romance but rather relating the sights is their function.

A number of visitors have struck up conversations at the ballet, puppet theater, or circus with Russian girls who have accepted invitations for ice cream. Many Russian young ladies, though, are hesitant about dating foreigners.

Dating works two ways, and occasionally Russian men will ask young women tourists out. We know of one particularly persistent Russian who took three days off his engineer's job to accompany an American girl, despite her feeble protests, from Moscow to Leningrad. They still correspond. The only advice that can be offered when a Russian "wolf" turns his attention to the traveling lass is that she act just as she would if the same thing happened at home.

A likely spot for meeting young non-Russians is at American House, a private club run by bachelor members of the American Embassy staff.

There's a dance almost every Saturday night, bingo games on Thursday, movies two other nights of the week. There's a small bar, a juke box and pleasant company. Young people from various non-Communist embassies—secretaries, attachés, noncommissioned officers of embassy military staffs—gather there. If you're homesick, this may be the cure. Usually the club has extended hospitality to transient guests, but it might be better to ask about it when you stop in at your embassy to register. The address of the American House Club in Kropot Kinskaya Naberezhnaya 3. The telephone number is 46 05 89. There is also a similar club on the premises of the British Embassy at Sofiiskaya Naberezhnaya 14. The embassy telephone number is 31 95 55.

WHERE TO GO

The biggest problem in romance for Russians is "where to go." If romance comes your way in Russia this will be your problem too. Most Russian girls won't come to your Intourist hotel room, and visitors must be out of the hotel rooms by midnight. There's just too much of a gamut of curious eyes to run—the policeman in front, the administrator's desk downstairs, the elevator operator, the key desk custodian. Family apartments are crowded and few Russians own cars. *Love in a Taxicab* might be a title for a Russian novel someday. The lanes and benches of Gorky Park and other parks are often busy places at night. This is complicated by the fact that it doesn't get dark until past ten o'clock for most of the summer, and in the winter it is so cold that lovers risk frostbite if they hold hands without gloves on.

LADIES OF THE EVENING

Soviet authorities are proud to point out that they have eliminated prostitution in the U.S.S.R. This is almost true. But not quite. Girls can be seen plying their trade in various parts of Moscow, often on the sidewalks near the Moscow Hotel, less frequently on Gorky Ulitsa. It's obvious to even the casual observer that they lack the pertness of their Parisian counterparts. There are no houses of prostitution, but some of the practitioners have rental arrangements with taxi drivers.

Some tourists, especially those staying at the Ukraine Hotel, claim to have received suggestive offers by telephone during the night. A writer for the British magazine, *The Economist,* puts it this way: "Even a foreigner with only a limited grasp of colloquial Russian eventually gets the drift of the inviting phone calls made to his hotel bedroom around or after midnight."

CHAPTER TWELVE

Moscow: What to Buy and Where

One of Russia's most prominent movie directors told friends about a most unusual suit he had made at a time when fabrics were in much shorter supply in the U.S.S.R. than now. A general in the M.V.D. (the secret police), an acquaintance of boyhood days, had offered to help the movie director get a new suit. He gave him a note to a certain tailor who showed him some material, took his measurements, and soon the suit was ready.

A few weeks later the movie director was invited to a Kremlin party in honor of a visiting leader of a foreign government. Prominent figures of the Communist party were present, and there were many M.V.D. secret police agents interspersed in the crowd of diplomats, foreign correspondents, and theater folk in the huge Kremlin hall.

The movie director, proudly wearing his new suit, noticed with some surprise that a number of men (in fact, quite a large number) were wearing suits of the same pattern. He dismissed the matter from mind and found a place at a crowded buffet table lavishly covered with delicacies. As he was generously spreading caviar on bread someone tugged at his sleeve. There stood one of the men wearing the same suit as his. He whispered furtively in the movie director's ear, "The boss says we're not to eat any caviar. They're short of it tonight."

Only then did the movie director realize that the tailor was unusually well supplied because he was the outfitter for the M.V.D.!

However, things are changing in Russia. Although there still are secret police, there is an increasing selection of fabrics and other goods offered for sale in stores.

And speaking of caviar—on one of my first trips home from Moscow I brought along a dozen jars of caviar as gifts to friends. It seemed an ideal little present from Russia, a rare and expensive delicacy. The first person to whom I presented one of these jars accepted it casually. "Oh, caviar," he said, turning the jar in his hand. "It's the same brand that I get at the store around the corner."

This disillusioned me as to the merits of caviar gifts from Russia although less cosmopolitan friends received them with more enthusiasm. Despite this deflating experience, caviar *is* an excellent item to buy in Russia and bring home. There are, in fact, many other interesting and unusual things to be bought in the U.S.S.R. The next section of this chapter lists them. After that a section names the most important stores for buying these and other things. Finally there's a section on shopping hints.

WHAT TO BUY

Folk Art Dolls: There are various types of dolls and they make wonderfully decorative pieces as well as being fine gifts for children. There is an especially appealing set of fifteen dolls, four inches or so in height. Each is dressed in the traditional native costume of one of the fifteen Soviet republics. The boxed set costs about 40 rubles (as mentioned previously, there are ten rubles in one dollar and 28 rubles in one pound sterling).

Matryoshka is a particularly characteristic Russian doll of lacquered wood. Actually it is a nest of several dolls, one inside the other in diminishing size. These rounded, brightly painted figures come in various sizes from about five inches (with two dolls inside) to giants a foot high (with a score of graduated dolls inside). The price range runs from eight rubles to 150.

Clay Figures: These are among the most artistically imaginative souvenirs, known as *Vyatka* toys. Made in villages in the Kirov region, these small clay animals and people take quaint and delightful shapes—a sad-eyed rabbit holding an out-sized carrot, roosters with combs of rainbow colors bedecked with bits of gold paper pasted on, and peasant women carrying geese and other goods to the market. There are also reindeer, bears, and other animals. Recently the artisans have started to produce these figures in large sizes, but we find those in two- and three-inch sizes the most delightful. The small ones cost from 15 to 30 rubles each. One note of caution: these clay figures are easily broken in travel. We managed to cement a couple of broken heads back on, but careful wrapping would have prevented this decapitation in the first place.

Tea Cozies: These foot-high and higher dolls of sweet-faced, shawl-covered peasant women with long broad skirts are lovely to look at, and useful too. The skirts stand out stiffly with the help of an insulating material that also serves to keep a pot of tea remarkably hot when the doll stands over it.

Phonograph Records: More about these later when the names and addresses of record shops are given, but for now suffice it to say that we've found our Russian recordings of *Swan Lake*, of the Soviet Army Chorus, and of other Soviet performing groups to be among our most evocative souvenirs.

Vodka: Nothing, unless it be caviar, will mean "Russia" as much to a gift recipient as a bottle of vodka with a label in Russian. Of course, vodka can be purchased anywhere else, but somehow friends seem particularly pleased to have the genuine, original Russian product.

Balalaikas: For those with a bit of bohemia in their souls, a balalaika can make a fine wall decoration. This stringed instrument's unusual and attractive shape is a sure conversation piece. The price depends on the workmanship, but 40 rubles is an average cost. The problem is how to pack it for the trip home. I know of only one practical way, and that is to carry it as a hand luggage. Your fellow plane passengers will hate you, but you may consider it all worth while when you finally get it home.

Postage Stamps: This is the least expensive and often most appreciated gift from Russia, ranging in denomination from a few kopecks to several rubles. Russian stamps are works of art.

Folk Art Boxes: These are expensive. Small boxes an inch or two square that may be used for holding earrings or cuff links sell for about 50 rubles. The larger sizes cost as much as 1500 rubles and make attractive cigarette boxes. There are several kinds depending on the village in which they were made. The most popular type is known as the *palekh* box. Made of durable, strongly compressed papier-mâché, the boxes are painted with glossy black lacquer. The tops are ornamented, in ancient Russian style, by a village scene, an episode from folklore or figures of people. The older the boxes the better. Some of the newer creations have figures of ballerinas that are quite out of context with this art form.

Embroidered Wear: GUM and *Petrovsky Pasage* (described later) are the best places to try first for shirts, blouses, dresses, tablecloths, napkins, and pillow covers trimmed with Russian and Ukrainian embroidery. These are by no means inexpensive. A man's shirt of good quality will cost 240 rubles. Such a shirt can be worn as a sport shirt although it is very loose fitting; the Russian gathers it in at the waist with a cord in the tunic style of folk dancers. We've found that these long, full men's shirts make attractive and unusual pull-overs for women —both as maternity blouses and over bathing suits.

Bear Skins and Other Furs: Bulky to carry, but bear skins are cheaper to buy in Moscow than at home. Matched skins of other furs are hard to find; the best are exported.

Toys: There are some excellent toys in Russia. A construction toy in the shape of a Kremlin tower is our favorite. The child slides colored blocks and disks off a central shaft and then reconstructs the tower according to memory or imagination. There are also delightful hand-manipulated puppets, trucks, airplanes, games. Although it is not intended as a toy, the abacus—the ancient adding apparatus consisting of beads on a wire frame that still is used in Russia—is a unique made-in-Russia toy for the very young.

Tea Holders: If you take to the Russian custom of drinking tea from a glass you'll want to buy one of the metal holders into which the tea glass fits. The least expensive is in silver-colored metal with a Kremlin emblem.

Cloisonné Ware: Delicately colored cloisonné work is available in the handles of gold-bowled sugar spoons, tea holders, shot-size vodka cups, and other items. Expensive. For example: the small sugar spoons average about 120 rubles each.

Semiprecious Stones, Chinaware, Antiques, Paintings, Icons: Worth while for those with special interests and an experienced eye.

NAMES OF STORES

Stores worth visiting, both for the items we have described and for exploring on your own are:

GUM
Red Square 3
Telephone: 90 01 08
Extensions for information: 470 or 233 or 404

GUM rhymes with "boom." GUM is an abbreviation derived from the initials of the store's full name—Gosudarstveniy Universalniy Magazin meaning State Department Store.

This is the country's largest department store. When it was built in 1893 it was the largest store in Europe. It was then really an arcade that sheltered 240 small shops selling a variety of goods. For a period after the revolution it was converted to government offices. When Stalin died and a policy was introduced of greater emphasis on consumer needs, the building was renovated, the government offices moved elsewhere, and GUM was reopened as a store.

It still is basically a huge arcade with separate shops, although now all under one management. A rounded glass roof gives it the appearance of a railroad station. In the center of the store tiers of balconies look down onto the fountain which is a favorite meeting place for Muscovites. Lost children are brought here to be claimed by their parents.

GUM's statistics are impressive. The total length of its counters is 1.6 miles, 200,000 people shop in GUM every day, and 30,000 items are offered for sale. These include food, clothing, shoes, furniture, kitchenware, and electrical appliances. GUM is the place to come first when shopping for something. It is the Macy's and Gimbels and Harrod's all wrapped in one Russian package.

The sections within GUM that might be of greatest interest to the visitor are these:

On the first floor a phonograph record shop has one of the widest selections in Moscow. Like every other section of GUM it is usually very crowded.

On the first floor near the fountain there's a shop selling souvenir folk art of all sorts including gaily colored dolls, decorative lightweight, wood bowls for fruit and smaller ones for holding peanuts or candy, lacquered boxes, and small carved wooden bears.

Another ground floor counter sells serviceable and characteristic black metal trays decorated with flower designs.

On a second-floor balcony a counter offers a wide selection of real Russian-style fur hats. Nearby is a fur-skin department where bear rugs are sometimes available with price tags, depending on size, of about 1000 rubles ($100 or £35.14.–).

If you're in Russia around Christmastime be sure to visit the large section devoted to Christmas tree decorations. More accurately, these are intended to decorat the *yolka*, or Russian New Year's pine tree, because, of course, the Soviet state does not recognize religious holidays. Colorful and imaginative, these decorations are in the shapes of fruits, vegetables, teakettles, pocket watches, parachutists, dolls, and Grandfather Frost—the Russian counterpart of Santa Claus. They are quite sturdy, too. We've taken two large boxes of assorted decorations, carefully wrapped in Kleenex, home to New York, without a single crack.

TSUM
Petrovskaya Ulitsa (behind Bolshoi Theatre)

The initials stand for Tsentralniy Universalniy Magazin, or Central Department Store. This is not as large as GUM or as well stocked. But if you can't find what you want in GUM, the next best place to try is TSUM.

PETROVSKY PASAGE
Petrovskaya Ulitsa 10

This is an arcade with a number of shops opening off a central passage. We've found Petrovsky Pasage especially good for embroidered tablecloths, shirts, blouses and decorative pillow covers.

CHILDREN'S WORLD
Dzerzhinsky Square

This is Moscow's newest department store. Known in Russian as Detsky Mir, the "Children's World" reflects the growing attention given to consumer goods by the Soviet administrations that succeeded Stalin's. The Detsky Mir has many counters selling toys. There are racks of children's clothes, and, if youngsters are on your gift list, you might care to look at some of the dresses and suits for infants. Quality is poor, but the designs are unusual. Also sold here are musical instruments, household pots and pans, tea holders, and occasional surprise items such as skillfully woven, small straw baskets for serving bread.

PODARKI (Gift) SHOP
Gorky Ulitsa 4

As already mentioned, there is a big department in GUM devoted to souvenirs. Also most of the hotels including the National, Metropole, Moscow, Ukraine, and Leningradskaya have counters selling tea glass holders, dolls, boxes, kerchiefs, and other souvenirs for the tourist. The prices are the same in all the stores. Sometimes it takes some hiking between stores to find the item you are looking for. This two-story main gift shop on Gorky Ulitsa is a good place to try, although you may find that your hotel's smaller souvenir department offers a more tasteful selection.

PHONOGRAPH RECORD STORES

Phonograph records are heartily recommended as souvenirs or as gifts. Soviet government recording studios issue a great variety of phonograph records ranging from the Soviet version of jazz (you will find these to be of the 1930 vintage) to classical numbers. After you have seen *Swan Lake* danced or the opera *Prince Igor* sung on the stage of the Bolshoi Theatre you may well want to have a recording.

Phonograph records are reasonably priced, costing about 13 rubles ($1.30 or 9s) for a long playing 33-speed disk. Be careful, because in Soviet terminology many records which are 78 speed are called "long playing." Particularly recommended are phonograph recordings of groups of the national republics—Uzbek, Ukrainian, Russian, and others with their native and often exotic instruments.

Friends of ours have been pleased to receive recordings

of the Soviet Army chorus and of the stirring Soviet National Anthem. Although Soviet recordings are of good quality, they are not up to Western hi-fi standards, and the disks wear out much more quickly, because the material used as a base is not as hard. Here are the addresses of some of the stores in Moscow specializing in phonograph records:

Phonograph Record Store, number 18, Arbat Ulitsa 6/2

Phonograph Record Store, number 25, Dzerzhinsky Square 3/2

Phonograph Record Store, number 47, Kirova Ulitsa 17

Phonograph Record Store, number 54, B. Sherpukhovskaya Ulitsa 2/1

FOREIGN LANGUAGE BOOK STORE
Kuznetsky Most 18/7

If you want to buy a book published in Russia but written in the English language this is the store you are looking for. On its shelves are such titles as *The Soviet School of Chess, Sport in the U.S.S.R., Football, Students of Moscow University, The Quiet American* by Graham Greene, and *Khrushchev Speaks.* The last book is a collection of Khrushchev's speeches, interviews, letters, and declarations on foreign affairs. Also this store carries any number of works, either complete or selected, of Engels, Marx, and Lenin. There are excellent photographic books of scenes of Moscow, of Leningrad, and of treasures in various Soviet museums including a richly illustrated volume on Kremlin treasures.

There are probably more stores selling books than any other commodity except food. Russians do read a great deal. Many of the shops sell only current political tracts, but others can be fascinating to the foreign visitor with a special interest. For example, persons curious about pre-revolutionary editions of works by Tolstoy or Gogol may find a visit to Book Store number 14 dealing in second-hand books worth while. This and other specialized book stores are listed:

Book Store, number 84, House of Political Literature, Proezd Khudozhestvennogo Teatra 6

Book Store, number 1, Books of Peoples' Democracies (Communist countries) Gorky Ulitsa 15

Book Store, number 8, Scientific and technical literature, Petrovskaya Ulitsa 15

Book Store, number 14, Secondhand books, Proezd Khudozhestvennogo Teatra 5

Book Store, number 33, Literature on light industry, Kuznetzky Most 22

Book Store, number 47, Medical literature, Pushechnaya Ulitsa 4

Book Store, number 87, Literature on architecture, Zhdananova Ulitsa 11

Academy of Science Publishing House, Gorky Ulitsa 6

Books on Theatres, Gorky Ulitsa 16

Book Store, number 50, Literature on arts, Arbat Ulitsa 4

Book Store, number 79, Foreign secondhand books, Gertzena Ulitsa 24

STAMP STORE
Kuznetsky Most 20
Telephone: 94 49 69

This store is the stamp collector's delight. As a matter of fact, even if you are not a stamp collector yourself, your friends who are will appreciate no gift more than a batch of Soviet postage stamps. Stamps are sold singly and in packets containing a mixed variety. There are also stamp albums for sale.

Postcards are sold here too and include not only views of Moscow but also rather unexpected flower-bedecked greeting cards for Soviet Women's Day in March and cards depicting happy children in honor of the annual International Childrens' Day. Other postcards commemorate the Soviet May Day and Revolution Day. From time to time very colorful and attractive posters for such events as an International Youth Festival held in Moscow are for sale here. Although clumsy to carry without folding they do make decorative souvenirs.

(A good variety of stamps is available at the store at Gorky Street 15, telephone: 29 53 83.)

MAP STORE
Kuznetsky Most 9
Telephone: 28 61 09

A frequent incorrect impression of visitors is that it is impossible to buy a map of Moscow or of Russia. This is not so. If you care to take the proof home try this map store. The prices are low. A big map of the U.S.S.R. costs 1.35 rubles which is about 13 cents or 1s. A colored wall map of the world costs 4.45 rubles (about 45 cents or 3s).

These maps, by the way, indicate that Russians see the world quite differently from Westerners. To the Russian the world is divided through the Pacific Ocean unlike most maps published in the Western world where the line is drawn through Soviet Siberia.

It is also possible to buy a map of Moscow, but these are less often in stock than maps of larger sections of Russia.

ART STORE
Kuznetsky Most 11

Perhaps you may discover a new genius in the art world here. Personally I've never found anything that I would care to hang in our home, but several works came close to it, and Soviet art seems to be getting better as artists become bolder in departing from the postcard requirements of "Socialist Realism." In "Socialist Realist" art the subject matter must be easily and graphically understood, the topic must be optimistic, inspirational, patriotic, or all three. It may also be neutral as in a still life. Soviet artists exhibit their work at this store with a price tag set by the store's government management. Sometimes it seems that the price is set according to the size of the canvas rather than the quality of the work.

(Next door there is a store where paint brushes, paints, and other artists' supplies can be purchased in the event that painting in Russia is one of your interests.)

RUG STORE
Gorky Ulitsa 9, entrances 2 and 3

This store has the widest selection in town, but the price of a good rug is high even if you can devise a way to get such a bulky object home.

PRECIOUS STONES STORE
Stoleshnikov Pereulok 13
Telephone: 94 49 69

The name of this store is somewhat misleading because in fact *semi*-precious stones and the colorful minerals of the Ural Mountains (which separate Europe from Asia) are sold here.

Malachite, that highly prized, veined, bright-green mineral that is often seen in small inserts on urns and clock bases in Europe's palaces, is a specialty in this shop. It is very expensive. A casket about the size of a cigar box sells for about 15,000 rubles ($1500 or £535.14.3).

Even if you are not in the market to buy, but only to window shop you may find a brief look interesting. Malachite plays a prominent part in Russian folklore. The Soviet ballet *Stone Flower,* for example, concerns itself with a stonecutter's obsession with malachite.

Large clear topaz stones set as brooches or cuff links can be purchased at comparatively reasonable prices, and some visitors to Moscow have purchased topazes, although not liking the setting particularly, with the intention of having them reset later as earrings or in rings. Several friends of ours have been pleased and surprised to find that jewelers at home have appraised the stones at six to eight times the price paid in Russia. A medium-size set of topaz cuff links costs 300 rubles ($30. or £11). By the way, Russian topaz is crystal clear and not yellow as is the topaz generally known in western countries. Also be careful to distinguish between the real topaz and a cut glass also sold in this store at about one-sixth of the price, which are called "crystal topaz."

Other precious and semi-precious stones are sold here as well as ivory or imitation ivory figures including an owl with a light bulb inside. This owl and most other items in the store are not to our taste, but tastes vary.

Note for further shopping: On this same short street just a few doors from the Precious Stones Store are several excellent shops that sell Russian and Ukrainian embroidery-edged shirts of the white Cossack type. The colorful embroidery is sold by the yard here if you want to edge a dress or blouse for yourself at home.

FLOWER SHOP NUMBER 2
Oktyabrskaya Ulitsa 11

Flowers are much more appreciated as a gift by Russians as well as by foreigners living in Moscow than by people in many other countries. That's because flowers are so rare for most of the year. If someone has been particularly kind to you in Moscow and you want to express appreciation, flowers are a good way to do it. You will not always find the kind you want, but even during the bitter blizzards of January this state Flower Shop number 2 seems to have at least potted plants in stock. There's a 15 ruble charge ($1.50 or about 10s) for delivering in most parts of town. There are many other florist shops in Moscow, but this one is centrally situated and we've found their service satisfactory.

COLLECTIVE FARM FOOD MARKETS

There are still a few vestiges of "free enterprise" remaining in the Soviet Union. The "collective farm markets" or, as they're better known, the "free markets" are the best example. Goods are sold here at prices not set by the state as at state stores, but rather are fixed by the capitalistic economic law of supply and demand.

On collective farms (which are an amalgamation of once privately owned small farms into one farm under a single management with farm families sharing profit) each household is permitted to operate a plot of land independently, usually about a half acre in size. This is called a "household plot" or a "personal plot." The family can plant what it wishes and may keep its crops. These crops may be for the family's own use. But whatever the family can spare, it usually sells on the "free market."

Also, whereas state farms (farms on which workers receive daily wages as in a factory) must deliver their entire produce to the state, collective farms have certain quotas to fulfill. That is, they are obligated to deliver a certain amount of grain and other produce to the government. Whatever they produce beyond that, they can dispense in various ways. They can sell the surplus to the state too or they can sell it on the "free market" where prices almost always are considerably higher than those paid by the government.

There are "free markets" in every Soviet city and more than thirty in Moscow alone. These are busy places. Usually there is a cement or wooden building on the premises where meats and sometimes vegetables and fruits are sold, but a great deal of the commerce is transacted out in the open at counters. Women with shawls over their heads (and padded jackets in winter) sell produce for members of their collective farm. Some come from great distances, even from as far away as the Georgian Republic and the central Asian republics of the U.S.S.R. They come by truck or train or even, as with crates of newly picked grapes, by plane. The high prices of the "free market" make such long trips profitable.

Though you probably will not be shopping for food on a brief visit to Russia, you will find a visit to a "free market" fascinating. There is the bustle of the bazaar, faces of peasants that will delight the photographer, and strange sights such as the heads of animals on display to identify nearby cuts of meat.

There is also a so-called bird market operating only on Sundays where individuals sell pigeons and porcupines, goldfish, and goldfinch. This is a giant, outdoor pet shop.

Here are the names and addresses of some of Moscow's most lively "free markets":

Centralny (Central) Market, Tsvetnoy Boulevard 15.

Tishinsky Market, Bolshaya Gruzinskaya Ulitsa 50.

Yaroslavsky Market, Prospekt Mira 122.

Usachyovsky Market, Usacheva Ulitsa 36.

Bolshoi Kolkhozny Market, Khukhrikov Pereulok 8a.

Izmailovsky Market, 3d Parkovaya Ulitsa 24.

Ostankinsky Market, 1st Ostankinskaya Ulitsa 6.

Danilovsky Market, Mytnaya Ulitsa 78.

COMMISSION STORES
(Antiques)

For the antique, for the really unusual item from old Russia, for the occasional "find," these are the stores to explore.

The Soviet Commission Store is a unique combination of secondhand shop, rummage sale, junk shop, and rare antique dealer's. When a Soviet citizen wants to get rid of something he has had around the house for years, or when the Russian needs money, he most likely will go to the Commission Store. There are a number of such state-run establishments in Moscow, each specializing in one or several types of goods. Thus, there is a Commission Store dealing in photographic equipment, others which specialize in clothing, and, most interesting to the souvenir-seeker, those that handle *objets d'art,* knickknacks, paintings, chinaware, and jewelry. Each Commission Store has an expert appraiser who evaluates the item brought in by the Russian, and sets a price on it which the Russian may either accept or reject. If the price is agreeable, the Russian leaves his old lamp or samovar, and receives a receipt for it. Then he comes back every so often to ask whether his possession has been sold. When it has, he presents his receipt and receives the amount originally set by the appraiser minus seven per cent which is the store's commission for making the sale.

Commission stores used to be the places to buy icons. Strictly speaking, it is illegal to take art work of pre-1917 origin out of the U.S.S.R. Yet tourists were buying icons several centuries old, and only occasionally did Customs officers detect them. In order to completely stop the flow of art treasures from the country, the authorities have made it against the law for icons even to be offered for sale by Commission Stores. The only way to buy an icon now is to find an individual Russian who has one and wants to sell it. Beware of the few unscrupulous Russians who try to sell modern imitations as the real thing.

Also, more than one visitor has been disappointed to discover that pieces fashioned by the skilled artisans of the Faberge workshops of Czarist times are not readily available. Some foreigners come to Russia with the misconception that they can buy Faberge jeweled Easter eggs, charmingly carved and sometimes mechanically animated miniature animals of quartz, small boxes topped with cloisonné work or jewels. These can no longer be found in stores in Russia. It is much easier to buy Faberge on Fifth Avenue. I've heard second- and thirdhand of foreigners who discovered such valuable items, but even these unconfirmable reports are rare.

Nevertheless, there is much of beauty and of unusual character to be found in Commission Stores. It often takes time and patience, but you may be lucky on your first visit. You will have better luck in out-of-the-way cities like Riga than in Moscow, where diplomats and other foreigners have taken off the cream.

Friends who have persistently gone back time and again to Commission Stores have found exceptional items such as antique silver wine coolers; silver serving spoons; silver teapots; candlesticks; eight- to ten-cup china tea sets; odd demitasse cups for collectors; various decorative plates and other pieces of chinaware made by the Gardner and other once-famous Czarist china factories (including the much rarer Popov and Menshikov factory pieces; look for a Cyrillic alphabet G on the bottom to identify Gardner ware); Easter eggs of glass, quartz, or painted china; paintings of old Russian scenes; amber beads; framed miniatures painted on ivory, and a variety of other antiques, including of course big, and often ugly, samovars, if your baggage allowance is unlimited! Perhaps you will be lucky and uncover a really valuable antique.

You may be approached by Russians offering to buy articles of your clothing at high prices. Foreign-made goods are in demand. Although a few tourists have sold everything but the clothes on their back at enormous profit, we can only discourage anyone from engaging in this illicit commerce. At one time it was legal for foreigners to sell items to Commission Stores. Now even that is forbidden.

United States Customs regulations permit a returning traveler to bring in duty free $500 worth of articles purchased abroad if he has been abroad at least 12 days and has not claimed a duty exemption within six months prior.

These Moscow Commission Stores are worth trying:

Antique Commission Store, number 97, Arvat Ulitsa 19, *Telephone: 41 06 43*

Commission Store, Sretenka Ulitsa 37/10

SHOPPING HINTS

Unlike Italy and some other places in Europe, you can't bring down the price in a Soviet store by a bit of friendly bargaining. The price is fixed by the government. All stores are owned by the government and administered by the Ministry of Trade. The exception to this rule is the collective farm market.

If you've been shopping for a certain item and finally see it in a store don't say "I'll come back tomorrow." The chances are it will be sold by then. Products that are in short supply disappear quickly from store shelves. Buy an item you want when you see it or you may be disappointed later.

Standing in line is the chief characteristic of shopping in Russia. However, a foreigner, as in so many other ways, is shown great courtesy and is often motioned to the head of a queue. In most stores the method of shopping is this: You choose the item you want to buy and ask its price. Then you stand in line at a cashier's booth to pay for it and to receive a receipt. Finally you go back to the counter to present your receipt and pick up your package.

Most stores do not have names. There are exceptions like GUM and the Children's World. But for the most part stores and service shops are numbered. Thus instead of Harry's Barber Shop or the Top Quality Meat Market, in Moscow it will likely be Barber Shop number 12 and Meat Store number 423.

CHAPTER THIRTEEN

Moscow: Outside the City Limits

Russians who are cynical about the disproportionate investment of resources in machinery and missiles compared to the investment in consumer goods tell this little story. It seems that two Russians were discussing the prospects of the Seven-Year Plan for Economic Growth. One said to the other, "Just think of it. By 1965 every Russian family will have its own jet airplane."

Replies his skeptical friend: "What do I need a jet airplane for?"

Exclaims the first Russian: "For what? Why, when there are no refrigerators for sale in Moscow and you read in the morning *Pravda* that refrigerators are available in Sverdlovsk you can hop into your jet and fly out there and buy one."

Until this jet-in-every-garage age arrives, there are a number of interesting trips near Moscow that can be made in one day or even half a day by car, bus, or train.

OSTANKINO

This is mentioned first because it is the nearest to Moscow, and might in fact be considered to be in Moscow itself. The Palace of Ostankino, a unique example of Russian architecture of the late eighteenth century, was one of many mansions owned by the Sheremetyev family. It is on the outskirts of Moscow, near the Exhibition of Economic Achievements, and shares its grounds with the Soviet version of an amusement park.

The Sheremetyev family was one of the fabulously wealthy aristocratic families during the time of the Czars. Some of these had hundreds of estates all over Russia which were perpetually staffed and waiting for the owner's visits. Some of the families never had the time to see all of their homes and properties.

The main palace looks more like a huge library than a home with its columns and dome. The Ostankino estate had a private theater for the amusement of the Sheremetyevs and their guests. The actors and actresses were serfs owned by the feudal Russian lord. The theater is in the largest of the Ostankino Palace's many elaborate halls. It occupies a central position right under the palace dome. The theater had moveable ornamental columns.

The principal building, consisting of the palace-theater and two pavilions with galleries, has been preserved. On the western side there is a seventeenth-century church, and to the south, a large pond. To the north of the palace there is a park.

This palace is rather overdone for our taste, but is well worth the short ride if you haven't time to visit one of the homes mentioned later in this chapter.

ARCHANGELSKOYE

This is our favorite place to visit near Moscow. Sometimes spelled "Arkhangelskoye," this was one of the many estates of the immensely rich and influential Youssoupoff family of Czarist times. Less than an hour from the center of the capital, Archangelskoye is especially pleasant to visit in spring, summer or fall, because during the winter wooden coverings hide the statues in its stately gardens, stretching from the colonnaded mansion to the high bank overlooking the broad valley of the Moscow River. The vast park around the estate has many beautiful walks and magnificent giant fir and birch trees.

For a hint of what life was like for the most privileged class under the Czar be sure to spend an hour or two at Archangelskoye. Valuable paintings and other works of art are displayed in its tastefully lavish rooms. Remarkable pieces of Sèvres porcelain can be seen in glass cases and there is a particularly placid and appealing blue and white cow that we thought to be the most charming of the chinaware collection.

Besides the main building with its regal rooms there are a number of other interesting, smaller structures. A Youssoupoff prince built a temple in honor of Catherine the Great. When an oriental potentate, visiting Moscow, expressed the desire to visit Archangelskoye, the prince could not bear the idea that an infidel might look upon this temple. He had a wall, fringed in oriental designs, built in two days to conceal Catherine's temple from his guest.

There used to be a glass factory and a porcelain factory on the grounds, but they were destroyed by fire.

At the far end of the long formal garden are several buildings that the Youssoupoffs did not build. These are buildings of a Soviet Army rest home overlooking the Moscow River. Luckily these additions are far enough away from the old mansion not to seriously interfere with the general scheme of the estate.

To fully appreciate Archangelskoye the visitor should first read *Lost Splendor* by Prince Felix Youssoupoff, a member of the family who escaped after the revolution. His description of the estate in its original form applies today: "The park was laid out in the purest French style. Three long terraces adorned with statues and marble urns led down to the river. In the center, long hornbeam hedges bordered a sweeping lawn, and fountains played on every side. . . . A long, straight avenue led through a forest of pine trees to a circular courtyard round which ran a colonnade. On the ground floor of the château, great columned halls with frescoed ceilings were adorned with statues and fine pictures. Two rooms were specially reserved for the works of Tiepolo and Hubert Robert. In spite of their imposing proportions, all these rooms were friendly and intimate, thanks to the beautiful old furniture and a profusion of plants and flowers. A rotunda intended for receptions had doors opening onto the park. All the visitors who came to Archangelskoye admired the view from this room; terraces and a long green lawn lined with statues stretched to the horizon and seemed to fade into the shadowy blue of the forest."

The estate's theater is a gem of scaled-down opera house architecture. Prince Nicholas, one of the more buccaneering of the Youssoupoffs, who died at the age of 80 in 1831, staged a most unusual type of entertainment in this theater. According to *Lost Splendor*, Prince Nicholas "kept an incredible number of mistresses, dancers and peasant girls. An habitué of the Archangelskoye theatre used to relate that when the whole ballet was on the stage the Prince waved his cane and suddenly all the dancers appeared completely naked."

ZAGORSK

This is the most frequently taken short trip from Moscow. It should not be missed. To enter the walls at Zagorsk is to step back into ancient Russia. Zagorsk is about 45 miles from Moscow and at least a half day must be devoted to the trip there and back and to a brief look at the town's sights. This is one of the most holy places in Russia. The old walled city with its still active churches and monasteries inside are places of great beauty. The tomb of Boris Godunov is here. The old monastery named Troitskoye Sergievo dates its origins back to 1340. Other buildings with their star-speckled domes and cupolas date from the fourteenth to the sixteenth centuries. Monks with long beards and pale complexions still work and study at this Zagorsk monastery. There is also a museum of icons and other religious art work. Often overlooked by the tourists is Zagorsk's museum of toys.

KHIMKI

Khimki is Moscow's port. It may come as a surprise to learn that Moscow has a port since it is so far inland. However, because of a complex network of canals, Moscow actually connects with five seas—the White Sea, the Black Sea, the Caspian Sea, the Aral Sea, and the Sea of Azov. If you take a boat trip down the Volga River, as foreign tourists are now permitted to do, or if you take a short one-day trip through locks of the Moscow Canal, this is the place to start. Although Khimki is listed here under Moscow side trips because it is the starting place for such boat trips, Khimki itself is only a short ride from the center of the city and it has a restaurant where it is usually cool for summer eating.

KUSKOVO

The village of Kuskovo, situated about seven miles from Moscow, was another palatial estate owned by the Sheremetyev family. It is an excellent example of how lavishly the aristocracy lived before the revolution deprived them of their fortunes, their status, and, in some cases, their lives.

Kuskovo, Ostankino, and other palaces of the Russian nobility really are not palaces as we think of them in the Versailles, Buckingham, or Peterhof sense. Of smaller dimensions and less formal in furnishings, these aristocratic homes were mansions on a grand scale set on estates of even grander scale.

Kuskovo is about a half hour by car from Red Square. It is an interesting drive as the road leads past the "Hammer and Sickle" metallurgical factory, one of Moscow's biggest industrial complexes, and through small villages where unpaved side streets and outdoor water pumps are seen in the shadow of the show-place capital.

The palace is set on the shore of a pretty pond. In summer Russians rent boats and row around, eating picnic lunches and fishing.

A highlight of the Kuskovo Palace (which bears an architectural resemblance to Ostankino) is the collection, filling a series of large rooms, of china and porcelain. Some pieces were produced in kilns on this estate by serf artisans. The collection includes French, German, English, and Chinese pieces, as well as the native variety. There is every imaginable type of figurine, plate, cup, and dish. It is especially interesting to trace the Russian figurines from centuries ago to the Soviet "realism" in pottery that is being produced today.

Serfs (a class of virtual slaves—some of them skilled in arts and trades—who worked on estates and could be sold with the land, but who could under certain circumstances buy their freedom) played an important role in the history of Kuskovo. Kuskovo's Palace was designed by serf architects. One of the first serf theaters in Russia was organized by Count P. Sheremetyev. It had a company of 230 people, and had an influence on the development of Russian dramatic art.

In the park several houses built in various styles have been preserved. Among them are the "Hermitage," the

"Grotto," the Dutch and Italian houses and the hothouse.

On the shore of the pond there is also an interesting old church (1737) with an enclosure of wrought iron made by serf blacksmiths.

The museum is open daily except Tuesday. On Monday the working hours are from 11 A.M. to 5 P.M., on the other days from 11 A.M. to 7 P.M. On the last Monday of each month the museum is closed.

CHAIKOVSKY'S HOME AT KLIN

Allow a full half-day for a visit to this house and its wooded grounds where the great composer P. I. Chaikovsky spent the last two years of his life. For lovers of music this house in a town about 40 miles from Moscow is something of a shrine.

Not long ago the museum was visited by Van Cliburn, the young Texas pianist who won first prize and fame at a Chaikovsky international music competition in Moscow. Cliburn was invited by his hosts to play a few chords on Chaikovsky's piano. Reverently, Cliburn sat down and addressed his strong fingers to the keyboard. The notes rang true and loud—and several strings snapped!

Chaikovsky lived here during a period of grief and mental anguish. He suffered great personal losses. The people most dear to him had died—first his beloved sister, then several old friends. The ranks of his friends from the Conservatory were also becoming thinner and thinner.

Yet Chaikovsky overcame his grief. He was working so intensively that even in his dreams, he said, he was haunted by "some flats and sharps which would not do what they were supposed to do." These were the years of his greatest inspiration. It was in this house that he

completed or rewrote *The Nutcracker* and *Iolanthe,* his
Third Piano Concerto, over twenty piano pieces and
romances, and finally his Symphony No. 6 (the "Pathetic"), considered the greatest of all Russian sym-
phonies.

Today everything is kept as it was when Chaikovsky
lived there.

In the small circular room opening on to a veranda,
where he used to drink his morning tea during the warm
weather, his favorite cup, some music paper and an
inkpot can be seen. In the bedroom, near his bed which
is covered with a padded quilt, hangs his Bukhara dressing gown; nearby is a plain birch wood desk at which
he composed the "Pathetic" in 1893. Piled up in a corner
are trunks, suitcases and boxes—all evidence of the journeys he made.

Hitler's soldiers did much damage to the house. They
broke the statues, tore down and ruined photographs and
portraits, broke windows and doors.

Fortunately, all that was most valuable—the composer's documentary materials, the piano and a number
of valuable souvenirs—had been evacuated in time.

When the Nazis had been driven out of Klin, the
Chaikovsky Museum was restored. His most valuable belongings were brought back from the town of Votkinsk,
his birthplace, and on May 6, 1945, the museum reopened with priceless relics of Russian art: various drafts
of the scores for *The Queen of Spades,* the Sixth Symphony, *The Sleeping Beauty, Iolanthe* and *The Nutcracker.* In the bookcases are Chaikovsky's diaries, notebooks filled with musical jottings and over 9000 letters,
either written or received by him.

The house is open for visitors every day from 11 A.M.
to 6 P.M., except Wednesdays and the last Monday of
each month.

LENIN'S LAST HOME

The house in which Lenin spent the last years of his life and where he died is a pleasant one hour drive from Moscow, 23 miles to the south along the highway leading to the city of Kashira. Known as the Gorky Leninskiye estate, a small village nearby bears the same name. When Lenin lived here from 1918 to 1924 the village was called just plain Gorky. This rambling, two-story house is built in eighteenth-century Russian-style with six Doric columns, but its Grecian lines are destroyed by a second-story porch set behind the columns.

As in many Lenin shrines one room contains a glass-enclosed white plaster death mask set on a table covered with red cloth and overhung with palms. Lenin was partially paralyzed from a stroke during his last years and a double banister was built to enable him to support himself with both hands on the broad staircase. At the foot of the stairs, under the staircase, stands Lenin's battery-driven invalid car by which he propelled himself around the extensive grounds. A telephone of the original Alexander Graham Bell vintage (although the Russians claim that a Russian invented the telephone) is attached to a wall of a small first-floor room. Another period piece is an elementary movie projector on a table in the palm-filled winter garden. The inevitable white statue of Lenin looks down from one end of this long salon.

Lenin slept in a room of Spartan simplicity on a cot-size bed. His desk, oddly enough, stands in his wife's comparatively spacious connecting bedroom. A rose-colored glass screen separates his wife's bed from the rest of the room.

Although the rooms are filled with memorabilia of Lenin's last years—letters, documents, edicts, manuscripts, photographs—we "sacrilegiously" thought one of the most memorable objects in the house to be a ground-floor porcelain washbasin with a lovely blue floral design. It bore the inscription *Johnson Brothers and Hanley, England.*

When Lenin lived in Gorky he maintained contact with the Council of People's Commissars and the Central Committee of the Party. He looked after his mail, wrote letters and gave instructions and advice on a variety of questions on the work of the party and the government.

In addition Lenin worked on a number of theoretical problems. It was in Gorky that he wrote the book *The Proletarian Revolution and the Renegade Kautsky* and such articles as "Party Crisis," "Once Again on the Trade Unions," and "Fly in the Ointment."

SILVER FOREST BEACH

This is for summer visitors. If you want to see how Russians spend a day at the beach or if you are desperate for a dip yourself, try Silver Forest, or Serebryany Bor as it's known in Russian. A friend of ours had a small son who loved the Silver Forest—and as he pronounced it it had the impressive name of "Sir Ebony Bore." If you ask for the beach by this fictitious nobleman's name it sounds almost right and the driver will know just where you want to go. The beach here is not of California or Jones Beach, New York, quality. Not by a long shot. There are several stretches of stony, partially dirt "beaches" edged by grassy, pine-studded banks of the Moscow River. But, far from the ocean, Moscow has nothing better to offer. Wood slat "cots" are used by reclining sunbathers. Rowboats and "water bicycle" craft can be hired. Refreshments are sold at stands. Nearby are volleyball courts. There are bathhouses, but many Russians prefer to display their skill in self-concealment by changing right at the water's edge.

We can't recommend Silver Forest as a particularly pleasant or isolated retreat, but the temperature usually is a few degrees cooler than Moscow on a hot summer day, and it does provide the chance to see a different phase of Soviet activity when you become weary of trudging through museums.

It takes twenty minutes by car to go from the center of the city to Serebryany Bor. It is linked to the city by trolley and motorbus lines. If you prefer to go by water, you can take the "river tram" on the Moscow River, too.

There is a special spot of shallow water for children, separated from the rest of the beach by partitions.

KOLOMENSKOYE

Kolomenskoye, an hour's drive from Moscow, has more memories than monuments. This was an ancient estate of Russian princes and of the Czars who succeeded them. Of the numerous churches and palaces that stood here, little has survived. A part of the wall, the arch of the gate, the Kazan Church built in the seventeenth century, and the sixteenth-century Church of the Ascension (a unique example of Russian "tent" style architecture)—only these remain of what was once a wonder of old Russia. An indication of its lost grandeur is expressed in a visitor's notes written in the 1840s. Berlioz, the French composer, wrote of the Ascension Church: "Nothing has impressed me more than this relic of ancient Russian architecture in the village of Kolomenskoye. I have seen much in my life, I have admired many things, and many things have surprised me, but Russian antiquity, which has left its monument in that village, was a wonder of wonders for me. I have seen Strasbourg Cathedral, which took several centuries to build; I have seen Milan Cathedral, but I found nothing there but much ornamentation. But here I was confronted with beauty as an entity. My heart missed a beat; there was holy quiet and supreme beauty. I was seeing a new type of architecture thrusting forward. And for a long time I stood there dumbfounded."

The first mention of Kolomenskoye can be found in documents dating back to the first half of the fourteenth century.

Kolomenskoye has many historical associations. Prince Dmitri Donskoy of Moscow visited the estate in 1380 after his victory over the Tatars on Kulikovo Plain. Prince Vasily III marched from Kolomenskoye in 1528 and then in 1533 to fight the Tatar hordes. Ivan the Terrible passed through Kolomenskoye on his famous march to Kazan. Peter the Great spent his childhood there, and Catherine II had a palace on the estate.

Kolomenskoye's association with Peter the Great's childhood is the reason for an otherwise extraneous log cabin on the grounds of this museum. At one stage in his career Peter lived in this cabin at Arkhangelsk, many hundreds of miles from here. Much later the cabin was transplanted.

We can recommend a drive out to Kolomenskoye only if you have time on your hands in Moscow or if you are a student of Russian history or architecture. There is an exhibition in a museum building of Russian wood, iron and ceramic handicrafts. For most of us, though, Kolomenskoye has little to recommend it except for a grand, sweeping view of the Moscow River winding far into the distance.

YASNAYA POLYANA
Leo Tolstoy's Home

This is a full day's trip from morning until after dark. Count on at least three hours each way by car. One hundred and twenty-five miles south of Moscow, this estate where the great Russian writer spent most of his life is reached by a road that passes through Tula, once the foundry city of the Czars for making cannons and samovars.

We can recommend this trip only to those who have more than a week to spend in Moscow or to visitors with a special reverence for Tolstoy. Tolstoy lived here for fifty years of his long and productive life. It was here that his pen produced *War and Peace, The Kreutzer Sonata,* and a part of *Resurrection.*

Tolstoy loved the rambling, birch-wooded grounds of Yasnaya Polyana (which means "sunlit meadows") and he wrote of it: "Without Yasnaya Polyana I can hardly think of Russia or of my attitude to her." Tolstoy is buried here.

Many objects associated with the great writer are carefully preserved. There are portraits of Tolstoy done from life by Repin and Kramskoy, a tremendous library containing books in more than twenty languages (Tolstoy knew thirteen languages), a phonograph presented to the writer by Edison, a grandfather clock made by Eardley Norton, a British firm, which was brought from London two hundred years ago by Prince Volkonsky and still keeps good time, a rare portrait of Jan Hus, and many other relics.

First visit the museum, which has letters to Tolstoy from admirers in America, England, and France, as well as many family portraits. Then visit his home. It has been kept just as it was when he died. The large second-floor dining room was the gathering place for friends. The table is set, a piano stands in one corner, and the view is lovely. Look for the portrait of Anna Karenina, a neighbor whom Tolstoy borrowed in describing the lovely heroine of his great novel. She wasn't the type we had pictured, but perhaps you will feel you're seeing an old friend. Tolstoy's workroom has a large black-leather couch which he faithfully described in several of his books. His wife recopied his many drafts of *War and Peace* for him and her bedroom and desk are on this same floor. Some of his clothes hang in a wardrobe—the simple, peasant-type garb he favored. Outside the house stands a large tree. It was under this tree that Tolstoy would meet the peasants of the neighborhood, hear of their hardships, and give money to the needy.

The woods are especially beauitful in the autumn, when the birches are red-gold against the bright sky. We advise you to take a picnic lunch along on this trip.

CHAPTER FOURTEEN

Moscow: How to Plan Your Days and Suggested Walks

In walking around Moscow you are sure to see youngsters with red kerchiefs around their necks. This knotted red scarf is the badge of the "Pioneer" organization, the first rung on the ladder that can eventually lead to sought-after membership in the Communist Party. But with the privileges of Party membership go duties and discipline.

For example, the story is told of a young man being examined for entrance into the restricted (less than four per cent of the Soviet population) ranks of the Communist Party.

"Will you give up drinking?" he is asked.

"Yes, I will," he replies.

"Will you give up smoking? Will you give up women?"
To each question the candidate answers in the affirmative.

"Will you be willing to give up your life if your country asks you to?"

"Of course," he retorts, "with a life like this what difference does it make?"

A visitor to Russia can see and evaluate life best by getting out of the Intourist car and walking on side streets behind the imposing façades of broad avenues like Gorky Ulitsa. Although some interpreter-guides will stick to their charges like glue, many are delighted with an afternoon or a few hours off, so that it usually is not difficult to wander on your own. Almost any street will lead to revealing sights and interesting encounters, and this chapter recounts two walks that we enjoyed.

But first of all may we offer a few suggestions for planning out your days in Moscow? Five sample days are given. We realize of course that a visitor may have less or more time than five days in the city, but the detailed descriptions of sights given in previous chapters can help the traveler decide which to drop or to add depending on individual interests.

In charting these sample days an attempt has been made not only to include the most important places, but also to provide a "balanced" day between outdoor and indoor activities, between walking and sedentary sightseeing. To the extent that it is possible, we've tried to arrange the days with some consideration to geography so that not too much time is spent getting from one place to another.

Because a visitor may first of all want to know *what* to see and only later take the time to read *details,* a few words of description are given for every suggested sight. These proposed days cover only the highlights of what is dealt with in detail elsewhere in the book.

One more word of explanation: obviously your plans for the evening will depend on what's playing in the theaters. So, especially in the case of evening activities, consider these days as flexible suggestions to be adapted to your own preferences.

FIRST DAY

Morning:

(1) Intourist Service Bureau: Every Intourist hotel has a Service Bureau where English-speaking Intourist employees will help you plan what to see, order theater

tickets for you, and arrange for an interpreter-guide and a car. Even if it takes an hour or more you will save time in the long run by laying out your schedule the first morning, and especially by ordering theater tickets in advance.

(2) Tour of Moscow: A car or bus tour of the main streets and buildings will help you to orient yourself and to get a general impression of Moscow.

Be sure to see Red Square, the Kremlin, the Lenin-Stalin Mausoleum, Gorky Street, the Moscow City Hall, the Bolshoi Theatre, the Conservatory of Music, Moscow University, and stop for a view at the university of the Lenin Sports Stadium and the city beyond.

Afternoon:

(1) Lunch: It's best to have lunch the first day at your own hotel until you get the "feel" of the menu and of how to order. Waiters and waitresses at Intourist hotels understand some English.

(2) Tour of the Kremlin Grounds and Churches: Have your interpreter-guide take you through the Kremlin's walls, and see the Grand Kremlin Palace where the Supreme Soviet Parliament meets, the cracked Czar's Bell which is supposed to be the largest in the world, the icon-encrusted churches where the Czars were crowned and buried, and other fabulous Kremlin sights.

(3) Visit a Museum: There are a number of museums in the general neighborhood of the Kremlin. Depending on which subject interests you most here are several to choose from: the Lenin Museum (traces Lenin's life from his birthplace log cabin to the deathbed plaster impression of his face); the State Historical Museum (the history of the Soviet state from tribal community to Communism); the Revolution Museum (all about the 1917 uprising); the Technological Museum (exhibits of Soviet know-how from pick and shovel to nuclear pile); the

apartment of Nikolai Ostrovsky (the apartment in which a famous Soviet novelist spent his last years).

Evening:

(1) Theater: If the list of what's playing offers a choice, start off your Moscow stay with a performance of the Bolshoi Theatre Ballet, preferably *Swan Lake*. Otherwise, we recommend the Stanislavksy Theatre Ballet, the Branch Theatre of the Bolshoi, the Obraztsov Puppet Theatre, the Moiseyev Folk Dance Troupe at Chaikovsky Hall, or the Moscow Circus. Except for the puppet show and the circus you'll have time before the 7:30 P.M. curtain for only a quick snack at your hotel or for one-slice-of-bread sandwiches during intermission at the theater buffet.

SECOND DAY

Morning:

(1) Red Square: Go inside the four-century-old St. Basil's Cathedral, see the mound from which Czarist proclamations of old were read, and spend an hour in the GUM department store, buying souvenirs or watching Russians shop.

(2) Lenin-Stalin Mausoleum: Join thousands of Russians in their solemn procession into the Red Square tomb where Soviet leaders Lenin and Stalin lie embalmed under glass. From the tomb walk a few steps to the Kremlin wall to see the grave shrines of other Communist saints.

(3) Subway Ride: Take a trip on the Moscow Metro getting off at several stations to look at the elaborate decorations.

Afternoon:

(1) Lunch: Try an Intourist restaurant other than your own hotel. Your meal coupons will be honored at

the restaurants of these hotels: the National, the Metropole, the Berlin, the Ukraine, the Moscow, the Grand, and also at the Praga Restaurant if you tell the waiter beforehand that you want to pay in coupons.

(2) Art Gallery: The Tretyakov Museum has the finest collection of Russian art from icons of saints to portraits of Lenin. The Pushkin Gallery features a rich collection of French Impressionists including Gauguin, Renoir, and Matisse. Take your choice, but we recommend the Tretyakov first.

(3) Movie: The Moscow Panorama Movie is the next best thing to a tour in person by plane, car, sled, and water skis through the vast U.S.S.R. and other Communist countries.

Evening:

(1) Theater or a Leisurely Dinner: If your mood is theater attend one of the performances you didn't see in the list of first evening suggestions. If you prefer to slow down for a quiet (really not so quiet) dinner, we suggest the Aragvi Restaurant with cooking in the style of Stalin's native Georgia, U.S.S.R.

THIRD DAY

Morning:

(1) House of Worship: If this is a Sunday morning by all means attend a portion of the service at the Moscow Catholic Church, the Baptist Church, and at a Russian Orthodox Church. Addresses are listed in the chapter on churches. If this isn't a Sunday, we suggest you switch this activity with that listed for a previous or forthcoming day which *is* Sunday. The main service at the Jewish synagogue is Friday evening.

(2) Museum: It will take less than a half hour to see everything at the Underground Printing Press Museum in-

cluding the illegal press used by revolutionaries. This modest museum is our Moscow favorite.

Afternoon:

(1) Lunch: If none of the restaurants suggested for the previous days appeals to you, try the Sofia, the Baku, or the Kiev Restaurant.

(2) Short Trip: There are a number of mansions near Moscow's outskirts that reflect the style in which pre-revolutionary aristocrats used to live. It takes 45 minutes to drive to Archangelskoye, most interesting and beautiful of the estates, and 35 minutes to reach Kuskovo.

(3) Commission Store: To shop for secondhand items or simply to see an unusual Soviet enterprize, pay at least a brief visit to a Commission Store.

Evening:

(1) Theater: In addition to the performances listed under the first evening's choices there are other theaters including the Moscow Art Theatre (for drama from Chekov to Shakespeare), the Variety Theatre (after an evening here you'll *know* what happened to vaudeville), and the Maly Theatre (a miniature of the Bolshoi Theatre with full-size plays).

(2) Dinner: After the theater try a late dinner at the Ararat (Armenian type cooking), the Uzbekistan (for central Asian dishes), or the Peking (Chinese food). Whichever your choice, phone for reservations.

FOURTH DAY

Morning:

(1) Zagorsk: It takes an hour and a half each way by car to see this remarkable old monastery. It's an opportunity to witness a Russian Orthodox church service. In the summer you might ask your hotel waiter to pack a

picnic lunch of hard-boiled eggs, cold chicken, wine or bottled Narzan mineral water, bread and fruit. Otherwise there's a fair restaurant across the street from the entrance to the monastery. However you may prefer to return to Moscow for lunch.

Afternoon:

(1) Lunch: For a view of the city (although not the best food in town) we suggest the top of the Ukraine Hotel Café. For a view of the Kremlin (and better food) try the roof of the Moscow Hotel.

(2) Kremlin Museum: See the fabulous Czarist state carriages, ermine-fringed jeweled crowns, Faberge Easter "eggs," and other treasures to make even a millionaire's mouth water.

(3) Novodevichy Monastery and Cemetery: This is an ancient monastery right in town that is now a museum. It looks a bit like the Kremlin. In the adjacent graveyard is the Stalin family plot.

FIFTH DAY

Morning:

(1) Exhibition of Economic Achievements: This used to be called the All-Union Agricultural Exhibition, but now it has expanded to include a big display of industrial items, a Sputnik exhibit and a building in native architecture for each of the Soviet republics. You can spend a full day on these acres, but probably a couple of hours will exhaust your interest and your legs. During the winter months when the exhibition is closed this time might be spent in one of the walks suggested here.

(2) Ostankino Mansion: Right near the Exhibition of Economic Achievements is the former estate of an immensely wealthy Czarist era merchant. It's now a museum.

Afternoon:

(1) Lunch: Take your choice of the restaurants you missed in the previous days' suggestions.

(2) GUM department store: For last-minute souvenir shopping.

(3) Fashion Show: To see clothing that indicates what Russians *want* rather than what they actually *wear*, attend at least part of a fashion show at the GUM department store or at the Dom Modele (House of Fashion).

(4) Museum: See one of the museums listed under number three in the first afternoon's suggestions or one of the art galleries listed under number two for the second afternoon.

(5) Boat Ride: For a final view of Moscow take a "tram boat" ride on the Moscow River, buying a ticket for as many stops as your time permits. (The boats don't run during the winter.)

Evening:

(1) Dinner. After a hard day of walking you may not want to dance yourself, but for a view of Soviet night life try the Sovietskaya Hotel Restaurant, the Grand Hotel or the Praga Restaurant (the most elegant by Soviet standards and the most expensive by any standards).

WALK AROUND THE KREMLIN WALLS

If you have any time left over in these suggested days or if you are staying more than five days you will find it time well spent to take several walks either on your own or with your guide. The rest of this chapter is devoted to proposing walking routes, and the first suggestion is a walk around the Kremlin's wall. The wall roughly forms a triangle with one leg bordering on the Moscow River, a second segment bordering on Red Square, and the third on a strip of grass and trees known as the Alexander

Garden. The wall is one and a half miles long. Its height varies from 40 to 50 feet. Although the cupolas and buildings inside the wall lend the entire Kremlin a very Russian air, the wall itself with its crenelations resembles those surrounding Italian hill towns. The wall originally was built for defense. Later it acquired a secondary purpose—to protect the Czarist residence from perennial Moscow fires. The Kremlin has 20 towers.

Start this walk in Red Square at the Spasskaya Bashnya or Savior's Tower, now the main Kremlin portal. Built in 1491 and embellished in later years, it is the tallest Kremlin tower rising 221 feet from the cobbles of Red Square. Two guards stand at either side and a bell clangs to warn pedestrians when cars enter or leave. The upper story of the tower is in Gothic style and was the work of England's Christopher Alloway in 1625. A blank rectangle of stone above the portal shows where an icon of Christ used to be displayed, and until 1917 everyone passing the gate was supposed to cross himself as he went by. A huge clock marks the time, and bells ring out for each quarter hour. The Spasskaya Tower is one of five crowned by a red glass star which lights up at night. In Czarist times the towers' emblems were imperial eagles. The others with stars are the St. Nicholas, the Borovitsky, the Triple, and the Water Towers. The Water Tower has the smallest star with a span between tips of nine feet. The largest are on the Spasskaya and St. Nicholas Towers, measuring 11 and a quarter feet between tips.

Now walk on the sidewalk nearest to the wall into Red Square and the next tower is the Senate Tower. This stands directly behind the reddish granite mausoleum where Lenin and Stalin are preserved. Right behind the tower is the green dome of the building that used to house the Russian Senate. In niches in the wall on either side of the Senate Tower lie the remains of Communist heroes.

Reaching the end of Red Square you come to the St. Nicholas Tower. This used to be an entry to the Kremlin, but the gate is now sealed. It got its name from an icon of St. Nicholas which was removed in 1919 by the Communist authorities. This Nikolskaya Tower is 201 feet high. It was badly damaged in 1812 when Napoleon, retreating from Moscow, tried to blow up the entire Kremlin, but luckily failed. Its upper stories are comparatively modern, dating from 1816.

As you descend the hill from Red Square, the State Historical Museum is on your right and you see the National Hotel at the foot of the hill across Manege Square. It is up this hill (and the hill at the other side of the State Historical Museum) that troops and civilians march on May Day and the November 7 Revolution Anniversary to pass in review by the leaders standing on the Lenin-Stalin tomb. At the foot of the hill is the round Sobakina Tower which gets its name from a boyar (nobleman), Danila Sobaka, because this tower originally formed a part of his residence. Whereas the Savior's, Senate, and St. Nicholas Towers are majestic and decorative, the Sobakina Tower has the appearance of an unchallengeable fortification.

At the Sobakina Tower the wall bends to the left (to the southwest), and here you enter the pleasant Alexander Garden (where there are benches if you care to rest). By the way, under your feet flows the Neglinka River which long ago was piped underground. Alexander Park commands a dramatic view of the sloping Kremlin wall. The park is a favorite place for parents of the neighborhood to air their babies.

The next tower is the Arsenal Tower, so named because the long building directly behind it is the Kremlin's Arsenal.

The following tower may look familiar. It has much the same lines as the Savior's Tower but is nine feet lower and less lavishly embellished. It is called the Triple Tower or, in Russian, Troitskaya Bashnya. It is connected by a long bridge (which once crossed a moat) to the Kutafia Tower, a white, ornate round gem of a tower that would look right at home at Windsor Castle or in the time of King Arthur. It is the most decorative of the Kremlin's towers and the only one to vary the red-brick hue. The Triple and Kutafia Towers form another access way to the Kremlin, but it is usually open only to pedestrian Kremlin personnel and not to the general public.

The Commandant's Tower follows, and its name comes from the fact that the Kremlin's military commander used to have his headquarters here.

The Armory Tower, next to punctuate the wall along the Alexander Garden, is named for the Armory (now the Kremlin museum) building behind it. The mounds of earth that form an embankment at the foot of this tower are all that remain of fortifications built here by Peter the Great in 1707 when it was feared that the Swedish king, Charles XII, would march against Moscow.

At the end of the Alexander Garden stands one of the Kremlin's most interesting ramparts, the Borovitsky Tower. The word bor in Russian means "forest," and this area was once a dense wood. Standing 152 feet high, the tower is rather like a stunted pyramid in shape. It is on the site of the first Moscow settlement—the low hill overlooking the Moscow and Neglinka rivers where Prince Yuri Dolgoruky built a house in the twelfth century which later was expanded into a wooden fortification. The Borovitsky Tower was constructed in 1490. It was through this gate that Napoleon entered the Kremlin in 1812. Cars of the Kremlin leaders, of guests, and ordinary tourists on foot now walk into these historic grounds through the Borovitsky Gate.

From the Borovitsky Tower the wall follows a course downhill to, and then along, the Moscow River. The

Water Tower (Vodosvonaya Bashnya) is next. Russians say it resembles a chess rook, and indeed it does. It is 176 feet high. It was erected in 1488, and 145 years later craftsmen devised a way for raising water from a well at the foot of the tower and conveying it along an aqueduct-type chute into the Kremlin palaces and gardens. It thus won its name of Water, or Water-raising, Tower. The French blew up this tower in 1812, but the Russians restored it five years later.

The section of the wall facing south along the Moscow River is the oldest segment. It was built first because Moscow was most vulnerable to attack by invaders from the south. As you walk along this wall you can see the British Embassy across the river. The bank of the river nearest the Kremlin is called Kremlevskaya Naberezhnaya, Kremlin Embankment, and the opposite bank is called Sofiiskaya Naberezhnaya, Sophia Embankment. For photographers there is a fine view of the Kremlin from the Sofiiskaya Embankment.

After the Water Tower you will come to the Annunciation Tower, named after the Kremlin Church.

Next is the Secret Tower, built in 1485. It is the oldest tower, and it is here that the construction of the present Kremlin walls began. A secret underground passage was built from the tower to the riverbank to ensure a supply of water in case of a prolonged seige.

The British Embassy is almost directly across the river from this tower.

In 1773 Catherine II ordered the Secret Tower torn down in order to make room for a palace she planned to build on this site. Lack of money in the treasury forced her to abandon the plan, but not until this tower and its neighbor, the First Nameless Tower, had been destroyed. Both were rebuilt later, but in much less elaborate form.

The First Nameless Tower is followed by the Second

Nameless Tower. These rather inauspicious turrets were designed by men whose identities are lost in history and hence the strange names for them.

The Petrovskaya Tower, with three stories and a cupola-type top, completes the stretch of wall facing on the river, and now you walk a little further to round a corner onto the broad street that leads up a hill to St. Basil's Cathedral and Red Square. At this corner stands the imposing Beklemishevskaya Tower. It was built in 1487 by the Italian architect Marco Ruffo and is 138 feet high. Only the peaked top is "new," having been added in 1680. This pinnacle was badly damaged in the fighting in 1917, but was completely restored five years later.

Walking uphill you arrive at the Konstantino-Yeleninskaya Tower, named after a Kremlin church inside the walls. In an earlier era it had a gateway from which a retractable bridge spanned the now covered Kremlin moat. In the sixteenth and seventeenth centuries the tower was used as a prison and it became known as the Pytoshnaya (Prison) Tower. The word *pytka* means "torture."

A few steps farther is the Nabatnya Tower. It was built as a watch tower and its bell was rung to warn the people of the approach of enemies. The word *nabat* means "alarm."

Finally, there is the Czar's Tower which is the smallest, least elaborate, but most charmingly contrived Kremlin tower. It resembles a canopy. One of the most "modern" Kremlin turrets, it was added to the wall in 1680.

At the top of the hill is the Spasskaya Tower where this walk began and now ends.

WALK ON SRETENKA STREET

Sretenka Street is a representative Moscow thoroughfare. There is a variety of stores and a constant bustle of people, residents of apartment houses on Sretenka's side streets, doing their daily errands.

Start at Kolkhoz ("Collective Farm") Square where Sretenka Street intersects the Sadovaya avenue, a broad circle around a major part of the metropolis. Enormous stone reliefs of farm workers in heroic pose decorate corner buildings.

Number 1 Sretenka Ulitsa is a flower shop, state-run like all other commercial enterprizes. As mentioned elsewhere in this book, flowers are an especially appreciated gift in Moscow because they are so rare during the long winter.

At number 6 there's a toy store. If there are children on your gift list this may be the shop you've been looking for. There are construction toys, blocks, dolls, and games not unlike lotto, dominoes, and Monopoly.

Number 40 is a small department store, but the shop across the street is far more interesting. This is a Commission Store specializing in (according to the sign outside), *"Bronze, Crystal, China, Porcelain, Fabrics, Clothes, and Trickotage."* It is at number 37/10 Sretenka. A Mecca for the hunter of antiques and rare items, this store is open daily from 9 A.M. to 9 P.M., with an hour off for lunch from 3 P.M. to 4 P.M. Sunday is a workday too from 9 A.M. to 7 P.M. without any lunch hour. The lunch hour on Saturdays is from 2 P.M. to 3 P.M. And, finally, to add to this typically Soviet confusion of work hours, Monday is the store's day off. Commission Stores are described in greater detail in the chapter on shopping.

Another unique Soviet establishment is a Kulttovari Store at number 36 Sretenka Street. This is a combination sports and "culture" shop. Chess and checker sets are the cultural items. Bicycles, balls for various games, track shoes and athletic clothing are some of the sports items in stock. Nearby is a little fur shop. Rather straggly pelts are on display. Furs are not sold here. Rather this is a fur tailor shop.

Number 30 is a bank. There's only one banker in the U.S.S.R.—the government. There are various neighborhood branches and also branches to deal with specialized banking functions. This bank is up one flight of stairs. For the sake of complete exposure to Soviet everyday life, you should see at least the inside of a bank which, in its barren, Spartan simplicity, is quite a departure from chrome-plated, modern U.S. banks and the wood-paneled, dignified London variety.

Across the street from the bank is a quick-snack restaurant.

At number 18 Sretenka Ulitsa is Moscow Bakery number 344. Bakeries, like other commercial establishments, seldom have a name in Russia, usually only a number. This busy bakery has a wonderful scent of freshly baked bread. Glass cases are full of pastry of all kinds, but the most revolutionary item sold here is *sdobny khleb*. This is white, leavened bread. Unusual in itself in a country which favors dark or black bread, the *sdobny* (meaning "leaven") loaf caused a ripple of excitement when it was first produced in 1959 because it actually is *wrapped*— in a kind of red waxed paper. All other bread is sold without any wrapping and *is* touched by many human hands. Some Westerners in Moscow considered this wrapped loaf as a greater development than the Sputnik, but more cynical members of the foreign colony pointed out that the Russians *still* had not developed a *pre-sliced* loaf.

Stop in at number 19 Sretenka to see a Soviet cigarette shop. The brand names of government-manufactured cigarettes are alone worthy of examination: Sputnik, Shipka (a Bulgarian city where Russian troops fought), Droog (meaning "friend," with a picture of a dog on the package), Yava (which is the Russian way of spelling

"Java"), Sever ("north"), and Troika (a characteristic Russian team drawn by three horses). A ten-kopeck piece placed in an automatic dispensing machine will produce a box of matches. Match boxes are often used for conveying state propaganda. Users are urged to increase the cotton crop, or to co-operate with census-takers, or to do their utmost to fulfill the goals of the Seven-Year Economic Plan. If you're a cigar smoker you can buy some here, although few Russians use them. Cigars are available in a variety of grades; the least expensive is 2.75 rubles for a box of ten.

There's another florist shop (this one is Moscow Flower Shop number 29) at 16 Sretenka.

At number 9 is a general bookstore. It has a wide selection, including picture books on Leningrad, illustrated books of the works of famous Russian artists, single prints of masterpieces, postcards, and placards.

Number 7 is a state savings bank.

At number 6 there's a particularly well-stocked toy shop. Here are some of the toys on display the last time we looked: bears, camels, monkeys, trucks, mushrooms, dolls in native costumes of the various republics, accordions, a miniature dining room set, and toy telephones. The only mechanical toy was a trapeze that flipped a toy acrobat.

Number 5 is a state repair shop. The sign outside indicates that it has the most versatile employees in town—any town! This shop accepts for repairs the following: vacuum cleaners, pocketbook handles, umbrellas, and cameras. What's more, duplicate keys are made here. Personally I'd take my camera elsewhere if it needed to be fixed.

As you crisscross Sretenka to look at these various representative stores, be sure to choose a side street or two to walk down. Many of the apartment buildings are dreadfully run-down. The crowded housing conditions are obvious. This is near the center of the city, but far enough off the beaten Intourist track to enable the visitor to better evaluate the show-place housing he may be shown elsewhere in the city.

CHAPTER FIFTEEN

Leningrad

A recent illegal enterprise in Moscow capitalized on the average Soviet citizen's understandable hesitation to resist official orders—or, in fact, anything that even *seems* to be an official order. An ambitious operator took photographs of the Moscow Agricultural and Industrial Exhibition. Every day he sent sets of these photos to several scores of collective farms throughout the country. With each he enclosed a slip of paper reading simply, "Remit 200 rubles to post office box 402, Moscow." The money poured back by mail. What collective farm chairman, receiving an envelope bearing a Moscow postmark, would stop to question whether the imperiously worded note was an order or a request? What Russian would stop to question the source of the solicitation? The promoter received hundreds of thousands of rubles and had several bank accounts before the authorities finally arrested him for illegally running a profit-making business in a country where only the government is supposed to be in business. It's interesting that the tip to the police came from a collective farmer in the Leningrad district.

The people of Leningrad are different, and they are the first to say so. Leningrad has been compared to Boston and Moscow to Chicago. There is validity in this, because Leningraders consider themselves the most cultured and cosmopolitan of citizens in this Communist state. They dress more carefully and with better taste than Muscovites. They display a pride in their city and a conviction that it is by far the most superior place of the Soviet Union.

Leningrad certainly is the most attractive city. It retains an imperial quality from the time when it was the capital of the Czarist empire. Originally founded in 1703 as St. Petersburg (renamed Petrograd in 1914 and Leningrad in 1924), this city was intended by Peter the Great as a "window on the west." He was eager to expose his backward country to the ways and achievements of the Western world, and he began with the architecture of the new capital. Glimpses of Amsterdam, Paris, Copenhagen are revealed in its squares and structures. There is much ugliness in Leningrad, but certainly a greater percentage of this city of 3,000,000 inhabitants (second largest in the U.S.S.R.) retains more genuine beauty and grace than any other Soviet metropolis.

Peter was determined to build his new capital quickly, but work progressed more slowly than he anticipated because of a shortage of materials and skilled workmen. On September 9, 1714, Peter issued a decree forbidding the construction of stone buildings anywhere in Russia except in St. Petersburg. This decree, which stayed in effect for several years, was soon followed by another which obliged anyone who traveled to the new city to carry with him stones to be used for paving roads.

Peter's typically Russian, fanatic, all-out approach to a problem has been inherited by his Communist successors in their methods of coping with priority projects. In Peter's case at least it brought results. As Alexander Pushkin wrote in his poem "The Bronze Horseman":

> A century—and that city young,
> Gem of the northern world, amazing,
> From gloomy wood and swamp upsprung,
> Had risen, in pride and splendor blazing.

Not only did St. Petersburg produce great buildings; it also produced great men. Mikhail Lomonosov, the famous Russian scientist whose name has been bestowed on Moscow University, spent most of his life here. Pavlov, the physiologist who made a science of the conditioned reflex; Mendeleev, who gave the world the table of elements; Popov, the man Russians say invented radio; literary figures including Pushkin, Gogol, Turgenev, and Gorky all worked in this city. Chaikovsky, Glinka, Rimsky-Korsakov, Musorgsky composed here.

The Bolshevik revolution began and was fought in its streets.

Leningrad suffered greatly in World War II. The city was under siege for 900 days. Along with Stalingrad, Odessa and Sevastopol, Leningrad has been bestowed with the title of "hero city" for the endurance and courage of its inhabitants in battle. It is difficult to find a family in Leningrad which did not lose someone in the war. Many died from artillery fire. Others died of starvation. The city was supplied only intermittently, mostly over the ice of frozen Lake Ladoga to the north. A railroad was built on the ice. With German forces besieging the city from three sides, this frozen life-line sustained the fighting forces and the equally courageous civilian population.

Leningrad is situated as far north as Canada's Hudson Bay. In June the city experiences its unforgettable "white nights" when it is possible to read a book without artificial light at any time of night or day and the tennis courts are busy until after midnight. It is eerie to witness a night passing without darkness. Because of the angle of the earth's axis the sun never drops very far below the horizon at that time of year. By contrast, winter days are depressingly short. In December street lights go on before 4 P.M. and people go to work in the morning in darkness.

If you can visit only one city in the U.S.S.R., we suggest that you see Moscow. If time and budget permit you to visit two, make your second city Leningrad.

It's been our experience that a traveler will get the most out of a stay in Leningrad if he has seen Moscow first. Try to do it in that order. Coming directly from Copenhagen or Helsinki, the visitor may find Leningrad drab, run-down, shabby. But after a few days in Moscow for acclimatization to the Soviet scene, the tourist sees Leningrad in its proper perspective and context.

HOW TO GET THERE

Leningrad can be reached by airplane from Helsinki or Copenhagen (with a change of planes in Riga). There are planes several times a day from Moscow including a jet flight that covers the 400 miles in about an hour. However, we'd like to recommend strongly that you go by the Red Arrow Express, a train with unique characteristics that put it in a class with both the Paris-Istanbul Orient Express renowned in spy thrillers and the aristocratic Blue Train linking Paris and the Riviera.

The Red Arrow departs around midnight (check the schedule which is altered occasionally) from Moscow's Leningradskaya Station, a remarkably clean terminal with a glass roof and a classic statue of Lenin gazing down the tracks. Its polished blue cars bear a seal with the letters OK. This may startle the traveler by its jaunty familiarity in an unfamiliar setting. But OK here is simply an abbreviation for *Oktyabr*, meaning "October" in Russian; this government-run railroad is known as the Great October Line, in honor of the month of the revolution.

There are several classes of sleeping cars. All are built in the European style with a narrow corridor running down one side of the train and compartments on the other. Depending on the class, two or four persons sleep in a compartment. It is possible to buy a compartment for one person, and in the case of a woman traveling alone it is a good idea to do so, because the Russians think nothing of assigning a man and a woman, complete strangers, to the same sleeping compartment. Usually, after a certain amount of fuss and reshuffling of tickets, the female traveler from a strange foreign land is assigned to a compartment by herself or with another woman. But not always.

The berths are clean and reasonably comfortable. A washroom is shared by two compartments but can be locked from the inside when occupied. The toilets at the end of the cars are kept more sanitary than most Soviet public facilities. Each compartment has a small table with a lamp and a radio loud-speaker overhead carrying the music and news of Radio Moscow. The car attendant—a woman on most other trains, but usually a man on the Red Arrow—brews tea in a modernized samovar and serves it in a glass, sometimes with biscuits. The charge is a few rubles.

The Moscow-Leningrad railroad line was built during the reign of Czar Nicholas I and completed in 1851. Although you may jounce and jiggle during the overnight ride, you will not find centrifugal force tugging at you, because there are no curves for the Red Arrow to round. The Czar had his own concept of what Russia's first railroad should be like. He would tolerate no arguments from engineers and surveyors or keepers-of-the-treasury. The result is a perfectly straight line.

There are other comfortable trains on this Moscow-Leningrad route, but the Red Arrow is the best. All keep strictly to schedule; Soviet trains are rarely late.

A round-trip ticket on the Red Arrow costs 452 rubles ($45.20 or just over £16) for an international class sleeping car (the best) or 394 rubles ($39.40 or £14) for the less comfortable ordinary sleeper. A round-trip airplane ticket is 300 rubles ($30 or almost £11). This is the tourist-class fare—the only class available on this short hop.

For the really leisurely traveler who scorns time, there is yet another way to get to Leningrad. A Soviet ship, once named after V. M. Molotov but renamed the *Baltika* when Molotov fell out of favor, sails from London about once a month. Travel agents can give you the precise schedule of the voyage which takes about a week with brief stops at Baltic ports. Faubion Bowers, writing in *The New Yorker* magazine, recommends the *Baltika* approach to Leningrad with these enthusiastic words: "Leningrad, like most port cities, should first be seen from the water. Arriving by ship, you avoid the inevitable characterless industrial suburbs and come straight into the heart of Peter the Great's capital. There, all around you, are the imposing prospects, the wide avenues, the vast plazas, the palaces and cathedrals, spread across a hundred islands in the delta of the Neva River, crosshatched with tributaries and canals and strung together with countless bridges . . ."

WHERE TO STAY

There are two very good, up-to-Moscow-standards hotels in Leningrad—the Astoria and the Europa. The Astoria has acquired a reputation (perhaps because it has been an Intourist hotel longer) as *the* place to stay in Leningrad. Personally we prefer the Europa. Both are old, ornate, with large, high-ceilinged rooms and tasseled lamp shades.

The Astoria's ground-floor dining room has a good-size dance floor and a band that is one of the best in Russia.

One night in 1955 the Astoria restaurant rocked with some of the hottest jazz ever heard in the Soviet Union. Members of an American troupe performing *Porgy and Bess* (the first such group to come to the U.S.S.R.) borrowed the Russians' instruments and put on an informal jam session. The Astoria's musicians still talk about it.

Service Bureaus in the Astoria and Europa Hotels take care of cars, theater tickets, sight-seeing tours, and other Intourist arrangements. Both hotels have souvenir counters.

WHAT TO SEE

Tour of Leningrad: Start off your day in Leningrad with a tour of the city's landmarks by chauffeured car or by bus. The guide will point out the gold-spired Admiralty building, the statue of the Bronze Horseman, St. Isaac's Cathedral, the Neva River, the astoundingly rich Hermitage Museum, the city's spacious squares, the Kazan Cathedral which has been converted into a history of religion museum, the Nevsky Prospekt avenue and the Peter and Paul Fortress. These and other highlights are described below:

The Bronze Horseman Statue: This is a trademark of Leningrad much as the Eiffel Tower is pictured to denote Paris. It was unveiled in 1782 to commemorate the centenary of the coronation of Peter I, or Peter the Great, if you prefer that title. This equestrian statue, showing Peter (in Roman toga, no less!) on a rearing charger, was sculptured by E. M. Falconet. The sculptor began by making preliminary sketches of a Russian cavalry general, resembling Peter in height and figure, who posed on the finest steed owned by the royal stables.

After considerable search, a suitable block of granite was found near a village called Lakhta, not far from St.

Petersburg. Then came the problem of how to transport this 1600-ton block. A reward of 7000 rubles (worth a great deal more than it is today) was offered to anyone producing a solution. A Russian blacksmith whose name has long been forgotten suggested using brass balls on specially laid rails. It worked; he got the prize, and Peter and his horse got their pedestal which bears an inscription (in Cyrillic letters on one side and Latin on the other): *"Peter I, Catherine II, 1782."* Willful Czarina Catherine made sure that she got a credit line along with Peter because the statue was erected during her reign.

The statue inspired a poem "The Bronze Horseman" by Pushkin which in turn inspired a ballet of the same name.

Decembrist Square: The statue of Peter stands in the grassy park called Decembrist Square which used to be called Senate Square. Its name comes from the Russian word *Dekabrist*, roughly translated as "man of December." It was on December 26, 1825, that 2000 soldiers of the Czarist guard staged an attempt at a *coup d'état*. It was unsuccessful because of lack of leadership and of clear purpose, and the soldiers did little more than mill around this square outside the Council of State until artillery fire was directed on them. However, later they came to be regarded as martyrs and participants in one of the first acts of the drama of the Communist revolution.

The Admiralty: Its golden roof and spire can be seen from many parts of Leningrad. It was one of the first buildings Peter had constructed; it was built in 1704 on the same left bank of the Neva as the Winter Palace. As headquarters for Peter's navy, the Admiralty symbolizes the importance of St. Petersburg (and to a lesser extent Leningrad, under comparative Communist isolation) as

Russia's main port for commerce and contact with the West. The tower is 230 feet high, it is crowned by a weather-vane ship, and now houses various Soviet Navy offices as well as a Navy Museum.

Peter and Paul Fortress: This is one of Leningrad's oldest buildings. It was begun in 1703 and completed seven years later. Peter I intended it as a fortress, but as the city grew, it soon lost its strategic position and was converted into a prison. The first prisoner to be held within its bleak, bastioned walls was Peter's son, Czarevich Alexis, who was put to death on his father's orders for plotting with certain nobles to seize the throne. Russian history is full of such intrigue and all kinds of homicide ranging from patricide to fratricide. The Fortress became a favorite place for imprisoning political opponents, and it acquired the reputation of being the Russian Bastille.

Smolny: This yellow-squash colored, large building set on a broad lawn with the inevitable statue of Lenin in front used to be a girls' school for aristocratic families. It became the headquarters for the 1917 revolution. Lenin had his office here. It now houses the Leningrad Communist Party Central Committee. It's worth the time to drive past and look at this building, but there are far more interesting sights in Leningrad. The name Smolny comes from the Russian word for "tar." This area was used by Peter I to store highly combustible tar for caulking his ships.

The Aurora: This old, three-stack cruiser looks like an American or British Navy destroyer of World War I vintage. It played a historic role in the 1917 Bolshevik revolution, and now rides at anchor in the Neva River at the shore opposite the Hermitage Museum. It certainly should at least be seen by the visitor to Leningrad.

The *Aurora* was a cruiser of the Czar's fleet, inherited by the provisional government which took power when the Czar went into exile in Siberia. On October 23, 1917, three members of the ship's crew were summoned to the Smolny Institute where the Communist revolutionaries had their headquarters. One of the trio was named A. V. Belyshev, who still lives in Leningrad and is a chief mechanic at the Lenenergo Factory. In an interview Belyshev recalled that when he got to Smolny, "the entrance was crowded with workers, soldiers, sailors, and delegates from the villages going in and out of the building. Detachments, parties, watches, and patrols were coming and going all the time. All around the Smolny were artillery pieces, machine guns and armored cars. Everything indicated that big events were in the air.

"We were received by Comrade Sverdlov, one of the revolutionary military leaders," recalled the old *Aurora* crew member. "He first asked us to tell him about the situation on the cruiser, the mood and the thoughts of the sailors and then he said: 'The Revolutionary Military Committee has authorized me to appoint a commissar (revolutionary leader) for the *Aurora*.'" Belyshev was appointed and returned to his ship. Two days later a messenger arrived by boat at the *Aurora* with a message for Belyshev. It read: "The Provisional Government is to resign at 9 P.M. If it refuses to do so, a signal light will appear over the Peter and Paul Fortress. And then the *Aurora* should fire a blank signaling that the time has come to storm the Winter Palace."

Nine o'clock came and passed. Finally three-quarters of an hour past the appointed time a red flare appeared above the fortress. Belyshev shouted: "Fore gun, stand by, fire!"

"There was a flash," recalled Belyshev, "and the shot roared across the Neva. We heard shouts of 'hoorah,' and bursts of machine-gun and rifle fire. And then finally a signalman waved his cap and shouted to us: 'Aurora! Stop firing! We have taken the Winter Palace.'"

Palace Square: This square is portrayed in many paintings by Soviet artists. In October 1917 rebellious troops and workers gathered here and attacked the former Czar's Winter Palace, by that time the headquarters of Alexander Kerensky's provisional government. The Winter Palace (now part of the Hermitage Art Gallery) stands on the north side of Palace Square. On the other side is a horseshoe-shaped building of the Czarist military General Staff. It is now occupied by Communist military offices. A copy of a Roman triumphal arch intersects the building, and you can pass through it. It is called the Triumphal Arch of the Red Army. In the center of the vast square stands Alexander's Column, more than 150 feet high and weighing 600 tons. It was erected in 1834 to commemorate the victory over Napoleon. Atop the column is the figure of an angel holding a cross. Palace Square bears some resemblance to Place de la Concorde (mainly because of its great size) and to Place Vendome (mainly because of its column monument).

The Hermitage: This is one of Leningrad's greatest wonders. The Hermitage is among the world's most distinguished art galleries, ranking with the Louvre in Paris, the National Gallery in London, and the Metropolitan Museum of Art in New York.

The Hermitage occupies four connecting Czarist palace buildings; the oldest is the Winter Palace where, as the name implies, the Czars spent the winter months. The Winter Palace, built between 1754 and 1762, was designed by Bartolomeo Rastrelli, an architect of Italian parentage who was born in Paris and moved to Russia. The official Soviet guidebook for the Hermitage has appropriated Rastrelli as Russia's own. It refers to Rastrelli simply as "the prominent Russian architect" and mentions nothing about his origin.

The Hermitage was built in 1765, after completion of the Winter Palace, as a comparatively small, secluded retreat (speaking in regal proportions of course) for Catherine the Great who reigned from 1762 to 1796, after usurping the throne from her ineffectual husband, Peter III. Catherine used the Hermitage for social activities with a restricted circle of members of the court in order to escape the formality and ceremonious pomp that attended activities in the nearby Winter Palace. She gave this annex the name of the "Hermitage" which more closely describes what she sought than it does the building that she got. Catherine moved her private art collection into the Hermitage. The collection grew and expanded during the century and a half left to the Czars, and under the Communists too, and today the entire, spacious art gallery has taken the name of Catherine's original mansion.

One side of the Hermitage faces on the tree-lined Neva River. On the opposite side is Palace Square. Constructed in baroque style with statues lining the stone edges of its flat roof, the Hermitage is a remarkable color—an intense and yet powdery blue-green mixture. Although the Hermitage has three floors, the columns that contribute to the regal quality of its façade are divided into two tiers; the lower tier extends from the ground to the top of the first story, and the upper set of corresponding columns extends past the next two stories to the roof balustrades. This tends to give the palace buildings a heightened appearance.

For those with a penchant for statistics it may be of interest to note that the Winter Palace has 1050 chambers, 1945 windows, 1786 doors, and 117 staircases.

But more important than the architectural history or appearance of the Hermitage is what's inside. Certainly works of art should not be described in terms of *quantity*, but it is difficult to resist counting. In one ill-lighted room alone there are 27 Rembrandts, the greatest collection outside of the Netherlands. There are 40 pictures by Rubens, 14 by Poussin, 11 by Cézanne. There are masterpieces by Rubens, Vandyke, Titian, Tiepolo, Cellini, Veronese, Monet, Pissarro, Renoir, Rodin, Gauguin, Matisse, Cézanne and many, many others. A 113-page *Short Guide* to the Hermitage Museum is sold for 10 rubles ($1 or about eight shillings) at the book counter in the lobby. It lists the paintings, statues, and other items of the Hermitage collection from exhibition hall number one to 117 of the Hermitage's 322 rooms, including Czarist living quarters. With its monochrome reproductions, it is a worth-the-price souvenir, and is especially useful in helping the visitor decide what to see and what to skip. We recommend that in a two-day visit to Leningrad you plan to spend a full morning or afternoon at the Hermitage, and proportionately more for a longer visit. Plan to see these highlights of the Hermitage: the suite of four rooms (numbered 111, 112, 113 and 114) on the top floor facing Palace Square with works by Renoir, Matisse, Gauguin, and other Impressionists including the original of Pablo Picasso's famous and now propagandized "Dove of Peace"; two of the 14 works in existence of Leonardo da Vinci on display in room 11, the "Madonna with a Flower" and the "Madonna Litta"; nine works by Titian, the great master of the sixteenth-century Venetian school should be seen in rooms 25 and 31 unless you've been to Italy and seen enough Titians there to last you for a while; room 35 assembles marvellous masterpieces by El Greco, Diego Velázquez and other Spanish artists from the mid-sixteenth to the mid-seventeenth century; no fewer than 42 paintings and statues by Peter Paul Rubens, head of the school of Flemish art of the seventeenth century, are on display, most in room 42; the next hall, room 43, holds one of the world's most extensive collections of the works of Anthony Vandyke (1599–1641) including a portrait of his contemporary Rubens with his son Albert; and last but obviously not least, room number 50 contains the staggering storehouse of Rembrandts.

For the visitor with time to spare there are sections of the Hermitage of lesser interest including: a room (number 19, second floor) with pieces of malachite stone by Russian artisans of the first half of the nineteenth century; room 60 with Russian silverware spanning four centuries; and rooms 65 through 67 with mementoes of the military past of the Russian people such as the saddle used by Peter I in the Battle of Poltava and the silver trumpets awarded by the Czar to the Russian troops who captured Berlin in 1760.

Besides the paintings, the rooms of this former Czarist residence themselves are of great interest. A fire in 1837 caused considerable damage to the Winter Palace. While having the palace rebuilt, Czar Nicholas I issued a decree that all privately owned houses in St. Petersburg were to be at least seven feet lower than the Winter Palace. This decree of autocratic vanity was not remanded until 1905.

The exterior of the Winter Palace was restored after the fire to conform to Rastrelli's design, but only a few of the rooms retained their original baroque character after this reconstruction work. The main stairway by which you enter the museum looks as it did when counts, dukes, and czarinas swept up its broad stone steps under the priceless ceiling frescoes. The small throne room (now room number 64 containing paintings by Johann Heinrich Tischbein and other late eighteenth and early nineteenth century German artists) was restored to its original form. It is known as Petrovsky or Peter's Hall in honor of Peter the Great. In the appropriately lavish words of the Soviet guidebook: "The picturesque panels, the elaborate frescoes on the vaulted ceiling, the old velvet hangings stitched in silver thread, the rich moulding and gilding, the use of colored stones and the beautiful parquet of rare varieties of wood combine to create an impression of majestic splendor."

One small section of three rooms in the Hermitage is known as "The Treasury." It is not open to the general public. A special ticket is needed. This usually can be obtained from the Intourist Service Bureau at your hotel by requesting it a day before you plan to visit the Hermitage. The Treasury contains a rare collection of jewelry and other objects of lacelike gold work of the Scythian culture dating back 700 years before the birth of Christ and of the Greek civilization of the fifth to third centuries B.C. These remarkable pieces were discovered in excavations on Soviet territory. Here too is a collection of Czarist jewelry of the sixteenth to the nineteenth centuries A.D. which dwarfs displays of gems at even such outstanding museums as the Vatican's. We particularly liked a collection of jeweled and enameled watches of all sorts and shapes owned by various Czars. There are three jeweled Faberge pieces in this Leningrad collection. By all means, try to make arrangements through the Service Bureau to include The Treasury on your tour of the Hermitage. Don't be offended if you are asked to leave your purse with an attendant before entering The Treasury. The official explanation is that a carelessly carried purse might crack a showcase.

An unfortunate note: the illumination of some rooms of the Hermitage is disgraceful. There's little daylight and the visitor is reduced to squinting and crouching to try to get a view of a masterpiece. The management of the Hermitage recognizes this deficiency and in a recent article published in a Soviet newspaper, Professor Mikhail Artamonov, director of the Hermitage, wrote: "It must be said that facilities in the various halls of the Hermitage are not all up to the same standard, and in many cases are not up to date. Furthermore many of the rooms contain too much material. In the next few years we intend to change and modernize our equipment, and radically reconstruct the lighting system, making wide use of daylight lamps."

Let's hope so.

Youssupov Palace: Here is the scene of the murder of Rasputin, the mad monk who exerted tremendous influence on the last Czar's family. He was killed by Prince Felix Youssupov and several nobleman colleagues who thought Rasputin's passing might energize the Czar into action in the nation's pressing problems. Invited for a drink by Felix, who had won his confidence, Rasputin was given a dose of poison in wine that should have been lethal for an ox. Rasputin remained unaffected. Fearing that Rasputin would escape, Felix then shot him. The monk fell to the floor, but with superhuman strength he managed to stagger to his feet, climb a flight of stairs from the basement room, and lurch out the door into the night. More shots felled him, and the conspirators stuffed his body into a sack and threw him into the Moika Canal on which the Youssupov Palace fronts. The address now is 94 Decembrists' Street, and the building is part of an educational institution. Much of the enormous Youssupov art collection is now in the Hermitage Museum.

Lenin's Secret Room: "V. I. Lenin hid here," might be the descriptive note for this typically Soviet sight. It is in the Electrical Engineering Institute. This was a particularly clever hiding place, because the Institute was under the auspices of the Czarist Ministry of Interior, the secret police headquarters. This would have been the last place that Czarist authorities would have expected to find Lenin. Fellow conspirators rigged up a blackboard on pulleys so that when lowered it hid a door leading to a cubbyhole-size room. A plaque in lecture room 10 where the sliding blackboard hides the secret door reads: *"V. I. Lenin (Ulyanov) used this room as a hiding place in 1905–07."*

Pulkovo Observatory: If you arrive in Leningrad by air your plane will very likely circle over the domes of an observatory. You can also see the buildings on a rise of ground from the airport. These hills, ten miles from the city, were German artillery positions during the war. The area is known as Pulkovo Heights and the observatory, the biggest in Russia, is respected by astronomers throughout the world. Founded in 1893 by a Russian astronomer, Professor Vassily Struve, the observatory has contributed to scientific knowledge about the universe. Although it has modern equipment, the meridian telescope installed when the observatory was founded still is used with, say the Russians, absolute accuracy. A principal Pulkovo activity nowadays is Sputnik and Lunik observation. The meridian on which the observatory stands is known as the Pulkovo Meridian and Moskovsky Prospekt, a street in Leningrad, is constructed as a straight line along it.

Leningrad Metro: If you've seen the Moscow subway, you can save time by skipping this. However, the chances are your Intourist guide will insist. The Leningraders are as proud of their underground system as are Muscovites of theirs. The Leningrad version is somewhat simpler and in better taste, we thought. See the Autovo Station if you have time for only one.

Resurrection Church: This is a rather cut-rate version of Moscow's St. Basil's Cathedral. Most of all it seems to prove that St. Basil's was a miracle of ornate, imaginative architecture that can not be duplicated. What Leningrad's Resurrection Church lacks in architecture it makes up for in its history. In 1881 Czar Alexander II, who sought to introduce an element of constitutional government into still almost feudal Russia, was being driven in his royal carriage, protected by mounted bodyguards, when a bomb was thrown at him. This plot on his life had been organized by his principal adviser, Sophia Perovsky. Historian Sir Bernard Pares describes the event this way: "Alexander was driving along the Catherine Canal when at the signal of Perovsky's kerchief a young Nihilist Rysakov threw a bomb at his carriage. The Emperor was not touched, and dismounted to speak to some of the Cossacks of his suite who were wounded. He even spoke not unkindly of the criminal, who had been arrested. At this moment a second assassin, Grinevetsky, with the words, 'It's too early to thank God,' threw a second bomb between his feet. His legs were crushed, his stomach torn open and his face terribly mutilated. He could only say: 'Home to the Palace to die there,' and passed away unconscious an hour and a half later. The bomb that killed Alexander put an end to the faint beginnings of Russian constitutionalism."

The church was constructed from 1883 to 1907 on the spot of the assassination. It is a "working" church with daily services

Kazan Cathedral: This is a church of quite another sort. No services are held here. Rather, since 1929 its purpose has been to *discourage* people from worship. A uniquely Soviet institution, it is Leningrad's Museum of the History of Religion, or more accurately, its Anti-Religious Museum.

Completed in 1811, the domed Kazan Cathedral is a miniature of St. Peter's in Rome with the arms of its colonnades reaching out into a park instead of around a piazza. At the time of its construction, this was said to be the third largest cathedral in the world.

Where altars and crucifixes once stood exhibits now are intended to evoke contempt, indignation or rage at religion. One display of pasteboard figures shows a peasant being executed in ancient times because he refused to give a sufficient portion of his crop to the church. In the museum's basement a realistic torture chamber has been re-created with three corpulent monks seated at a table. Branding irons of crosses are being heated in a fireplace. The wax figure of an infidel is shown suffering in a stock. Another is undergoing torture in a chair of nails. Still another is being crushed under a series of weights being lowered on his head. The sign over the exhibit reads: *"Headquarters of the Inquisition of the sixteenth century."*

Elsewhere in the Kazan Museum are the paintings of leering priests, words of denunciation of the Vatican quoted on cards, and caricatures of church figures. The intent is to show the history of religion as one of human oppression.

This museum may infuriate you or amuse you, but don't miss it! An hour is enough to cover the exhibits once over lightly.

Peterhof: Plan to spend a half day for the automobile trip to this remarkable palace near Leningrad. If you have more time, it is an interesting one-day outing by boat on the Neva River from Leningrad. Built by Peter the Great in 1709, it is the Russian equivalent of France's Versailles. The Soviet Government changed the name of Peterhof to Petrodvorets; it means Peter's Palace either way, but the former is in German, the latter in Russian. Everyone still calls it Peterhof.

The drive to Peterhof is in itself instructive because this is a road on which the German army advanced toward Leningrad in World War II. On the outskirts of the city stands a Russian tank. It participated in the breaking of the 900-day German seige and traveled all the way to Berlin with the Soviet armies. There is also a marker on the road to indicate the closest point to the city approached by the German armies.

A light cream color palace, built by a Russian Grand Duke named Constantine, can be seen along the way. It is now a Soviet officers' club.

Peterhof itself is situated about 25 miles from the center of Leningrad. It was captured by the Germans. The main palace building, on a hill overlooking a long lagoon leading to the Bay of Finland, was destroyed by the Germans. After the war, in reconstructing the palace, the Russians first erected a stage setting-like façade (without anything behind it) in order to provide a proper backdrop for the fountains and lagoon. Only later, when men and materials became available, was the palace itself, now a museum, reconstructed.

Peterhof consists of about 300 acres of formal gardens, wooded land, and most remarkable of all, 129 fountains. These fountains include a splendid cascade, which tumbles down from the palace level to the lagoon, as well as amusing trick fountains so much enjoyed by Peter the Great. Today Russians of more common stock also are vastly amused by these fountains. Benches spray water on unsuspecting persons who attempt to sit down. There is a pretty and realistic "tree"; its metal leaves suddenly spill water. Another fountain is a big umbrella; the trick is to escape from under its shade when the curtain of water that falls from its edges momentarily ceases. The trick fountains are controlled by operators hidden in the bushes.

Sphinx: Situated on the banks of the Neva River, two Sphinx statues were brought from Egypt in 1825 by Czar Nicholas I.

Statue of Czar Nicholas: Constructed in 1859, this statue shows the figure of the Czar, but is of particular interest because of the supplementary figures of four women. These women were modeled after the Czar's wife and his three daughters. They are supposed to represent Faith, Justice, Wisdom, and Power.

Lenin's Armored Car: This is situated in the courtyard of the Lenin Museum, a splendid marble palace which was a gift by Catherine the Great to one in her succession of lovers, Prince Orlov, who participated in the plot that brought her to power.

When Lenin arrived at St. Petersburg's Finland Station from exile to take charge of the revolution, he delivered a speech from this sturdy, old-fashioned armored car with its impractical, exposed rubber tires. The car now stands on a stone pedestal and the words painted in purple in 1917 on its black turret read, *"Enemy of Capitalism."* The clock in the tower of the Lenin Museum is stopped at 11 minutes to 7. This is the time that Lenin died. The clock commemorates that historic event of January 21, 1924.

Palace of Pioneers: The "Pioneers" in Leningrad as well as in every other Soviet city and hamlet is the organization for training, rallying and organizing school children. The Pioneers' Palace of Leningrad was a former palace of Czar Alexander. You should visit a Pioneers' Palace somewhere on your Soviet travels and this one is larger and more attractive than most.

Pushkin Theatre: This is the Leningrad equivalent of the Moscow Bolshoi Theatre. Bright yellow in color, the Pushkin Theatre and adjacent buildings form a symmetrical architectural complex that looks bright and cheerful even on dull days. The Pushkin Theatre fronts on the Square of Art which is the cultural, theatrical center of this city. See the Intourist office of your hotel for a schedule of what is playing in Leningrad theaters. There is, as in most Soviet cities, a circus in Leningrad.

Leningrad Library: One of the largest libraries in the Soviet Union, it claims to have 10,000,000 volumes on its shelves. Another Leningrad library is that of the Academy of Sciences with 8,000,000 volumes.

Czarskoye Selo: This means "Czar's Village," and that is just what it was—a community for members of the Czarist court when they tired of St. Petersburg. Preserved as a museum, its imposing architectural monuments are a short drive from Leningrad.

Summer Palace of Peter the Great: Situated along one of Leningrad's many canals (which remind some visitors a bit of Venice or Amsterdam), this is a comparatively modest but beautifully proportioned Czarist structure, and is one of the most attractive buildings in Leningrad. It stands in a Leningrad park known as the Summer Garden. The paths are lined by trees and marble busts. We thought that the big blue and white tile corner stoves were among the most interesting features in this building. We recommend a visit.

Nevsky Prospekt: This is Leningrad's broad main street. In the evening Leningraders are fond of strolling along the Nevsky Prospekt and looking at shop windows and at each other. You may care to join in this activity for at least a few minutes on one evening of your stay.

Other Sights: For the tourist with sufficient time in Leningrad there are other places to visit including the Natural History Museum, St. Isaac's Church, the stock exchange (now a museum), and the Pavlov Institute where the renowned Dr. Ivan Petrovich Pavlov, who made the conditioned reflex famous, worked. If you are in Leningrad in the summer you will find it enjoyable to take a boat ride on the Neva River in one of the small tram boats which ply this broad stream.

WHERE TO EAT

Astoria Hotel Restaurant: The menu here and at the Europa Hotel is in English, and if you've been eating in Intourist hotels in Moscow it will look like an old friend. As in Moscow, the menu is printed in four languages—Russian, German, Chinese, and English. The best meal we had at the Astoria consisted of crab salad, Kiev cutlet, fried potatoes, cucumber salad, and ice cream. The service at the Astoria is agonizingly slow. Take a handful of postcards to the table with you if you tend to fret about wasted time.

Europa Hotel Restaurant: There's little to choose between the Europa and Astoria as far as décor, food, and service. The décor is Victorian—more so at the Astoria which has marble statues under its winter garden, greenhouse-type roof. The food is hearty, unimaginative, filling. The offensively slow waiters are likely to make you feel like an intruder. Try caviar, roast chicken, and compote for a fairly quick (by Europa standards) and satisfying meal.

Kavkaz Restaurant: We think this is the best restaurant in Leningrad. As you face the Kazan Cathedral Museum it is on the corner at your right. There are several small dining rooms, down a short flight of stairs. No attempt at fancy decorations. It has a reputation for the best meal in town, is often crowded, and it is preferable to have the hotel Service Bureau telephone for a reservation. Although Russian dishes are served too, this restaurant, as the name implies, specializes in Middle Eastern cuisine. As is the case for any such regional restaurant, you usually can't go wrong with spicy roast lamb, *pozsharsky shashlik*. Try any of the dishes mentioned under the Aragvi Restaurant in the chapter on Moscow restaurants. The Kavkaz is the place to go for a leisurely meal—lunch or dinner.

Café Sever: On the city's main street, the Nevsky Prospekt, this popular restaurant has an off-tune band but quick service which brings the food piping hot. Try *blinchatye pirozhki* which are pancakes rolled up with chopped meat inside. By the way, there is a Sever *Restaurant*, too, which we can't recommend, but the *Café* Sever may be just the place you're looking for for a fast meal before going to the theater.

Lakomka Restaurant: This means "sweet tooth" in Russian, and is principally a children's restaurant. There are pint-size tables for youngsters as well as normal-size furniture. On the Nevsky Prospekt, it's a fine spot for a snack—not a full meal. Good pastry, tea, and coffee. In fact, this is representative of a type of restaurant that Moscow lacks—a place to drop in with a friend for a cup of coffee and a little gossip. This is the closest that Russia has to offer to the cafés so popular in Vienna.

A distinguishing feature of Leningrad restaurants is that paper napkins are usually *full* size. This is in contrast to restaurants in Moscow and elsewhere in the U.S.S.R. where paper napkins placed on restaurant tables are often cut in half or even into quarters. Perhaps this largesse may be one of the things which Leningraders have in mind when they claim that their city is more elegant than Moscow.

CHAPTER SIXTEEN

Kiev, Odessa, Tbilisi, Sochi, and Other Cities

Even simple things are often very different in Russia.
Whereas a Western child learns that dogs bark "bow
wow," the Russian child is taught to hear "gav, gav." To
the Russian the frog's croak sounds like "kva, kva," and
a pig goes "khru, khru."

With such simple differences as a dog's bark and a
pig's grunt, it's to be expected that more important
aspects of daily life will bear only small resemblance
to home. This is especially true as the traveler leaves
Moscow and journeys to other cities.

Besides Moscow and Leningrad which are covered
in previous chapters, these are the most important cities
usually open to foreign tourists: Ivanovo, Kiev, Minsk,
Riga, Lvov, Odessa, Kharkov, Stalingrad, Chernovtsy,
Gorky, Kazan, Ulyanovsk, Uzhgorod, Kuybyshev, Saratov,
Rostov-on-Don, Tbilisi, Gori, Sochi, Sukhumi, Yalta,
Borzhomi, Batumi, Baku, Ordzhonikidze, Yerevan, Tash-
kent, Alma Ata, Samarkand, and Stalinabad. The last
four are mentioned in a separate chapter on central Asia.
Others of importance are discussed here.

Most cities outside of Moscow and Leningrad have
only one hotel which accommodates foreign tourists.
There are fewer sights for tourists to see, fewer restaurants in which to eat. There is a sameness in architecture
to many Soviet cities, although there are notable excep-

tions. The tourist who has a week would do well to spend his time in Moscow and Leningrad. The traveler with more time should try to visit other cities. Two days is usually ample for the once-over-lightly visitor to any of the cities listed alphabetically in this chapter.

BAKU

Baku is the capital of the Azerbaijan (often spelled Azerbaidzhan) Republic of the U.S.S.R. which is situated on the western shore of the Caspian Sea. Baku is a busy port and is the center of an important oil production region. It is the Soviet Union's fifth largest city with a population of about 900,000.

Tourists who have traveled to Baku have found their movements restricted to an area near the hotel. The authorities seem particularly sensitive to foreigners' wanderings near the port section. More often than not, when a tourist tries to stroll toward the port area he is halted by a courteous policeman or plain-clothes agent who "suggests" that he turn back.

Worth seeing in Baku:

Oil Derricks: Like a Texas off-shore oil town, Baku has oil wells sticking right out of the sea. On occasion, travelers with authenticated knowledge of oil operations have been taken to the site of an oil well or to an oil refinery.

Academy of Science: This Azerbaijan institution has a number of schools, research centers and institutes engaged mostly in technical and scientific work.

Theaters: Baku has its dramatic theater and its ballet theater. The performances are below Moscow standards, but are worth seeing when a national (rather than Russian or Soviet) work is being staged.

Mosque: Baku and Azerbaijan are predominantly Moslem, and a visit to Baku provides an opportunity to witness a Moslem service.

BATUMI

Batumi is the terminal point of tourist cruises on the Black Sea which begin at Odessa. Most tourists, however, get off along the way, usually at Yalta. If you take the entire cruise you will find Batumi (population 82,000) to be a small but active port with a climate warm enough for swimming six months of the year beginning in May. Batumi is the capital of the Adjarian Autonomous Republic which is one of the political subdivisions of the U.S.S.R. An Autonomous Republic has no real autonomy, but the title simply is a form of official recognition that people of unique language and culture inhabit the region and are no longer independent.

Situated near the border of Turkey, Batumi's streets are lined with palm trees and the local pride is a seaside boulevard bordered by parks. This embankment area includes an outdoor theater, sports grounds, and leads to a large beach. The Batumi Botanical Garden was founded in 1912 and is one of the largest in the country. There are many "rest homes" and "sanitoria" in and near Batumi. One day is more than enough for the tourist who is not looking for a rest. Batumi's Hotel Intourist is a four-story comfortable building on Lenin Street.

GORI

If you visit Tbilisi, try by all means to spend a day (it can be done in a half day if you hurry) in the town of Gori where Stalin was born. The drive from Tbilisi is along a winding, black asphalt, two-lane road which, like most Soviet highways, lacks a white line to mark the center. The road follows the Kura River for a while, twists around mountains, passes the ruins of ancient fortresses. Occasional Russian language signs read GLORY TO THE COMMUNIST PARTY and PEACE TO THE WORLD. Near villages children sell grapes and cherries decoratively tied to short sticks. At intervals along the road there appear unexpected statues: a deer nuzzling a baby deer; a husky Soviet mother with a child on her shoulder; a father with one arm outstretched, a young son on his other shoulder and a toy plane in the child's hand, and, in front of a school, a statue of a young boy reading a book. These decorative statues apparently are the Soviet substitute for gasoline stations and refreshment stands of which we saw none.

We made the trip in a small Pobeda car. It was uncomfortable and breathlessly hot in June. We suggest you ask the Intourist Service Bureau for a bigger car, preferably a ZIM.

The two hour drive brought Gori into view—a grayish, dusty town in a broad valley backed by green, steep ridges. The word *gori* means "small mountain," and it is easy to see how Stalin's native town got its name.

Stalin was born and lived for four years in a rented room in a small Gori cottage. Stalin's mother was still alive when the house was converted into a museum in 1935 and the furnishings were restored as they had been when Stalin was a child. If the restoration is to be accepted as accurate, Stalin, his mother, and father slept in one narrow bed. The other furnishings in the small room are a table, four square stools, two chests, a samovar, and a wall mirror flanked by two candle holders. It was a modest beginning for a man who was to become the world's most powerful dictator.

In 1937 a grotesque stone pavilion was erected over

the wooden house to protect it from the elements. It has also succeeded in effectively blocking the house from view.

Behind the birthplace, an ornate museum in the same style as the protective pavilion has been built to glorify Stalin's memory. Paintings on the walls depict Stalin as a leader even when a child. He is shown reading revolutionary literature to other eight-year-olds on a hilltop and leading youngsters on a fishing excursion. Plaques and exhibits and the guide assure the visitor that Stalin was always an outstanding student. Stalin is shown in Siberian exile in 1902 and leading a railroad workers' strike in 1905.

An interesting mockup shows an illegal printing press operated in a cave which was entered through a tunnel dug in the side of a well shaft.

A gigantic sign that lights up at night in neon letters emblazons the side of Gori's background ridge. It spells out the words in Russian GLORY TO STALIN FOREVER.

There is a small Intourist hotel in Gori which provides lodging for the tourist whose itinerary provides for him to stay overnight, and its restaurant serves the best meals in town.

KHARKOV

Whatever other distinctions Kharkov may enjoy, it can lay claim to having the noisiest hotel in the U.S.S.R. The Intourist Hotel is right on a main street and only the space of a narrow sidewalk separates the hotel's front rooms from rattling, clanging trolley cars. (A quieter hotel out of the center of the city is the Kharkov Hotel.) Unless you have some special reason for wanting to visit Kharkov, we suggest that Kiev, Odessa, or Stalingrad has everything that Kharkov can offer and a good deal more.

Kharkov was 300 years old in 1955. It was founded as a fortress town on growing Russia's southern perimeter. During World War II more than half of the city's housing was destroyed. Kharkov is now an important industrial center in the agricultural Ukraine, with the population of the city proper approaching 1,000,000. It was the capital of the Ukrainian Rejublic until 1934 when Soviet authorities decided to restore the honor to the ancient city of Kiev.

These are some of the places to visit in Kharkov:

The Kharkov College of Agriculture: Founded in 1816, the school trains agricultural specialists.

Kharkov Tractor Factory: It produced its first farm tractor in 1930 and now turns out almost 20,000 tractors a year. Fifteen thousand workers are employed and 50 per cent are women. Like many big Soviet factories, this tractor plant has its own housing projects, hospitals, kindergartens, and theaters. There were 36 apprentices from Communist China learning trades when we went through this factory.

Ukrainian Scientific Research Institute: For anyone interested in cattle-breeding this establishment, spread over many acres, offers a chance to become acquainted with such Soviet breeds as Red Kazakh, Red Steppe, and Gray Ukrainian.

Lysenko Seed Selection Institute: The work of the biologist Trofim Lysenko, respected by Stalin and Khrushchev and discredited by most Western scientists, is carried on here. Pretty dull stuff for anyone who is not a specialist.

Collective and State Farms: There are many in this region, and a visitor to the Ukraine certainly should try to visit at least one. We visited the 4000-acre Karl

Liebknecht Farm where 3800 people live and share, among other things, two passenger cars and sixteen trucks.

Other Places: The Ballet and Opera Theatre and the Shevchenko Dramatic Theatre present performances below the Moscow standard; the State Museum of History is in the mold of similar museums in other cities which trace history from subhuman to Soviet; an enormous statue of the poet-philosopher Shevchenko; the Lopani River Embankment, a pleasant terrace overlooking the city, and the inevitable childrens' railroad so much favored by provincial cities. There are also art galleries, concert halls, sports stadiums, and a pretentions railroad station.

KIEV

Kiev, with more than one million people, is the third largest city in the U.S.S.R. It is in many respects the most beautiful city in the country. Leningrad easily surpasses Kiev in architectural beauty. But Kiev's charm lies in landscape and vegetation. Kiev's tree-covered hills rise steeply from the banks of the broad Dnieper River. Many of its streets are lined with giant chestnut trees and in the springtime it is wonderful to see them in blossom.

Kiev is the capital of the Ukraine, one of the 15 Soviet republics. It is in the fertile "bread basket" of the U.S.S.R. with rich, black earth known as *chernozem,* a word which has found its way into English to describe that desirable type of soil. The Ukraine, and Kiev in particular, also have important industry.

The native language of the region is Ukrainian which differs greatly from Russian. However, Russian also is now taught in all schools.

Kiev and the Ukraine suffered greatly in World War

II. The silver lining in this case has been that Kiev's reconstruction is in better taste than much of that elsewhere in the U.S.S.R.

Kiev is one of the country's oldest cities. It was the center of an important civilization when Moscow was not yet founded. Kiev dates back to the ninth century.

The Ukrainian people tend to be friendlier, more outspoken, more animated than the Russians.

Kiev offers these sights to see and things to do:

Pechersk Monastery: This is one of the holiest places in the Soviet Union. Sometimes called the Lavra, this ancient monastery dates from the days when Kiev was the greatest city-state in Russia. The most outstanding architectural masterpiece on these grounds *was* the Uspensky Cathedral, built between 1073 and 1089. In 1941 the Nazis wantonly demolished the cathedral, but worshipers still pray beside the ruins.

There are many other elaborately decorated buildings on the monastery grounds. One outstanding monument of ancient Russian architecture is the Troyitskaya Church which was erected at the beginning of the twelfth century over the main gate of Pechersk. With its golden cupola and its elaborately and beautifully decorated walls it is truly an exceptional building.

The belfry is almost 300 feet in height, it has four stories, each of them decorated with columns and cornices and crowned with a gilded dome. A model of late baroque style, it was erected between 1731 and 1745.

The Vsyekhsvyatskaya Church is built over another gate and is also a notable structure. It displays the typical Ukrainian architecture used in wooden churches.

However, the catacombs are the outstanding sight here. It was from these caves (*pechery*) that the monastery got its name. During the centuries the network of caves was extended and underground churches were built. Many monks died within the very underground cells in which they worked. Because of a combination of lime soil and atmosphere their bodies were naturally mummified and have become objects of worship. In prerevolutionary days and even today many pilgrims journey to this place which they consider sacred. Monks acting as guides now take tourists through as is done in the Roman catacombs.

It was, by the way, in these subterranean cells that the famous Kiev chronicler Nestor wrote and edited his ancient accounts which form so much of our basis of knowledge of the days when Kiev was a great state.

In olden times a monk might choose to remain in his cell. The door would be sealed and only a small window for receiving food would remain open. When the monk no longer appeared at the window to accept food it was assumed that he had died and the window was sealed too. These openings are now covered with small glass panes, flecked with wax from the tapers of persons going through the tunnels. We tried to peer through such a window, but it was too dark inside to see anything.

At intervals along the underground corridors there are glass-covered caskets, no longer than four or five feet, where naturally mummified bodies lie. These are sanctified monks; golden threaded cloth conceals their faces and bodies. In some cases a brown, shriveled hand, like that of old parchment, is exposed through an opening in the brocade.

Outside on the monastery grounds, during a summer visit, we saw old women clothed in black sitting under the trees. They were waiting to go into the tombs on religious pilgrimages. One came up to an American who was smoking and said sternly, "God will punish you for smoking here."

In 1917 at the time of the revolution there were 6000

monks at this monastery. Seventy-three monks are buried in the catacombs.

There are still about 150 monks at the Pechersk Monastery. They are permitted by the government to continue their religious pursuits, and they also act as guides. They arise at 4:30 in the morning, pray from 5 until 8. Some write music, but their ancient function of recording history is no longer pursued because, as one monkguide told me, "now there is no history of the Pechersk Monastery to write about."

The Monastery Museum, created by a state decree in 1926, has a number of interesting displays. A shrunken, mummified body is preserved in a glass case. Charts are hung with the intention of evoking contempt for the church. For example, one chart attempts to belie the church's claim that only the poor can become saints. Entitled "The Composition of Saints in The Church in Percentages," this unique chart claims that of those granted sainthood by the church 13 per cent were kings, 2.8 per cent had been nobles, 45.1 per cent bishops, 32.7 per cent monks, and only 0.3 per cent had been peasants. (Other individuals of undefined background comprised 6.1 per cent of the saints.)

Sofievsky (or St. Sophia) Cathedral: Now a museum, this cathedral was founded in 1037. It was wrecked by the invasion of the Tartars about 200 years later, and was restored in 1636. With its cluster of gold domes, its pure white color and its proud, ornate blue bell tower, this is one of the memorable sights of Kiev. Inside is the tomb of Yaroslav the Wise, one of the great princes of Kiev, who built the cathedral. Yaroslav was buried here in 1054. There are many interesting frescoes, mosaics and other icons on the walls of this venerable structure. Unlike such art work in other churches, some of these in St. Sophia's portray hunting parties, court entertainment,

and art museums. The Opera and Ballet Theatre is a round-shaped building of unusually modernistic lines. Stalin Prospekt is the city's main street and leads to the road to Moscow.

Its present population is 400,000, but Minsk, like so many other Soviet cities, had to rebuild from the ruins of World War II. Pillage is nothing new to Minsk; it was on the invasion route of the Tartars and of Napoleon before Hitler. Like Odessa and Kiev, Minsk was a center of Jewish population before the war. Most of its Jews were deported to German concentration camps or exterminated in Minsk.

For the souvenir shopper stores in Belorussia and in the Ukraine offer colorful, large sheet notebooks of embroidery designs. Some of these, in the form of imaginative, exotic birds and animals, are attractive enough to be framed.

ODESSA

Odessa gets its name from the ancient Greek colony of Odessus which is supposed to have existed here. Construction was begun on Odessa as an important naval port in 1794 by the great Russian military leader Alexander Suvorov. Previously it had been the site of a small village called Kotsyubievo.

Odessa today has a population of more than 600,000. It is a base for Soviet submarines and warships. It is the most important Soviet Black Sea port, and ships of many nations dock here. If you arrive in the U.S.S.R. by ship this is where you will land.

During World War II Odessa withstood enemy siege for 69 days. It sustained heavy damage. After the war it was given the title of "Hero City" by a decree of the Presidium of the Supreme Soviet of the U.S.S.R.

Just outside the city there are beaches. Seventy resort

hotels ("sanitoria" or "rest homes" are the words preferred in the Soviet lexicon) are situated in Odessa. Annually more than 150,000 Soviet citizens spend their vacations here.

Gunther wrote that "Odessa is the dingiest, most dog-eared city I saw in the U.S.S.R.; it looks as if mold were growing all over it."

A Soviet Government tourist booklet described Odessa this way: "Odessa is one of the Soviet Union's most beautiful cities. Lush greenery covers its parks, gardens, boulevards and its nearby resorts and suburbs."

We found Odessa to fall somewhere between these two descriptions. It certainly is a more attractive city than Kuybyshev or Rostov-on-Don. It has few of the attractive qualities of Kiev or Leningrad. We'd recommend a visit to Odessa only if it doesn't mean sacrificing Moscow, Leningrad, Kiev, Tbilisi, or cities in central Asia.

The names of many famous Russians are associated with Odessa. A number of streets bear the names of renowned citizens. Among the people who lived and worked in Odessa are Pushkin, Gogol, Chaikovsky, Mendeleyev, and Maxim Gorky who was a stevedore on the waterfront. The present-day musicians David Oistrakh and Emil Gilels were educated in Odessa.

The local Intourist hotel is called the Odessa; it is only moderately comfortable but stands on Primorskaya Boulevard with a good view of the port. We were unable to get a room with bath and had to use toilet facilities down the hall. Tourists are sometimes put up at the Krasnaya Hotel which is less comfortable and in the center of town.

These are Odessa's main attractions:

The Port: A boulevard overlooks the amphitheater-shaped port area. The Potemkin Stairs, 425 feet long, form the main entrance to the port from the city. My Intourist guide said that picture-taking of the port was not permitted, but some travelers have been allowed to photograph the area.

Richelieu Memorial: A monument to this French duke stands on the boulevard at the head of the Potemkin Stairs. Richelieu served the Russian Government as Governor-General of Odessa from 1803 to 1814, a period of rapid development for the city. This is one of comparatively few monuments in the U.S.S.R. to a foreigner.

Farms: There are many collective farms near Odessa. Visits can be arranged through the Intourist Service Bureau at the hotel. The Budënny Collective Farm, 40 miles from Odessa, which I visited, covers 8500 acres and has 1172 people living on it.

Other Sights: Odessa's Opera and Ballet Theatre (with double dome and classic columns, it bears a resemblance to the famous Vienna Opera House); the Concert Hall of the Odessa Philharmonic Society (it was the Stock Exchange in Czarist days); the Lysenko Institute (named after the controversial biologist Trofim Lysenko, this institution carries on agricultural research); six museums display objects of Russian and Western art; the Ukrainian Experimental Institute of Eye Disease (notable research in eye disease begun by a well-known Russian scientist, Professor V. Filatov, is pursued in this institution which will particularly interest the traveling medical man), and six parks of "Culture and Rest."

Black Sea Cruises: Odessa is a port of departure for a cruise on the Black Sea. I made the trip on the *Pobeda* (meaning *Victory*), a former German ship taken as war booty. This is one of the Soviet ships used for taking groups of Russian tourists on one-month vacations around Europe, starting at Odessa, sailing through the Black Sea to Turkey and Greece, through the Mediterranean to Italy and France, along Europe's west coast and into the Baltic to end the voyage at Leningrad. On the Black Sea cruise the *Pobeda* and other ships make stops at Yevpatoriya (a resort with a fine sandy beach), Yalta, Novorossiysk (a dismal seaport town), and Batumi. This voyage takes three days. It's a most pleasant way to travel and we recommend it enthusiastically. The ship has a swimming pool, a big dining room, and small but comfortable staterooms.

RIGA

Only very recently opened to tourists, Riga, capital of the Latvian Republic, is one of the most European of Soviet cities in architecture and in the attitude of its people. Latvia enjoyed independence from 1918 to 1940. Then it was overrun by the Russians, and the United States has never recognized this Soviet acquisition of territory. The impression obtained by many visitors is that substantial numbers of Latvians have not accepted it either.

The hotel for tourists is called the Riga, and is quite comfortable.

Founded in the thirteenth century, Riga still retains a medieval character in some of its narrow, charming streets. The sights to see include the Palace of Pioneers which originally was a fourteenth-century castle and the Riga Museum which formerly housed a monastery.

A busy port, Riga is especially worth visiting during the summer months when a tourist can swim in the Baltic Sea from Riga's white sand beaches, among the best in the U.S.S.R.

Because comparatively few foreigners have visited Riga, its Commission Stores (an establishment described in the Moscow chapter on shopping) have proved particularly productive of unusual antiques.

ROSTOV-on-DON

The city's full name is used to distinguish it from another Russian city simply called Rostov. Situated near the mouth of the Don River at the Gulf of Taganrog which is part of the Sea of Azov, Rostov-on-Don is a major industrial center. It has little to recommend it to the tourist except as a place to start or end a trip on the Volga-Don Canal. One day is time enough to spend in Rostov-on-Don.

Rostov-on-Don is called the "Gateway of the Caucasus" because an extensive network of railroad lines extends southwards from it into the Caucasus Mountain regions along the Black Sea coast and in the Republics of Georgia, Armenia, and Azerbaijan. Not far from Rostov-on-Don lies a broad belt of excellent agricultural land known as the Kuban which is second only to the Ukraine in natural fertility.

Although not as pretty as Kiev on the Dnieper River, Rostov on the Don River also looks most attractive when seen from the river. On Saturday afternoons and Sunday during the summer small sailboats (some privately owned, others owned by sporting clubs) skim over the broad river.

This city can be reached by plane, train or ship, but I traveled there by car from Krasnodar (in the center of the Kuban agricultural area), about 150 miles to the south. It is a good two-lane road through farmland with very little traffic except for an infrequent truck. As on other highways, occasional billboards advertise government slogans to increase meat and milk production or to announce "Glory to the Communist Party!"

As for the inevitable statistics: Rostov-on-Don (population 560,000) has 23 research institutes, seven institutions of higher education, 30 vocational schools, a botanical garden, several theaters, museums, a library with more than a million books, and a big recreational park on an island in the middle of the Don. In addition to these places, you may care to visit a factory or a farm.

Rostov Tractor Factory: This huge industrial plant near the center of town produces enormous combines, tractors and other agricultural machinery. Working on three shifts, the 17,000 employees (30 per cent of them are women) earn an average wage of 780 rubles ($78) a month.

Lenin Collective Farm: There are many collective and state farms within a two hour drive of Rostov-on-Don. This particular one covers more than 8000 acres and its widely diversified activities include breeding hogs and cattle, raising chickens and keeping bees. Two hundred and forty families totaling 1100 people live on the farm. Of these only two own their own cars, 30 own motorcycles and 100 have bicycles.

Hotels and Restaurants: There's no choice of hotels. The Moskovskaya Hotel is *it* and is comfortable as provincial hotels go. The hotel's restaurant is good. On a trip from Sochi to Moscow our plane put down at Rostov-on-Don and we had an excellent meal with chicken croquettes as the main course at the airport restaurant. Black bread, which is tasty everywhere in the Soviet Union, seemed especially delicious in Rostov.

SOCHI

Sochi and Yalta are our two favorite places on the Black Sea. Nestled at the foot of the luxuriant green Caucasus Mountains, Sochi basks in six-month sunshine

the night at Lake Ritsa's excellent hotel, but can be made in one day.

Other Sights: Sochi also has a fine opera and ballet theater, an open-air theater seating 1763 people, a botanical garden, and souvenir shops (a unique item available in Sochi is a sun hat of white felt, shaped in the form of a cone and edged with woolly fringe, which is remarkably cool in the blistering summer sun). Even if you don't want to swim, be sure and visit one or two of the many "rest homes" or "sanatoria." Built high in the hills, several have private funiculars for transporting guests to the beaches. The dining rooms are cavernous, and serve special health foods to those requiring it. A good way to get a glimpse of many of these rest homes as well as the lovely coast is by hiring one of the small, chauffeured speedboats that line the city harbor, and having an hour's spin along the sea.

STALINGRAD

Stalingrad is a dull city with an exciting history. It was a turning point in World War II. The city was almost completely demolished and literally has been rebuilt from the ground up.

Until 1925, the city was called Tsaritsyn. During the so-called de-Stalinization campaign of 1956, an attempt was made by Soviet newspapers to encourage people to use the old name. However very few did and there has been no official action to change the name that gained such great fame during World War II. (The names of other cities *have* been changed. For example, the city of Molotov has assumed its old name of Perm.)

Stalingrad is on the Volga River and is an important shipping port as well as an industrial center. Its piers and smoke stacks stretch along 35 miles of river bank.

Stalingrad is situated along that portion of the Volga
River which is the nearest to the Don River. The Volga
and Don Rivers were linked by a giant "ditch," the
Volga-Don Canal, which was opened on July 27, 1952.
Stalingrad has a population of over a half million.

Nazi tanks appeared near Stalingrad in August 1942.
The siege of the city began in early September. For
nearly 200 days soldiers and civilians fought the Battle
of Stalingrad from street to street, from house to house,
from room to room. The Soviet counterattack began on
November 19, 1942. A pincer was closed on the Germans, trapping huge Nazi armies in the jaws of a trap.
On January 8, 1943, the Soviet command sent the Germans a demand to surrender unconditionally. Two days
later the Russians began their drive to exterminate or
capture the entrapped men. The last shots of the war
were fired on the Mamai Hill; it is remembered as the
bloodiest battle of the Stalingrad campaign.

In this dramatic counteroffensive 330,000 German officers and men surrendered or were taken prisoner. Scores
of generals and other high-ranking officers were among
them.

The destruction was more total than that suffered by
any other Soviet city. With their fondness for statistics,
Soviet Intourist interpreter-guides will tell you that Stalingrad today has about 25 per cent more living space
than before the war. The city has 120 schools, almost 200
kindergartens, 25 hospitals, 36 clinics, and 82 libraries.

There are several ways to reach Stalingrad. There is
regular airplane and train service from Moscow. However, it is preferable to arrive in Stalingrad by ship. A
Volga River cruise which is available to tourists starts
at Moscow, proceeds through the Moscow-Volga Canal,
and down the Volga River to Kazan, Ulyanovsk, Kuybyshev, and Saratov. The other river route is via the Volga-

Don Canal, which connects Stalingrad and the city of Rostov-on-Don.

The Volga-Don Canal is sixty-three miles long, and was built in two and a half years, using German prisoners of war for a major part of the labor force. The first ship to enter the canal and begin regular passenger and freight service was named the *Joseph Stalin*. The Volga-Don Canal is Soviet architecture on the grand scale. It is also a testimony to Soviet engineering skill.

Besides providing a link between the Volga and Don Rivers, the canal also created lakes whose waters are the source of hydroelectric power. This electricity made big, new industrial projects possible along the canal route. The man-made lakes are contained by thirteen hydroelectric dams and dikes. The largest lake is called the Tsimlyanskoye Sea. It inundated former villages and farm lands covering 1400 square miles, an area somewhat smaller than the Great Salt Lake in Utah with its area of 2000 square miles. Thirteen thousand people were moved from their homes before the flood took place. The valleys of the submerged terrain make for depths of seventy-five feet in some parts of the Tsimlyanskoye Sea. By comparison with the Volga-Don Canal's sixty-three miles of length and fifteen locks, the Panama Canal is fifty miles long and has five locks.

Most of the ships on the Volga-Don Canal are sidewheelers, reminiscent of the showboats which once plied the Mississippi.

On the trip from Rostov-on-Don, the canal begins at a bend of the Don River. The entrance is marked by a white stone monument shaped like a towering lighthouse, with black metal ship prows jetting out in the four directions of the compass. For a half mile or so the canal consists of a ditch, scarcely wider than the ship itself, paved with white stones. Meadowland stretches to the horizon on either side. The portals of the first lock are marked by a stone tower decorated with statues of hard-riding Cossacks. Traveling from Rostov-on-Don to Stalingrad a ship is raised 132 feet by the first eight locks of the canal, and then is lowered 270 feet by the seven remaining locks to the level of the Volga River.

Except for the traveler with time to spare, one full day in Stalingrad is enough for a tour of the city's highlights: a drive through this newly constructed metropolis, a visit to Mamai Hill, an hour in the Museum of the Defense of Stalingrad, and a boat ride to the Stalingrad Dam. These and other sights are described below:

Museum of the Defense of Stalingrad: This is a small museum but one of the most moving I've visited in Russia. The events commemorated in its halls are mostly not of the distant past. The photographs, maps, weapons, and documents are evocative of the heroism of the soldiers and civilians who fought for Stalingrad. Unfortunately, the first few rooms are devoted to early Soviet events which are totally out of place here. The first room is devoted to the 1917 revolution. The second room depicts events during the civil war that followed the revolution. The most interesting item here is the original telegraph key on which Stalin in Tsaritsyn (Stalingrad's original name) sent Lenin (in Moscow) a message pleading that food be sent to the starving populace. According to the guide, Lenin did so. The rest of the rooms are more interesting. There is the rifle and the photograph of a sniper who is supposed to have killed more than 300 Germans in the streets of Stalingrad.

A scroll dated May 17, 1944, bears a message signed by President Franklin D. Roosevelt. It reads: "In the name of the people of the United States of America, I present this scroll to the City of Stalingrad to commemorate our admiration for its gallant defenders whose courage, fortitude and devotion during the siege of September 13, 1942 to January 31, 1943 will inspire forever the hearts of all free people. Their glorious victory stemmed the tide of invasion and marked the turning point in the war of the Allied Nations against the forces of aggression."

The museum also displays a jeweled sword presented by King George VI of England as a token of congratulations for the Stalingrad victory.

House of Architecture: A table top model of the city of Stalingrad is used by a lecturer in this institution to describe the destruction and rebirth of Stalingrad. More impressive, though, is the movie shown in the auditorium. It consists of actual battle film and is a heartrending reminder of the Battle of Stalingrad.

Stalingrad Tractor Factory: It is often easier to arrange to tour a factory in the provinces than in Moscow or Leningrad. This plant, founded in 1930, destroyed during the war (when it was making tanks), and rebuilt in 1944, now turns out farm machinery. It employs 14,000 workers. Twenty-five per cent of them are women. The assembly lines produce more than 25,000 big tractors a year, but some aspects of the process (especially the transfer of parts from one assembly line to another by human heft) are outdated.

The Port: The main river gateway to the city is in a style of architecture which may best be described as "Soviet-Grecian." A monumental flight of stone steps, 120 feet from river to road level, is finished in red and gray polished granite. The broad stairs with decorative columns and statues stretch along the bank of the Volga. If you arrive by ship, you will climb these steps to get into a car for the drive to the hotel. If you arrive by train or plane, be sure to drive past this area.

Mamai Hill or Mound: This was the scene of some of the fiercest battles in the western outskirts of Stalingrad. Today it has been converted into a memorial park with a good view of the city. There is a monument dedicated to the memory of those who died in Stalingrad's defense. It still is possible to find empty bullet and artillery shells and even helmets of German soldiers on the scrub-covered slopes of Mamai Hill, but souvenir hunters are quickly depleting this source of macabre mementoes.

Stalingrad Hydroelectric Project: This new, gigantic dam with its auxiliary projects is situated about fifteen miles from the city. The trip usually is made by boat although it can be reached by road. At full operating capacity the hydroelectric station supplies 11,000,000,000 kilowatt hours of electricity annually. (By comparison, the Grand Coulee Dam on the Columbia River in the State of Washington, the largest dam in the U.S.A., is capable of producing 14,698,303,400 kilowatt hours per year.) Even if dams and electricity are not your strong points you may find a visit to this enormous power plant —one of the biggest in the U.S.S.R.—interesting as an example of Russia's rapid industrialization.

Other Sights: The Planetarium (Stalingraders are proud of this, but it will interest only the astronomy-minded tourist); the Central Square of Fallen Heroes (which crosses Peace Street and honors the memory of the war dead); the railroad station (in "Stalingrad-grandiose" architecture), and the Opera and Ballet Theatre (in "provincial-Bolshoi" style).

Hotels and Restaurants: There are two hotels for tourists in Stalingrad. The newest and most comfortable is the Intourist Hotel at Mira Ulitsa 16. Older, less comfortable, and gloomy is the Stalingrad Hotel at Mira Ulitsa 12. Both hotels have fair restaurants.

SUKHUMI

Sukhumi (population 55,000) lies at the foot of snow-peaked mountains on the eastern shore of the Black Sea. It is a favorite summer resort for the Soviet people and claims to have the most moderate climate in the whole U.S.S.R. with swimming from April to October. Oranges, lemons, and tea grow in this subtropical climate.

In the characteristically lavish words of a Soviet travel folder: "The city stands on the shore of a broad, calm bay. Long rows of graceful palms, cypresses, eucalypti and magnolias line its bright, sun-flooded streets and esplanade. The background formed by their luxuriant foliage accentuates the beauty of the snow-white sanitariums, apartment houses and municipal buildings."

For our taste, Sukhumi has too much of a city atmosphere for a seaside resort and we recommend Sochi or Yalta for your Black Sea stop. If you do go to Sukhumi, these are some of the sights you might care to see:

Monkey Colony: Soviet scientists have a remarkable research station near Sukhumi, founded in 1927, where generations of monkeys are studied for information about various diseases. A number of visiting physicians and journalists have received permission to tour the colony. The full name is Medical-Biology Station of the Academy of Medicine of the U.S.S.R.

Botanical Garden: For those interested in species of trees, plants, and flowers.

Mount Sukhumi: A pleasant short trip from town.

Beaches: Ask the Intourist office at your hotel to arrange for you to swim and sunbathe at a "sanitarium" beach rather than at the public beach. It is cleaner and less crowded.

Lake Ritsa: Accessible by car either from Sochi or Sukhumi, this spectacularly scenic mountain lake is well worth the side trip.

TBILISI

This is a fascinating city in an engrossing section of the U.S.S.R. Tbilisi is the capital of the Soviet Republic of Georgia, for centuries an independent kingdom, a land of proud mountaineers, the region where Stalin was born and still is greatly admired. Droopy, Stalin-type mustaches even now are favored by many of Georgia's dark-skinned men. More Middle Eastern than Russian, the Georgians have their own alphabet and language, their national costumes, drama, songs, food, and fiery temperament. The Georgian name for the city, Tbilisi, is now used by Soviet authorities in deference to Georgian pride. Tbilisi means "hot springs." Tiflis is the Russian word for the city and still is used sometimes. The population of Tbilisi is almost 800,000.

Dramatically set among mountains in the valley of the Kura River, Tbilisi is one of the oldest cities in the world. Founded in the fourth century B.C., Tbilisi was for hundreds of years a trading post between Asia and Europe. From the twelfth to fifteenth centuries the Kingdom of Georgia held sway over almost the entire Caucasus Mountain land bridge between the Caspian and Black Seas.

We stayed at the Intourist Hotel on Rustaveli Street. There is no elevator and the high ceilings make for a long climb on the broad stone staircase. The rooms are large and airy which is a lifesaver in Tbilisi's hot weather lasting from spring to autumn. On the second floor lobby hangs a painting of Stalin bidding farewell to Lenin who is fleeing into exile from the shore of the Bay of Finland. This is a departure which Stalin did not witness, but it is not uncommon for Georgians, who were favored during Stalin's rule, to glorify their hero's role.

A gift shop in the hotel's second floor lobby sells various items including a small Georgian stringed instrument which would make an exotic souvenir.

The hotel's ground floor restaurant seems disorganized but the food is good. See the section on the Aragvi Restaurant in Moscow for Georgian dishes. A local drink is *Kruschon,* a concoction of two bottles of Georgian Wine number 1 (known as *Tsinondoli*), one bottle of flavored soda water (the flavor depends on individual preference), a half tumbler of cognac, lemon slices, and sugar according to taste.

There is much to see in Tbilisi and the traveler would do well to set three or four days aside for the visit including a one-day trip to Gori, Stalin's birthplace.

Rustaveli Street: This is Tbilisi's main street, named after a Georgian poet. Broad and tree-lined, it is the address of important government buildings (including the Supreme Soviet legislature and the Council of Ministers) and many stores. An unusual souvenir to buy in Tbilisi is the national Georgian vessel for drinking wine. It looks just like the animal horns slung over the shoulders of American frontiersmen in olden days for carrying gunpowder. Trimmed with ornamental silver, one of these horns makes an attractive decoration for a wall or mantelpiece.

Palace of Pioneers: A low, gray stone building, this was once the residence of the Czarist governor general (Georgia came under Russian suzerainty in 1801). After 1921 this mansion on Rustaveli Street became a government headquarters and more recently it was converted into an elaborate center for youth activities.

Metakhi Castle: This structure traces its origins back 1500 years. Dramatically poised on one of the high ridges overhanging the swift, gray, muddy Kura River, this multi-sided, cone-shaped tower used to be the residence of the Georgian kings. It is mentioned in the epic poem, "Knight in Tiger Skin," by the poet Rustaveli, translated into many languages, about Queen Tamara (a woman, as the name implies) who ruled Georgia in the late twelfth and early thirteenth centuries. This building was used as a prison by the Czars during the nineteenth century.

Narinkala Fortress: On the steep bank of the Kura River opposite the Metakhi Castle, this ancient fortification dates back to the fourth century. Its name is roughly translated as "the fortress which cannot be taken" and supposedly was so named by the Persians who assaulted it without success. The castle and the fortress dominate the approaches to Tbilisi at a point where the Kura River flows around a curve in a deep, narrow gorge.

Cioni or **Zion Cathedral:** This is the main cathedral of the Georgian Orthodox faith which differs in many respects from the Russian and Greek Orthodox. Services still are held in this cathedral which was constructed in the fifth century and repeatedly destroyed by foreign invasions. It is on Lasaledze Street, and our guide explained that this and other Tbilisi streets were purposely laid out by the ancient Georgians to be very narrow for two reasons. First, in order to deny enemy cavalry room for maneuver and secondly, to provide shade from the brutal summer sun.

The most treasured relic in this cathedral is a cross woven with vines and the hair of the now sainted woman named Nina who is said to have brought Christianity to Georgia in 327 A.D. Georgians managed to hide this cross from capture by Turkish, Persian, and other invaders. Worshipers now kneel and kiss the small shrine where the cross is kept.

Mtatsminda Mountain or **Holy Mountain** or **Mount David:** Known by several names, the summit of this ridge which dominates the Tbilisi skyline is reached by an enclosed funicular car. The view from the funicular and from the recommended restaurant on top is spectacular and should not be missed.

The National Museums of Georgian History and of Georgian Art: A plaque on the wall outside this building reads: "Great Stalin, the leader of the Communist Party of the Soviets and of Proletarians of all the world lived and studied here in a former religious seminary from September 1, 1894, until May 29, 1899, leading the illegal workers' circles in the city of Tbilisi."

It is a fact that Stalin's early education was in the seminary once housed in this building, but it is doubtful whether Stalin at that early age was the leader of the local revolutionary activities.

The seminary, despite its distinguished alumnus, has long ago been shut down and now two museums are housed here. By far the most interesting is the Museum of Georgian Art. It includes one of the most impressive collections of icons to be seen anywhere in the U.S.S.R. including the Tretyakov Museum in Moscow. A visit is strongly recommended.

Mtskheta: This may seem unpronounceable, but Georgians have no trouble with it. Mtskheta was the ancient capital of Georgia until the fifth century when it was moved to Tbilisi, about 25 miles away. A church on the site of the old capital dates from the eleventh century and several Georgian kings are buried here.

Other Places of Interest: There is the usual opera and ballet theater (don't miss a chance to see a performance of the *unusual* Georgian ballet version of *Othello*); the Georgian National Theatre (it presents works of Georgian as well as of Soviet origin), and the Georgian University.

UZHGOROD

If you travel by car from Czechoslovakia, Uzhgorod is the Soviet border city you will pass through. We've never been there ourselves, but those who have say it is only a place to drive *through* on the way to more interesting places. Uzhgorod belonged to Czechoslovakia until the end of World War II when the U.S.S.R. acquired it. Lumber, cut in the wooded mountains of this Transcarpathian region, and cattle are its main activities. Uzhgorod's sights include a castle (built in the 1200s on a hill overlooking the city and the Uzh River) and a children's railroad in the main park.

YALTA

Yalta is best known for the wartime conference held there by Stalin, Roosevelt, and Churchill in 1945. It is also a beautifully situated town in a mountain-ringed cove where a salubrious climate provides sunshine and flowers six months of the year.

Yalta is on the southern shore of the Crimea. The Crimea is a peninsula that almost ended up as an island. It is connected to the mainland by the narrow Perekop Isthmus which is only a half-dozen miles wide. The Crimea has a long and often bloody history. The Greeks settled here in the fifth century B.C. and it was a Roman colony during the time of the Caesars. It was overrun by the Tartars. In more recent times the Crimean War was fought on its territory from 1853 to 1856; during the days of the Civil War of 1918–1921 it was a last refuge of many aristocratic families owning mansions here. Some of these people finally fled in ships. The Crimea also was invaded by the Nazis.

Nowadays Yalta is one of the principal summer resorts of the U.S.S.R. In a Riviera-like setting with rugged mountains rising sharply behind stony beaches, Yalta has 200 "sanitoria" and "rest homes" for Russians on holiday. We recommend a visit either to Yalta or Sochi, especially if you want to interrupt an arduous tour with a few days of comparative rest.

Yalta has a year-round population of 35,000, but ten times that number of Soviet citizens visit it anually. Russians are guaranteed vacation time by law. In most cases it is from two to four weeks a year. In 1919 Lenin issued a decree ordering that all confiscated mansions and palaces of the Czars and the rich in favorable locations be converted into vacation resorts. An obelisk monument in a Yalta park is inscribed with the words of Lenin's decree.

The main hotel for the foreign tourist is the Yushnaya, adequately comfortable with an average restaurant.

Besides sunbathing and swimming there are these sights to see in and around Yalta:

Livadia Palace: Once a summer residence of Czar Nicholas II on a promontory overlooking the Black Sea, Livadia Palace has been converted into a vacation sanitorium for workers with respiratory complaints. They lounge on wooden benches along the paved paths of the estate often wearing striped pajamas, a customary Soviet vacation garment. Russians not only wear pajamas to bed but also on trains, on the beach, on ship deck and when strolling on the streets of Yalta or other resort towns.

A month at Livadia costs a worker (who is able to obtain a scarce ticket from his trade union council) 1400 rubles ($140), but the worker pays only 35 per cent of this amount; the trade union pays the rest.

The main Livadia mansion and its outlying buildings consist of 68 rooms and, with dormitory sleeping, can accommodate 750 guests. The staff includes 550 maids, waiters, waitresses and cooks. There are 54 doctors employed at Livadia.

The large room in which the actual Yalta Conference took place is now a dining room furnished with small square tables with four chairs at each. A ground-floor reading room, its walls covered with deep-red damask, was Roosevelt's study. A nearby room, with a brick fireplace and walls decorated in orange, was Stalin's study. It serves as an annex to the dining room. The room in which the Czars once played billiards is now a bathroom. The Czar's chapel no longer is used for religious services. The Czarina's private rooms now serve as sleeping quarters for Livadia's women guests.

The imposing, columned buildings with broad porches are constructed of gray Inkurmen stone quarried near Sevastopol, not far from Yalta on the Crimea Peninsula.

Massandra Winery: Steep, narrow roads that climb from Yalta's shores lead to the state-run Massandra Wine Cellar where grapes, grown on the shores of the Black Sea, are made into wine for sale in government stores. It is a most interesting place. In racks along the walls of seven deep underground tunnels totaling 500 feet in length are stored thousands of bottles of wine. Some are of recent vintage. Others are aged from two to five years in barrels and for ten years in bottles before being sold. Among the Massandra's "museum" items is a bottle of

Spanish wine corked in 1775. This is the oldest, but the racks also hold 200 bottles which are a century old. These are wines taken from the Czar's cellars. The Czarist seal can be seen on the bottles which, if opened, would probably now yield vinegar rather than wine.

The father of the Massandra manager, Constantin Saitzsev, worked in vineyards for the Czar. Saitzsev proudly explained that Massandra's main product is a *muscat,* a light dessert wine. He added that the writer Maxim Gorky once said that *muscat* concentrates the energy of the sun and introduces that energy into the stomach of man when he drinks it.

This winery produces 15,000 barrels holding 1,500,000 gallons of wine annually. Visiting tourists usually are offered a glass.

Drives: There are many attractive health resorts within a short drive from Yalta's palm-lined main street. Among them are Gurzuf, Mishkor, Gaspra, Koreiz, Simeiz, and Alupka.

Other Sights: The Nikitsky Botanical Garden (between Yalta and the village of Gurzuf commands a fine view of the sea and offers the visitor with an interest in plants and flowers a splendid collection of local flora); the Chekhov Museum (the house in which author and playwright Anton Chekhov lived for a number of years); the Vorontsov Palace (in which Winston Churchill's delegation stayed during the Yalta Conference), and excavations of Stone Age dwellings and of an ancient naval fortress of Roman times.

YEREVAN

This remote capital of the Armenian Republic of the U.S.S.R. is visited by few tourists, but almost everyone who does get there reports meeting at least one Armenian with a relative in the U.S.A. Yerevan's origins date back to 660 B.C., and there still are many remnants of the city's antiquity. Armenia has its own church which differs greatly from the Russian Orthodox faith.

Yerevan, with its population of almost 400,000, lies in the shadow of Mount Ararat (just under 17,000 feet high). Mount Ararat is only one of the many towering peaks in this country of great rugged beauty.

The Hotel Armenia is the local Intourist Hotel, and the dishes to order in its restaurant are described in the section on the Ararat Restaurant in Moscow.

CHAPTER SEVENTEEN

Central Asia: Tashkent, Stalinabad, Samarkand, Bukhara

The story is told of the initiation of a group of youngsters into the "Pioneers," the grammar-school-age Soviet organization which includes almost all of the nation's youth. Every youngster was asked the same set of questions.

"Who is your mother?"

"The Communist Party," replied each boy and girl in turn, "because it takes care of all my needs."

"Who is your father?" was the next question.

"Nikita Sergeyevich Khrushchev," came the ritualistic answer from each "Pioneer" candidate, "because he is working for my welfare."

"And what do you want to be when you grow up?"

There is some latitude in answering this question. One boy says he wants to be an engineer, another dreams of being a soccer star, a third aspires to be a scientist.

Finally comes the turn of little Ivan.

"Who is your mother?"

"The Communist Party," answers Ivan, "because it takes care of all my needs."

"And who is your father?"

"Nikita Sergeyevich Khrushchev," replied Ivan, "because he is working for my welfare."

"And what do you want to be when you grow up?"

"An orphan," replies little Ivan.

369

This story may well come to mind if you journey into the central Asian region of the U.S.S.R. This is an area that differs from Russia in the color of the people, their language, their religious background, their history, their culture, and in their clothing. This is a region remote from Moscow, incorporated into the U.S.S.R. by force of arms. It's no wonder that not a few of its inhabitants feel like little Ivan in his attitude toward his "maternal" and "paternal" bonds.

A FEW BASIC FACTS

This is a region of fabulous history. The legions of Alexander the Great and of Tamerlane trod its soil. Its cities lay astride the great ancient silk and spice trade routes between Middle East and Asia. As late as the first quarter of this century a cruel despot, the Emir of Bukhara, who sometimes subjected foreign envoys to cruel tortures including death by imprisonment in pits inhabited by giant bugs, ruled over a kingdom that included much of what has now been carved up into separate Soviet republics. In our travels we have found this to be the most fascinating region of the U.S.S.R., although it is in no respect *typical* of the rest of the country.

Central Asia is the heartland of Asia, a land-locked region that includes Mongolia, provinces of China, and a part of the U.S.S.R. Five Soviet republics lie completely or partly within that loosely defined region. The republics of Uzbekistan, Tadzhikistan, Turkmenistan, Kirghizia and most of Kazakhstan are within central Asia.

Soviet central Asia borders on Iran, Afghanistan, and China. It covers an area almost equal to India and Pakistan.

The population of about 30,000,000 consists mostly of Uzbeks and Tadzhiks, but very many Russians have been transported to the area, originally as administrators, teachers and overseers, but now in a broader spectrum of jobs. There are other nationalities here, too—Kazakhs, Kirghiz, Jews, Kalmuks, Tartars, and others. The Moslem faith is predominant among the people of central Asia.

The cities open for tourist travel in central Asia are Tashkent, Stalinabad, Samarkand, and Alma-Ata (meaning "Father of Apples," a modernized city against a backdrop of snow-capped mountains, the capital of Kazakhstan, with less of interest to offer than the other central Asian cities). On my trips I found Bukhara to be the most memorable city of this region; it *has* been visited by tourists, but is not on the usual list. It is such an unusual place that I cover it in this chapter in the hope that it will open up or that you may be able to convince Intourist to let you in; some important visitors have, such as Supreme Court Justice William O. Douglas.

By the way, almost every spring, usually late in March, central Asia is closed for about two weeks to all foreigners—diplomats as well as tourists. This seems to be the season for military maneuvers and Soviet authorities do not want foreign eyes catching sight of the movements of military equipment or foreign ears hearing the launching "whoosh" of missiles. It's best not to plan to travel in central Asia during late March and early April. Remember, too, that summer comes early here. In March, while often still glacial weather in Moscow, fruit trees and flowers are in full bloom in Samarkand. Take along appropriate, lightweight clothing.

TASHKENT

Tashkent is the capital of the republic of Uzbekistan, and is the largest city in the central Asian region of the Soviet Union. Its population is about 1,000,000.

It takes four days by train to travel the 2000 miles from

Moscow to Tashkent, but only four *hours* by the new swift Soviet jet passenger plane.

In some respects the city of Tashkent is as far from Moscow as the four-day train ride and in other respects as close as the four-hour jet.

The imprint of 30-odd years of Soviet rule is as unmistakable as the hammer and sickle flag that flies over public buildings in Tashkent, but Asiatic Tadzhik women still wash clothes in streams flowing near their mud-hut villages.

Some women still conceal their faces behind thick veils, turbaned men with dark skins and Oriental features ride on ridiculously small but sturdy donkeys, and modern plumbing and sewerage are projects for the future in the ancient city of Bukhara, a short plane ride from Tashkent.

Tashkent, whose history goes back to the seventh century and includes such colorful episodes as its capture by Genghis Khan in the thirteenth century, is fast becoming a modern city. The farther into the countryside one travels from this capital the farther one is transported into an earlier age of tiny gray mud huts, barefooted children and women following respectfully behind the male on burro-back.

Tashkent once was a famous commission city where merchants on the ancient trade route between Samarkand and Peking came to trade their wares. Now Tashkent is on a route of another sort. Airplanes from India, China, Pakistan, and Afghanistan put down on the long runways of its modern airport (where the clocks keep Moscow time although it's three hours later here). These aircraft, many of them now Soviet TU-104 jets, carry a steady influx of delegations of students, writers, teachers, parliamentarians, and persons from many other walks of life, all invited to the U.S.S.R. To a traveler from the United States, Canada, or Britain—or even from Moscow

—Tashkent may seem drab, provincial, but to the visitor from a poor Indian village or from illiterate Afghanistan, Tashkent must seem like the promise of a better life under Communism.

The word "Tashkent" means "stone fortress" and before the eleventh century it was pronounced Shashkent; the ancient name of the whole area was Chach and that of its center was Chach, Chachkent, or Shashkent.

Tashkent is located in an oasis in the mountains. It is one of the sunniest places in the U.S.S.R.; in fact it is claimed that the number of sunny days is equal to those in Egypt.

RUSSIAN INFLUENCE

To this heartland city of Asia the Russians have brought their language, their culture, their statues of Lenin and Stalin, and their army.

Most of Tashkent's main streets now bear Soviet rather than the indigenous Uzbek names. Kirov Street is lined with the same grandiose eight-story apartment houses as is Moscow's Gorky Street or East Berlin's Stalinallee. Lenin Street is crossed by Karl Marx Avenue (one of the few instances in the Soviet Union where Marx and Lenin follow divergent lines).

Like Moscow's main park, Tashkent's bears the name of Maxim Gorky, the revolutionary poet and author. Tashkent's Gorky Park of Culture and Rest is landmarked by a brown-brick clock tower and Uzbek intellectuals with a cosmopolitan frame of mind refer to it as Tashkent's "Big Ben."

A steady stream of Russians have been sent to Uzbekistan as administrators, educators, doctors, and technicians, and the influx has raised Tashkent's population to its present status as the Soviet Union's fifth largest city after Moscow, Leningrad, Kiev, and Stalingrad. The population of almost 1,000,000 is about evenly divided between Russians and peoples of central Asian origin such as Uzbeks, Tadzhiks, and Turkmens. One-eighth of the total population of the republic of Uzbekistan lives in Tashkent.

The guides assigned to show the travelers around emphasize that under Communism illiteracy has been all but wiped out among people below sixty years of age, a school system of compulsory education has been introduced, sanitation and a free public health system has reduced disease and lengthened life expectancy. A vast network of irrigation canals has made Tashkent a cotton-growing center.

The Soviet guides deny that any effort to eliminate the native culture and to impose Russia's was involved in the 1946 decision to substitute the Russian (Cyrillic) alphabet for the Arabic script of the Uzbek natives of the region. It's pointed out that newspapers are published in both Russian and in Uzbek (with its new alphabet), that there are plays and movies in both languages, and that schools and courts are conducted in both tongues. It's indignantly denied that this implies two systems of justice, one for the native Uzbek and another for the Russian newcomer.

Youngsters wear the Soviet school uniform at Russian language schools, but at the schools taught in Uzbek and preferred by much of the native population, little girls make up their faces—in characteristic Uzbek style—with a thick green line connecting their eyebrows.

WHERE TO STAY IN TASHKENT

The Tashkent Hotel is where Intourist puts up most travelers. Occasionally a delegation will be billeted in a government-owned villa at the edge of town. The Tashkent Hotel is one of the most modern in central Asia although it is below Moscow standards. Luckily, the rooms have high ceilings which is a life-saver in Tashkent's summer heat. There's a post office, a newspaper stand, and a souvenir counter in the lobby.

WHAT TO SEE IN TASHKENT

Supreme Soviet Building: This is the republican legislature of Uzbekistan. It passes local laws in conformance with broader laws passed in Moscow. By the way, each of the Soviet republics has its own Ministry of Foreign Affairs. This is intended to lend an aura of sovereignty, but none of the republics can assign its own ambassadors or conduct its own foreign policy. This is done only by the Soviet Union's Ministry of Foreign Affairs in Moscow. However, on the basis of this pretense of sovereignty, the U.S.S.R. has three delegations at the United Nations—one for the U.S.S.R. as a whole, one for the Ukraine, and one for Byelorussia. In front of this Tashkent legislature stands a larger-than-life-size statue of Lenin on a pedestal of the same red granite and of similar pyramid design as the Lenin-Stalin Mausoleum in Red Square in Moscow.

State Museum of Art: Its most interesting exhibits are of centuries-old tile work that decorated the domes and walls of buildings in an era when central Asia was a bustling center of civilization. Tapestry, rugs, and wood carvings are shown. The museum is housed in a former theater, and its slanted floor introduces the added element of possible vertigo to the other risks (sore feet, eyestrain) of museumgoing. There is also a History Museum run by the Uzbek Academy of Sciences in Tashkent.

Old Quarter: This is the most interesting section of Tashkent with its *gualah* (the Uzbek language word for baked clay) native homes. This is a rapidly constricting quarter of the city as new construction sweeps it away. The broad main streets of Tashkent's more modern areas are named with signs in two languages, Uzbek and Russian, and traffic is directed by signal lights of the customary red, green, and amber colors. But in Tashkent's old section tortuous lanes are scarcely wide enough for a single car to pass. Central Asian peoples live here much as they did before the Communists incorporated the area. Children peer out of openings in mud walls. A youngster of school age stepped forward in a market place to ask this traveler where he was from. When the reply was "the United States," the boy clapped his forehead and gasped, as if it had been Mars. But, deep in central Asia, the United States seems no nearer in many ways than Mars.

Bazaar: For the taste and scent of the Orient, be sure to visit the market place in the old section of Tashkent. Uzbek women with brightly colored shawls over their heads sell vegetables, strange cuts of meat, and *non*, the native round bread, freshly baked and with highly spiced crusts.

There are some truly beautiful striped native Uzbek fabrics sold in small shops around the bazaar. These can be made into striking dresses once you are home. Characteristic men's coats are also for sale here. They are quilted, often in blue calico patterns with contrasting piping—a little below knee-length—and make splendid winter lounging robes for either men or women.

Statues: Besides the statue of Lenin in front of the republic legislature building, there are others worthy of note such as a starkly sculptured figure of Alisher Novayi, Uzbek poet-philosopher of the fifteenth century. Most statues are of Russians. There are statues of V. Kuybyshev, M. I. Kalinin and M. Frunze, all of whom played a role in establishing Soviet rule in central Asia.

Theaters: Here's a chance to see performances of Uzbek drama, dance, and song. There are nine theaters in Tashkent. The leading one is the state Drama Theatre. Such classics as *Hamlet* and *Othello* are shown as well as Uzbek dramas. Worth seeing, but you may want to leave before it's over.

The Uzbek Opera and Ballet Theatre is the local "Bolshoi," but lacking in the talent of the Moscow company. The fine building was constructed in 1947. If you've missed ballet elsewhere on your trip in the U.S.S.R., see it here.

The Tashkent Circus, like others in the U.S.S.R., changes its program regularly, and draws its cast of state-employed performers from all over. Like other Soviet circuses, it is usually good fun.

Sports: The new Pakhtakor Stadium seats 50,000 people. Enthusiasm for soccer is as great in central Asia as elsewhere in the U.S.S.R.

Ancient Structures: Moslem architecture of the sixteenth century is preserved in a number of buildings: the Kukeldash Medresse (Moslem religious school), the Marakkhan Medresse, and the mausoleum of Kafali Shasi.

Mosque: We found a visit to a religious service at a mosque to be one of the most interesting parts of our central Asian trips. (Less strict than Moslems elsewhere, Uzbek Moslems usually permit women visitors to enter the grounds of the mosque and to watch the service from a respectful distance.)

Prayers are offered five times a day, at 6 A.M., 1 P.M., 6 P.M., 7 P.M., and 8:45 P.M. There are a number of mosques in Tashkent and, on request, your guide will take you to a service.

WHERE TO EAT IN TASHKENT

The restaurant in the Tashkent Hotel is supposed to be the best place in town, but we found the service agonizingly slow, the food mediocre and many items appeared on the menu only and were not available. A dreary orchestra added to the din in the hot dining room with its soiled tablecloths. You may be luckier, and if the service and fare in this restaurant have improved I'd appreciate hearing from you about it.

If you arrive at or are leaving the Tashkent airport at mealtime, the restaurant on the second floor of the terminal building has little to offer in the way of atmosphere (except for some exotic-looking fellow travelers), but the food is hearty and tasty. The Russian version of hamburger with fried potatoes served here is surprisingly good.

Here are some other Tashkent restaurants:

The Tashkent, Pravda Vostoka Ulitsa 16, *Telephone:* 3 14 16

Fergana, Karl Marx Ulitsa 27, *Telephone:* 34 74.

Odo, Engels Ulitsa 13, *Telephone:* 3 42 83.

Zeravshan, Leningradskaya Ulitsa 11, *Telephone:* 3 11 27

Vostok, Khamzi Ulitsa 27.

STALINABAD

This was a village within one hundred miles of the border of Afghanistan that has been converted into a metropolis in less than thirty-five years. It is an instructive place to visit in order to witness what can be accomplished by concerted and co-ordinated Communist effort.

Stalinabad is the capital of Tadzhikstan, a Soviet republic about the size of the state of Georgia. Originally, for many centuries, the town was called Dyushambe. It was a backward hamlet of dirt lanes trod by small burros. Even now if you drive ten miles outside of Stalinabad the road is only intermittently paved, and villages of mud huts cling like wasps' nests to hillsides.

Dyushambe means Monday in the Tadzhik language, a tongue of Persian origin. It seems that centuries ago the village from which the present city grew held a lively weekly bazaar on Mondays.

It was still a mere dot on the map when the Bolsheviks came to power. Dyushambe then consisted of about five hundred clay houses ruled by the remote, cruel potentate, the Emir of Bukhara. The Emir and his people, although a protectorate of the Czar, did not yield easily to the Communists. A long period of open civil war and guerrilla activity ensued. In 1924 only 42 houses and a population of 242 people remained in Dyushambe after the period of the most intense fighting.

The Communists virtually rebuilt and expanded Dyushambe from the ground up. On October 16, 1929, it was renamed Stalinabad and proclaimed capital of Tadzhikistan.

The growth of the village to town size and into a city has been astoundingly swift.

In 1926 the population numbered 5607 people.

In 1939 it had climbed to 82,540.

Now there are 300,000 inhabitants.

In an area of once almost universal illiteracy there are now 32 Stalinabad schools providing eight years of compulsory education. There is a university in Stalinabad and a number of institutes teaching such specialties as agriculture, medicine, and engineering.

Now that Stalin's reputation has been partially restored, Communist authorities of Stalinabad are relieved that they retained the city's name.

During the fervor of de-Stalinization, the name of Joseph Stalin was dropped from factories and townships, but, like Stalingrad, the central Asian city of Stalinabad resisted the trend.

The process of "Sovietizing" an alien Asian culture is clearly seen on Stalinabad's main street stretching in a straight line from mountain range to snowcapped mountain range, 10,000 feet high. The avenue bears the name of Lenin.

With few exceptions, the buildings along Lenin Avenue share the same ponderous lines that characterize all Soviet grandiose architecture. The Central Telegraph Office, the Academy of Science, a new yellow stucco secondary (high) school, all are clearly designed-in-Moscow. By now it is the buildings of native Arabic-Persian architecture that look out of place in this "Sovietized" central Asian setting.

Construction of two- and three-story square, characterless apartment houses is gradually razing the traditional low, adobe homes of the Tadzhik people. Eventually these apartments will provide more modern if not necessarily less crowded housing, but the price is total destruction of Stalinabad as an Asian town of whitewashed clay walls and minarets.

The clipped trees along Lenin Avenue contribute to the new provincial ugliness of Stalinabad. Besides being in an earthquake zone where tremors of force five (on a scale where twelve is maximum shock) are almost annually recorded, Stalinabad is in a region seasonally swept by strong winds. Swaying branches regularly knocked down recently installed trolley bus wires, so the decision was made to cut off the branches. This lends the main street the stark atmosphere of the Ardennes after artillery bombardment.

Tadzhikistan is changing and the authorities encourage the still rare visitor to see the new instead of the old. An old Tadzhik man was beating a stubborn sheep when I raised my camera. A guide provided by Intourist shouted to the man in native tongue to desist until the foreigner had passed. He quietly sat down on the curb and let the horned sheep have its way.

Like every other city in the U.S.S.R., Stalinabad has a housing shortage. An attempt is being made to overcome the shortage of space by encouraging private ownership of homes. This is a recent departure from universal government ownership of dwellings. Cheap government loans are now offered to those who undertake to construct their own bungalows. Several score of such two and three room bungalows are being built in one section of Stalinabad. However, it will be some years before the private owners of housing will have a sewerage system. Community pumps are the only source of water.

In the countryside, too, although less than in Stalinabad itself, Soviet industrialization is bringing Tadzhikistan abreast of the sputnik age. Against a backdrop of mountain villages, a smoky cement factory casts its pall on the road leading toward Tashkent, north of Stalinabad.

Three creditably large hydroelectric stations along the same mountainous road supply power to the Tadzhik capital city.

The Russians may have brought their schools, newspapers, industry, and power plants to Stalinabad, but the Tadzhiks still retain their own tastes in many respects. Whereas in Moscow, Russians buy ice cream at outdoor stands even when blizzard snow is falling, Tadzhiks buy ice cream only in midsummer. It was balmy spring in Stalinabad when I ordered ice cream for dessert. The waitress shook her head, explaining, "No, we are not producing ice cream now as it's too cold. Wait until it gets warmer."

Russians drink black tea from a glass; Tadzhiks, green tea from a bowl.

It's a two-hour flight from Tashkent to Stalinabad over rugged, picturesque mountains. Only the small type of two-engine Aeroflot plane seating 14 or 21 passengers flies into Stalinabad's crude field which has dirt runways.

WHERE TO STAY IN STALINABAD

There's only one Intourist hotel in Stalinabad. The rooms are small, but not uncomfortable, although Moscow's hotels will seem like the Waldorf in New York after a couple of nights in central Asia. We had a suite consisting of a five-foot-wide sitting room with a round table, a sofa with an arm that repeatedly fell off, and a desk in one corner, and a larger bedroom with narrow twin beds. As in many homes in central Asia, hotel bedrooms often have rugs hung on the walls. These are usually Bukhara rugs, rare and renowned. Our bathroom facilities were adequate but basic with a rough cement floor punctured by a drain in the center for a shower that stood at the far end of the room without so much as a curtain around it. There is warm water only a few hours a day.

In the hotel lobby a wall-size painting depicts a benevolent Nikita S. Khrushchev in light-tan topcoat inspecting a cotton field as a group of Tadzhik men listen with rapt interest to his words. A painting of equally dramatic proportions in the second floor corridor shows Stalin and Mao Tse-tung, the Chinese Communist leader, conversing.

WHAT TO SEE IN STALINABAD

The State Drama Theatre: Productions at this splendid theater, in Persian architectural style, are in the Tadzhik language. Its 700 seats are sold out for almost every performance. The permanent company presents *Romeo and Juliet* and *King Lear* in addition to Tadzhik classics. Some seats are provided with earphones for simultaneous translations into Russian from the Uzbek language used on the stage.

Ask to speak with the theater director, A. Kasimov, a friendly Tadzhik if you are interested in learning more about the theater. The farther the traveler gets from the suspicious bureaucracy of Moscow the easier it often is to get information.

Twenty-eight performances are put on each month at this Stalinabad theater except for the two months each year when the cast goes on vacation. The actors are well paid by Soviet standards, and director Kasimov receives 3000 rubles ($300 or £107) a month.

There is also a Russian language theater, a symphony orchestra, and a ballet troupe.

A Collective Farm: If you haven't visited a collective farm elsewhere in the Soviet Union, you really should see this important sector of Soviet life before leaving. Even if you have seen one collective farm, central Asia is a good place to tour another. A readily accessible farm, only 15 miles from Stalinabad, is the "Stalin Collective Farm," situated in a Colorado-like mountain setting. Spread over 150,000 acres (two-thirds of it is arable), this is an amalgamation of 43 smaller collective farms. There are 3461 households (or families) on this farm living in 71 separate villages, some of them many miles apart. Although this is one of the most prosperous farms in the region, there are fewer than a dozen privately owned cars among the farm's population. Twelve hundred people, though, own bicycles, and others have donkeys, still a favorite mode of transportation in this part of the world. If you visit this farm and are invited to a meal you will do well to accept. It is an experience of warm hospitality to a visitor from a distant land as well as a chance to taste the hearty, spicy food of the region.

The farm's main crop is cotton. The farm has 33 schools, a hospital with 53 beds, 56 teahouses, 26 nurseries, 16 one-room stores, and four small halls that serve as theaters for movies and for performances of the farm's dramatic groups.

The Stalin Textile Factory: This textile plant is one of the main industries of Stalinabad. It is an excellent example of the industrialization of this until recently backward area.

The factory employs 3300 persons; 85 per cent of them are women. About half of the employees are Russian, and half are central Asians. The Communist Party unit, which like all Party units in every institution and enterprize actually runs the plant, numbers 190—half Russians, half Tadzhiks, Uzbeks, and one Korean.

The one-story plant, a long series of low, shedlike buildings with most of the light provided by skylight windows, holds modern, automatic machinery. A single girl can attend a great machine of more than one hundred spindles that stops automatically when one of the strings breaks. However, at the pay-off end of the complicated series of machinery the final product is muddy red and black colored cloth of a drab variety that is not likely to add gaiety to the Soviet scene.

This year the plant will manufacture a half million feet of cloth, ten per cent more than last, in line with Nikita Khrushchev's latest program of providing more consumer goods—textiles, shoes, clothing—that still are in short supply.

All the equipment in the plant is Soviet-made. A decade ago one person could handle only two looms. Now 20 to 24 looms per worker is the average.

To run a plant of this sort, workers with some technical training are needed. The plant itself has a school for training specialists, and higher skilled technicians are sent to institutes in the Russian part of the Soviet Union.

All workers enjoy a paid holiday of from fifteen days to one month, depending on how difficult the worker's job is. Like many Soviet plants, the Stalin Textile Factory owns a mountainside rest home nearby which can accommodate 360 persons a month, or about 2000 each season. The other workers, not lucky enough to obtain a ticket for the rest home, must find scarce accommodations where they can, if at all. Tickets are, of course, given to workers considered the most deserving because of their contribution to fulfilling the plant's production quotas.

Educational Institutions: The Tadzhiks are justly proud of their educational plants, many of them built only since the last war. There is a state university as well as a number of institutes (the Soviet equivalent of colleges) for agriculture, medicine, and science.

Movie Studio: Here is the place to see films made in the Tadzhik language. Hollywood on a very small and provincial scale.

Frunze Stadium: This grandstand, named after the Russian general who played a great role in subjugating this region, has a mountain view and is the scene of soccer games. If you're especially interested in sports here is an opportunity to see how Soviet fans react.

Government Buildings: The Supreme Soviet Legislature building where laws are enacted for the Tadzhik

Republic, the city hall, the Communist Party headquarters, the law courts, the central telegraph office—these are edifices about which the local Intourist guides will gladly recite facts and figures.

WHERE TO EAT IN STALINABAD

The Pamir Restaurant is by far the best in Stalinabad. It's a bare, big hall with glaring lighting, only a short walk from the hotel, and, most important, the food is fine. There's dancing at night. We suggest that you begin with *mast-ava* or *shur-po*, robust, rich rice soups flavored with onions, meat and potatoes. For the main course try *chikh-am-bili*, goose cooked native Tadzhik style. Tadzhik *shash-lik*, chunks of lamb interspersed with onion, cooked on a spit is delicious. *Obi-non* is the local, pie-shaped, flat, tough but tasty bread. A sweet red wine favored by the Tadzhiks is called *jaus;* it's easier on the tongue in tasting than it is in pronouncing.

SAMARKAND

This is a magic city. It is steeped in legendary romance, in history, in majestic beauty of ruins of a once great civilization. An ancient proverb said that: "In all other parts of the world light *descends* upon earth. From holy Samarkand and Bukhara, it *ascends*." Of course Samarkand's days of glory, of rich trade, of heady conquest are far behind it. But the atmosphere lingers on in the proud beauty of green-tiled domes of its now well-preserved ruins, in the occasional camel caravan that lurches through Samarkand's narrow streets on its way from the desert, and in the tiny lanes that comprise the labyrinth of the *medina*, the clay-hut native quarter.

Samarkand is one of the oldest cities in the world. No

one really knows how old, but it was mentioned in chronicles four hundred years before Christ was born. Once conquered by Alexander the Great, three centuries before the birth of Christ, and later overrun by the Mongol Genghis Khan (in 1220 A.D.), Samarkand was a shrine city of the Moslem faith. The faithful of the ancient world made pilgrimages to its holy places. Samarkand lay astride the great silk trade route between the Near East and China. Under Alexander, when the stream of trade was at its flood, Samarkand became a meeting point between Western and Chinese cultures. It benefited from both.

Today, Samarkand, lying between two snowcapped expanses of mountain range, reflects a mixture of two *other* cultures—the culture of backward central Asia and that of Moscow's Communism.

Samarkand fell to the Communists in 1920 shortly after the Bolshevik Revolution, and the spread of Soviet influence into this region of bearded Asian men with turbans and some still veiled women has been gradual but relentless.

Of Samarkand's 200,000 people, about one-half now are Russians. Only half of the population are the native Uzbeks and Tadzhiks—whose features are a combination of Persian and Mongolian. Samarkand lies within the Uzbek Republic; it was the capital until 1930 when it was transferred to Tashkent.

To see Samarkand in its proper context it is probably better to approach it from backward Afghanistan—a land of illiteracy and without railroads—which lies 500 miles to the south, rather than from Moscow, 2000 miles to the north, a city of subways, skyscrapers, and ZIM limousines. Samarkand seems backward compared to Moscow; outdoor pumps supply much of the populace's water, narrow mud lanes stem from the main streets, and women balance huge bundles on their heads.

But to a delegation from Afghanistan it must seem like a city well on the way into the twentieth century. There are buses, a railroad station with silver-painted statues of Lenin and Stalin, a hotel with plumbing of sorts, and even a few television sets that pick up programs relayed from Tashkent.

The name Samarkand comes from two Uzbek words meaning "fruit" and "sugar," and the reason for at least the former is seen in the flowering trees in springtime.

Although Samarkand can be reached by car or train, that's doing it the hard way, even if permission can be obtained to travel by those means. The quickest and most comfortable way is by plane either from Tashkent or from Stalinabad.

In the summer months be prepared for debilitating temperatures well over 100 degrees Fahrenheit.

WHERE TO STAY IN SAMARKAND

There's no choice here either—just one hotel for tourists. One measure of the distance from Moscow is the plenitude of toilet fixtures. We had to go down the hall to a "community" toilet. Baths are "by appointment" made with the chambermaid who arranges for you to use the bathroom during the hours when hot water is available.

WHAT TO SEE IN SAMARKAND

Observatory of Ulug-beg: Some spell it Ulugh-beg or Ulug-bek. However it may be spelled, he was a remarkable ruler who lived from about 1409 to 1449. He was the grandson of the great Tamerlane. But whereas Tamerlane was a conqueror, Ulug-beg was more interested in science than in conquest. From this ancient observatory, built in the 1400s and excavated in 1908, Ulug-beg observed and catalogued 1018 stars. The Intourist guide told us that five centuries later, astronomers using improved instruments had found only fourteen additional stars in the heavens.

This singular ruin stands on a hillside a short distance from Samarkand. A steel rail, curved in an arc, on which Ulug-beg and his assistants traveled within their observatory to follow with their primitive telescopes the path of a star or planet, can be seen below ground through an opening. It's worth the short ride to see the view of the countryside from the observatory hill.

Shah-i-Zinda: Samarkand's most beautiful monument of a majestic past is the Shah-i-Zinda tomb. Shah-i-Zinda means "living shah," and it takes its name from a passage in the Moslem Koran which states that those who die for Allah have not really passed away. This was the burial place for members of the family of Tamerlane, whose empire in the 1300s stretched from the shores of the Black Sea in the European part of Russia to India. The Shah-i-Zinda consists of a series of incredibly beautiful temples, their glazed turquoise-tile domes brilliant against the bright blue sky. These mosques are set on either side of narrow, stone stairs that begin their ascent sharply and then taper gradually. Near the end of this long, staircase lane is the sepulcher of a Moslem saint who, it is said by the faithful, will rise some day and preach the faith of Islam. Having died in the service of Allah, he is the "living shah." This is a holy shrine to Moslems, and prior to the days of Communist rule pilgrimages were made here much as to Mecca. Even now Moslems can be seen on religious pilgrimage to the Shah-i-Zinda.

Restoration work is in progress at the Shah-i-Zinda as at other heritages of the past in Samarkand and elsewhere in the U.S.S.R. Workmen have secured the precious, delicately hued tile mosaics of marvellous blues and greens and shades between that were flaking off the façades of the Shah-i-Zinda mosques. Particularly since the death of Stalin the Soviet Government has shown a consciousness of the value of these treasures. Previously the official attitude seemed to be that if these monuments crumbled it might serve to extinguish the embers of nationalism burning in Moslem hearts. Now the Moscow attitude seems to be that evidence of Communist care for such shrines may prove a way of evoking the loyalty of the populace.

The Mosque of Bibi Khanum: This architectural wonder has suffered more from the ravages of time and earthquakes than most in Samarkand. It was built by Tamerlane for one of his wives who was Chinese. Legend has it that she fell in love with the architect who designed this gift from her husband. When Tamerlane returned from a military expedition and learned of the romance, he sent soldiers to kill the architect who climbed a high minaret, sprouted wings, and flew away to Persia. I don't know what Tamerlane did to his unfaithful wife. All that remains now of the Bibi Khanum (the name of the Chinese wife) is a graceful arch, half a dome, a minaret, a fertility stone, some tiles and the legend.

The Registan: This was once one of the great squares of the world. Registan means "public square." Travelers who visited it as late as the end of the 1800s described it as more noble than St. Mark's Square in Venice. This was the central square of the Samarkand of Tamerlane's time. It consisted of a main mosque and a number of *madresses,* religious schools, as well as some small supplementary structures. Even in its decayed state it still is possible to visualize the majesty and colorful beauty of the Registan of old. As extensive a traveler through Asia as Supreme Court Justice William O. Douglas wrote of the Registan: "I do not think it is as lovely as the Taj Mahal, which Tamerlane's descendants built in India. But it is more magnificent than any other structure I have seen in Asia or Europe. The Registan finds grandeur in mass and in simple lines rather than in ornament. It represents Persian and Arab genius at its best in the medium of brick and tile. It is a place where I could sit for hours."

One of the Registan's high minarets is leaning at an angle that challenges the Leaning Tower of Pisa. A girdle of chains is restraining the minaret from crumbling to the ground, undoubtedly it would be with a sigh after standing up so straight for so many centuries.

The Old Quarter: The *medina*, or old native quarter of Samarkand, is overlooked by many visitors. Intourist guides steer tourists away from it. But you can wander there on your own. We did one evening. It is situated just behind the Mosque of Bibi Khanum, away from the main road. This is a maze of low, gray clay homes hidden by thick walls from narrow lanes. Children peeped out of doorways. A mother with a cheerful but filthy child in her arms smiled proudly as we admired her baby. A trio of men crouched over a pail mixing a white, taffylike substance which they insisted we taste; it was an Uzbek candy. In courtyards behind the walls women were cooking the family's rice and meat on outdoor brick stoves. In the old town's market Asians squatted on the ground selling strange cuts of meat, including the heads and hoofs of sheep. Don't miss a visit to the old section of the city and to one of the markets. There's an interesting market where meats and produce are spread out on the ground on a rise across the road from the Shah-i-Zinda.

The Tomb of Tamerlane: This impressed us even more than the Registan. The ribbed tiles of its soaring dome have a more bluish shade than most of Samarkand's green glazed tiles. The tomb stands in a small court-yard in an unbuilt-up area that affords an unbroken view of the tomb's pointed arches and noble dome. Tamerlane's sarcophagus is made of black nephrite stone. Others are buried here too, including Tamerlane's religious instructor. Ironically, the underground chamber of this regal tomb was dimly lighted, when we visited it, by a single bare bulb hanging from a cord.

In 1941 Russian scientists received permission from the Moscow government to open Tamerlane's tomb to measure Tamerlane's dimensions, and in this way to try to reconstruct his appearance. A few days after the tomb had been opened Germany attacked, and the U.S.S.R. was at war. Moslems, who had been shocked at this sacrilege in the first place, were convinced that evil spirits, set loose by opening the tomb, had caused the Nazi invasion. The legend lives on in central Asia despite Soviet attempts to squelch it.

Uzbek State University: This is one of the leading Soviet educational institutions in this remote region. More than 7200 students attend classes here in physics, mathematics, literature and, of course, Marxism-Leninism. The university occupies a group of three-story, gray-stone buildings on a pleasant boulevard near the center of the city.

As in other universities in the Soviet central Asia, classes in each course are taught in two languages—Uzbek for the natives and in Russian for the newcomers. About 70 per cent of the student body are of central Asian origins. The rest are Russians.

The university's faculty numbers three hundred, more than half of them now Uzbeks and Tadzhiks, although in the early years after the university's founding in 1927 the faculty was almost entirely Russian.

Each year there are about 2500 applicants for admission to the Uzbek State University, but only 450 are admitted; of these, one-third as a rule are women.

WHERE TO EAT IN SAMARKAND

Samarkand is a place for romance of the past, but not for repasts. The only decent place we found to eat was the restaurant in the Intourist hotel. Try the *shaslik* (which is lamb on a spit, as we've mentioned before) and *plov* (rice with meat and bits of vegetables). Any of the dishes mentioned for the Uzbekistan Restaurant in Moscow originated in this region and are available in most restaurants.

BUKHARA

Time has passed Bukhara by. It's the most primitive city we visited in the Soviet Union. In many ways it is the most fascinating. The imprint of Russification has been slow in reaching this remote community. There seem to be more people astride donkeys than riding in Pobeda cars. Construction is starting on a "new Bukhara" in a large cleared area outside of the ancient part of the city. When that is completed the scrapers and steamrollers of progress may start encroaching on the ancient minarets, *madresses*, mosques, and markets, but for the present at least Bukhara is much as it was when it was ruled by an Emir in 1920, or as it was when slaves were sold in market places as late as 1870, or even as it was when Alexander the Great marched into its streets.

As seen from the road leading to the city, the minarets and gray-domed bazaars that characterize Bukhara lend it the appearance of a town of Biblical times. Actually Bukhara can trace its origins back more than 2000 years. Alexander the Great conquered the region in the fourth century before Christ. It came under Arab rule during the seventh to ninth centuries, A.D. Bukhara became, and for a long period remained, a center of Islamic culture. There were at one time one hundred *madresses* (schools for training Moslem priests) and three times as many splendid mosques.

Bukhara is famous for its rugs, but it is one of those quirks of fact that Bukhara rugs were not *made* in Bukhara but only were sold in its markets. The rugs were made in Ashkhabad and other nearby cities. It's still possible to buy Bukhara rugs, but the prices are high and they are difficult to transport.

Bukhara still is eight miles from the nearest railroad line. With a population of 80,000, Bukhara has no sewage system, but one is planned. Outdoor water pumps are the main source of water. There are few cars and trucks in Bukhara, and even electric trolley cars and buses are seen only on its few main streets. Uzbeks and Tadzhiks live in adobe homes built around courtyards as in ancient times.

There is almost no industry in Bukhara. Astrakan sheep are raised on the arid, near-desert land that lies for hundreds of miles around the Bukhara oasis. Silk growing, cotton farming in irrigated sections, and cattle breeding are the main activities. There is a butter factory, a silk winding and a knitting factory, but Soviet industrialization has yet to move into backwater Bukhara, once the capital of the region, with any intensity.

This is reflected in the comparatively small number of Russians who have come into the region as (if an epithet reserved by the Communists for the West may be employed) "colonizers." Whereas there are as many Russians as central Asian peoples in Tashkent, Russians in Bukhara number only 6000—a small percentage of the city's populace. These serve in many of the jobs of key political, military, and administrative importance.

A word of warning: try to avoid Bukhara in midsummer. Temperatures of 130 degrees Fahrenheit are not unusual in July and August.

The history and one-time glory of Bukhara are conveyed by its buildings and monuments which are described in the "What To See" section, a few paragraphs hence.

HOW TO GET TO BUKHARA

Bukhara can be reached by airplane, but we made the trip by train from Samarkand (taking about five hours) and we recommend this route. The train leaves the Samarkand Station, a typical, green-colored, Victorian style Russian building, promptly at 8 A.M. It arrives at Kogan, the town nearest Bukhara served by rail.

Almost immediately a woman selling *piroshki* (a hot doughy bun stuffed with chopped meat) made one of her periodic trips through the aisle. At one end of the car a samovar-type water heater produced tea which the attendant offered for sale.

The train passed first through rolling green country and then into semi-desert area with only occasional villages. It moved at about 25 miles an hour. Along the route a woman cleaned the compartments with a vacuum cleaner. At a stop called Kat Kagan a toothless Uzbek woman with a dirty child at her breast came through begging for money.

It was an opportunity to strike up conversation with fellow passengers. In the compartment with us a 23-

year-old girl from the Urals was on her way to a new farm in Uzbekistan. She was a devout member of the Young Communist League but when we asked her whether she might marry an Uzbek she showed signs of bigotry as she screwed up her face and blurted, "Not that!" She taught us to play a favorite child's card game called *Durok* ("Fool").

WHERE TO STAY IN BUKHARA

The Uzbekistan Hotel is Bukhara's "finest," and frankly it is awful. The rooms are small. There is no elevator, no hot water, no restaurant, no room service. The only running water is provided in a common washroom that opens on the lobby where Uzbeks may stand and watch a foreigner through the washroom's open door. Furthermore the washroom is "co-ed," no separate facilities for men and women. The "best" rooms in the hotel have a small tank of cold water attached to a stand that enables you to draw water through a dribbling spigot. Don't drink Bukhara's water!

The toilet facilities consist of an outhouse in back of the hotel. Be prepared for the worst!

Bukhara obviously is for the hardy, grin-and-bear-it traveler, oblivious to inconveniences.

WHAT TO SEE IN BUKHARA

The Great Minaret or **The Tower of Death:** A tapered, factory chimneylike minaret—its topmost balcony taken over by a stork for its nest—casts its long afternoon shadow across the narrow streets of Bukhara much as when Moslems constructed it in 1127. The tower is 135 feet high, built of brown bricks; there is a narrow interior staircase and slit windows at the top.

This tallest of Bukhara's many minarets was built for the purpose of summoning the faithful to prayer, but it served a supplemental purpose as a tower from which smoke signals could be sent to guide lost camel caravans across the surrounding desert.

Built during the time of rule of the Turkish dynasty in this central Asian region of the Soviet Union, it also was a watchtower to guard against the approach of unfriendly nomadic tribes.

Later, at the end of the seventeenth century and the beginning of the eighteenth, it was used as an execution tower—victims were forced to jump to their death by order of one of a series of despots who ruled the territory.

The Emir's Summer Palace: The cruelest despot of all was the last Emir of Bukhara. It was from him that the Communist Russians conquered Bukhara and its vast Emirate (kingdom) in 1920. His palace is fifteen miles out of town.

The Emir kept a harem of one hundred wives; some accounts say four hundred and fifty. The Emir escaped from the Communists to a bazaar in Kabul, Afghanistan, where he is said to have become a tea merchant.

The Emir's summer palace, completed only months before he fled, has now become a rest home for Soviet factory workers. Tours are taken through the grounds where haughty peacocks fan their tails and screech at the intrusions. Some of the low, wooden palace's rooms are constructed of squares of colored glass that lend it the appearance of nothing so much as that of a room in an amusement-park funhouse.

The Citadel: This is the ancient fortress of Bukhara from which the Emir ruled. Its high sloping walls give the impression of impregnability, but the assault by Communist forces under General Frunze brought the Emirate to an end and sent the Emir in flight from Bukhara.

The lavish bad taste in which the Emir lived and ruled is fully exploited by his Communist successors. The Citadel is now a catch-all museum with displays of flora and fauna of the region and of Communist accomplishment, but mostly of indoctrination on the dreadful conditions of pre-Communist days. Dungeons can be seen in the Citadel's walls with realistic wax figures cringing in chains.

There are paintings of the Emir's slave markets and diagrams and charts indicating how confiscatory were the Emir's taxes.

In the plot of green park in the center of town stands a statue of General Mikhail Vasilyevich Frunze who returned from Czarist exile in Siberia to lead Communist forces in the campaign to conquer central Asia. On September 1, 1920, Frunze sent a telegram—its text enshrined in the Citadel—to V. I. Lenin at the Moscow Kremlin reading:

THE FORTRESS OF OLD BUKHARA TAKEN TODAY BY ASSAULT THROUGH THE JOINT EFFORTS OF RED BUKHARA AND OUR UNITS. THE LAST BULWARK OF BUKHARA OBSCURANTISM AND REACTION HAS FALLEN. THE RED BANNER OF WORLD REVOLUTION IS TRIUMPHANTLY WAVING OVER REGISTAN. (The Registan is, of course, the square in front of the Emir's Citadel.)

Madresse: This is a seminary—a school for training Moslem priests. Opened in 1946, it is the first Moslem religious school permitted by the Communists since the 1917 revolution. Permission was given as a reward for the role of the Moslem church in rallying the faithful behind the Soviet World War II effort. Seventy-five students now are enrolled at the bare, Spartan premises of the madresse that originally dates back to the sixteenth century. Constructed around a courtyard, the building consists of two stories of arched cloisters. Each archway leads into a cell-like, small stone room which serves either as a class room or as crowded living quarters for four students.

It is a monklike existence for the novices during their nine-year course. Classes were already well in progress when we visited a madresse class at eight one morning. An old mullah (a learned Moslem teacher) with a wispy white beard hanging from his Chinese scholar's face listened to each of eighteen students in turn conjugate the verb "to write" in Arabic. The students sat at bare board tables, shoulder to shoulder, many of them wearing overcoats in the chill morning.

The only heat in the rooms in winter comes from a small earthen stove in the corner. A clean, ascetically undecorated one-room building behind the main madresse structure serves as a community dining room.

The Bug Pit: This is certainly one of the most bizarre tourist sights in the world. A favorite form of punishment inflicted by the Emir was to lower prisoners into deep, well-like pits infested with big, biting insects that would torture but not quite kill. This pit contains two wax figures representing British officers sent in 1843 to offer British assistance against Russian incursions. They spent two months in the pit and finally were beheaded.

Synagogue: Among the most ancient houses of worship in Soviet central Asia is the Jewish Synagogue on the narrow Street of the Jews in Bukhara. Like the other low, one-story buildings next to it, the synagogue is built of clay and straw on a frame of light wood. Age has given it a dull gray appearance. There is no sign outside to indicate that it is a Jewish temple. A high, blue-painted door leads to a small courtyard, and painted on the white washed walls is a blue Star of David. Windows on either side of the court look in on the rooms for prayer.

We attended an early morning service which commenced at 5 o'clock. Old men, their shoulders covered with *talisim* (tassled white prayer shawls) swayed gently as they chanted the service. The community of Bukhara Jews is believed to have come to central Asia about 2700 years ago. Bukhara Jews retain their Semitic features, their prayers and services are read in the traditional Hebrew. They speak no Yiddish, as do Jews of Russia and other European lands. Their native tongue is Tadzhik with its Persian origin. The Jewish population of Bukhara is about 3000 and, with 15 small neighboring communities totals about 5000.

Mosques: There are a number of splendid mosques in Bukhara well worth seeing.

Market Place: There are nine bazaars in Bukhara sheltered by gray, clay cupolas. Interesting for window-shopping, but it's doubtful that you'll see anything you'll want to buy except, perhaps, colorful head shawls.

WHERE TO EAT IN BUKHARA

We found only one restaurant we can recommend. It is situated two doors down the street from the Uzbekistan Hotel, just past the movie house. The menu offers sparse choice, but any of the central Asian dishes mentioned for Tashkent, Stalinabad, and Samarkand are worth trying here too.

Postscript

If the Russians (or more precisely, Soviet authorities) do not like this book it is regrettable because in one respect, if in few others, this book *does* see eye-to-eye with the Russian leaders. It seeks (as does present Soviet policy) to encourage travel to the U.S.S.R. in the belief that understanding can best be achieved by seeing.

However, if a book is 90 per cent favorable to Russia and only 10 per cent unfavorable the arbiters of Soviet taste in literature will not approve of it. The ten per cent that takes issue with the Soviet system is enough to make it "unfriendly" or "negative" or "malicious" in the estimate of official Soviet critics. In this respect the Soviet system is monolithic and uncompromising.

Don't be surprised if your Intourist guide expresses criticism of *Travel Guide to Russia*. I won't be. However, judge for yourself. That's the important thing to do on a trip to the U.S.S.R. Obviously, in order to judge for one's self, it is desirable to have as much material at one's disposal as possible. The more reading the traveler can do before setting out the more qualified he will be to evaluate what he sees and hears. It is easy to jump to conclusions on a brief visit, but this is dangerous in a place as complex as the U.S.S.R.

Travel Guide to Russia has tried to avoid politics. That's not easy to accomplish when suggesting that the visitor see churches which have been converted to museums, behind-the-tourist-façade housing that is slum standard, radio jamming towers, Lubiyanka Prison. But these *are* sights which lead to an understanding of the country as much as the Bolshoi Theatre or the Pushkin Art Gallery.

The objective of this book is to help the visitor see the sights of interest and significance in the U.S.S.R. If it also helps the traveler to better understand and evaluate what he sees in the Soviet Union, the author's most earnest hope will have been realized.

Understanding is important in these times. The ultimate use that man will make of the jet plane, the missile, the Sputniks and the Luniks may depend in part on how well man understands his neighbor, brought ever nearer by science.

Tourism helps understanding. If we are to have war, the person who has seen Russia will know what we are fighting against. If we are to have peace, a bridge of tourists between nations will be important in maintaining it.

Acknowledgments

The word "we" is used frequently in this book. This is neither poetic license nor an editorial use of the word. "We" refers to my wife Nancy as well as to myself. Nancy and I visited museums, factories, schools, farms; we experimented with various dishes in restaurants, shopped in stores, talked with hundreds of tourists to find out what interested or puzzled them. For her companionship in travels through Russia and for her invaluable assistance which helped make this book possible I happily acknowledge my debt to Nancy.

I would like to express appreciation to my employers and editors at the National Broadcasting Company for the opportunity to represent NBC News in Russia for four years and for their support in the writing of *Travel Guide to Russia,* Brigadier General David Sarnoff, chairman of the board of the Radio Corporation of America, has always been generous in sharing his knowledge and judgment of Soviet affairs. Robert W. Sarnoff, chairman of the board of the National Broadcasting Company, and Robert E. Kintner, president of NBC, have given unfailing encouragement in my work. A special word of thanks is extended to William R. McAndrew, vice-president in charge of news at NBC, who is a thoughtful mentor and friend.

My thanks, too, to Lee Barker, Doubleday editor, for his encouragement, patience, and great help. For his services I want to express appreciation to Gerald Dickler.

Gabriel Reiner and Sid Reiner were generous in helping with portions of the book which deal with making arrangements to go to Russia; the long experience of their Cosmos Travel Bureau was most useful. Miss Maria Delicati and Mrs. Edmondo Ricci gave important assistance.

To numerous associates, both Russian and American, who shared their knowledge and experiences to try to make the road smoother for future travelers to Russia, a heartfelt *Spasebo*.

Rome, October 14, 1959

Index

405

The Center of
MOSCOW

TO DYNAMO STADIUM;
HORSE RACE TRACK;
SOVIETSKAYA HOTEL

1 Kremlin
2 Red Square
3 St. Basil's Cathedral
4 GUM Dept. Store
5 Bolshoi Theatre
6 Maly Theatre
7 State Historical Museum
8 Moscow Hotel and Restaurant
9 National Hotel and Restaurant
10 U.S.S.R. Council of Ministers
11 Metropole Hotel and Restaurant
12 Manege Exhibition Gallery
13 Central Telegraph Office
14 Lenin Library
15 Pushkin Art Gallery
16 Zoo
17 Moscow City Hall
18 Aragvi Restaurant
19 Museum of the Revolution
20 Central Lenin Museum
21 American Embassy
22 British Embassy
23 Moscow University (old campus)
24 Conservatory of Music
25 Moscow Art Theatre
26 Museum of Author Ostrovsky
27 Stanislavsky Theatre
28 Chaikovsky Concert Hall
29 Central Collective Farm Market
30 Circus
31 Panorama Movie Theatre
32 Variety Theatre
33 Peking Hotel and Restaurant
34 Praga Restaurant
35 Children's World Store
36 Berlin Hotel and Restaurant
37 Polytechnical Museum
38 Moscow's Reconstruction
      Museum
39 Tretyakov Art Gallery
40 Gorky Park
41 Lubyanka Prison
42 Catholic Church
43 Leningradskaya Hotel and
      Restaurant
44 Leningrad Railroad Station
45 Yaroslavl Railroad Station
46 Kazan Railroad Station
47 Foreign Ministry
48 American House Club
49 Outdoor Swimming Pool
50 Skyscraper Apartment House
51 Kursk Railroad Station
52 Skyscraper Apartment House
53 Planetarium
54 Manege Square

TO ARKHANGELSKOYE;
SILVER FOREST BEACH

GERTSENA ST.

ARBAT ST.

TO UKRAINE HOTEL
AND RESTAURANT

TO LENIN STADIUM;
NOVODEVICHY MONASTERY;
UNIVERSITY

MOSCOW R.